ESSAYS
ON THE
American Revolution

The Institute of Early American History and Culture is sponsored jointly by The College of William and Mary in Virginia and The Colonial Williamsburg Foundation.

ESSAYS
ON THE
American Revolution

EDITED BY
Stephen G. Kurtz
and
James H. Hutson

*Published for the Institute of Early American History
and Culture
Williamsburg, Virginia
by
The University of North Carolina Press
Chapel Hill
and
W. W. Norton & Company, Inc.
New York*

The conclusions and views of the authors do not
necessarily reflect those of the National Endowment
for the Humanities or other sponsors of the Symposium on the American Revolution.

Manufactured in the United States of America
Cloth edition, The University of North Carolina
Press, ISBN 0–8078–1204–8
Paper edition, W. W. Norton & Company, Inc.,
SBN 0–393–09419–7
Library of Congress Catalog Card Number 72–81329

Library of Congress Cataloging in Publication Data
Main entry under title:

Essays on the American Revolution.

Papers originally presented at a symposium on the
American Revolution held at the Institute of Early
American History and Culture, Williamsburg, Mar.
8–12, 1971.
    1. United States—History—Revolution—Addresses,
essays, lectures. I. Kurtz, Stephen G., ed. II. Hutson,
James H., ed. III. Institute of Early American His-
tory and Culture, Williamsburg, Va.
E208.E83   973.3'08   72–81329
ISBN 0–8078–1204–8
ISBN 0–393–09419–7 (pbk)

CONTENTS

[*v*]

PREFACE

In the fall of 1969 the staff of the Institute of Early American History and Culture met to consider appropriate ways in which we might observe the forthcoming bicentennial of the American Revolution. It was incumbent upon us as historians and editors to do what we could to reach as wide an audience as possible while at the same time upholding high standards of scholarship that are often laid aside in the rush to find commercial advantage in national observances. Our deliberations resulted in a four-day symposium on the American Revolution held in Williamsburg between March 8 and March 12, 1971, and ultimately in this volume of original essays. They are presented by their authors and by the Institute as a serious response to the bicentennial celebration and with the hope that reading and reflecting upon them will inspire others to join us in attempting to comprehend the meaning and importance of our Revolutionary heritage.

The symposium was made possible by a grant from the National Endowment for the Humanities, which was matched in part by grants from the American Antiquarian Society, the Elis Olsson-Chesapeake Foundation, the Robert Earll McConnell Foundation, and the Noland Company Foundation. We wish to express our appreciation to our two sponsors, the College of William and Mary and the Colonial Williamsburg Foundation, for their generous cooperation and hospitality and especially to Davis Y. Paschall, president of the College of William and Mary at the time of the symposium, and to William R. Emerson, director of the Division of Research and Publication of the National Endowment for the Humanities, for their patient efforts to assist us in bringing a memorable scholarly meeting into being. Our debt to the many historians who offered suggestions for the program cannot be adequately expressed, but to our colleagues on the Institute staff—Norman

S. Fiering, Sung Bok Kim, John E. Selby, and Thad W. Tate —who worked with us as a program committee and who gave so much of themselves to making it a success, our thanks are warmly expressed.

Williamsburg, Virginia   STEPHEN G. KURTZ
March 15, 1972   JAMES H. HUTSON

INTRODUCTION

The eight scholars whose research and reflections are presented in this volume were asked to interpret the Revolution and to summarize for educated readers the results of their studies in aspects of the Revolution best understood by them and for which they have gained the respect of their professional colleagues. It was decided by the Institute staff acting as a program committee for the symposium that two scholars who had ranged widely in their writing and research should be asked to speak on the causes of the Revolution and on its consequences and that these essays should be delivered in the form of public addresses that would open and close the four-day meeting. Bernard Bailyn and Edmund S. Morgan, both acknowledged masters of the historian's craft, undertook and carried out with rare eloquence and precision this difficult task. Their essays constitute, as they did in the program, the opening and closing interpretive summary statements.

During the intervening three days thirty-five scholars criticized and debated the findings of six historians whose essays had been distributed well in advance of the conference. At individual sessions three or four of the participants were asked, on the basis of their own closely allied work, to comment on each essay with the hope and expectation that close, expert scrutiny would lead to revision and a final version of the paper as substantial and well honed as human effort could make it. These scholars, then, are fellow editors of these essays and deserve mention. Jack P. Greene's essay on the underlying causes or preconditions of the Revolution was examined and criticized by Thomas R. Adams, Daniel J. Boorstin, Benjamin W. Labaree, William H. Nelson, and Gordon S. Wood; Richard Maxwell Brown's discussion of violence as a conditioning factor in the Revolutionary era, by William W. Abbot, Winthrop D. Jordan, and Page Smith; John Shy's examination of the effects of war upon the civilian population, by George A. Billias, Don Higginbotham, Piers G. Mackesy, Howard H. Peckham, Bradford Perkins, and William B. Willcox; H. James Henderson's essay on the formation of voting blocs in the Continental Congress, by Merrill Jensen, Cecelia Kenyon, James Morton Smith, Clarence L. Ver Steeg, and Alfred F. Young; William G. McLoughlin's analysis of the religious settlement that emerged during and after the Revolution, by Richard L. Bushman, Sidney E. Mead, Edmund S. Morgan, and Donald G. Mathews; and the provocative thesis of Rowland Berthoff and John M. Murrin on the social effects of the Revolution, by James M. Banner, Jr., Kenneth A. Lockridge, Jackson T. Main, and Merrill D. Peterson.

Adding greatly to both formal and informal discussion that continued unabated during the course of the symposium were special observers, Lester J. Cappon, director emeritus of the Institute of Early American History and Culture and now editor-in-chief of the Atlas of Early American History, and four others, all distinguished in their own line of work but "outsiders" or laymen as they relate to the writing of history—Alain Clement, feature writer for Paris's *Le Monde*; Dan Lacy, senior vice president of McGraw-Hill Book Company; James E. Mooney, editor on the staff of the American Antiquarian Society; and the distinguished news commentator Edward P. Morgan, of the American Broadcasting Company. Those who participated in the symposium will remember distinctly the summary comments of these perceptive men and especially their plea that historians write for a wider audience than the handful of reviewers and professional colleagues who seem so often uppermost in their minds.

Critics may find much to contest in this volume, and we are aware as we bring it to press that such major themes as great men in history, economic causation, the structure of British politics, and foreign policy are not the subjects of individual essays. The adherents of a radical approach to the history of the American past will notice, moreover, the absence of an avowed disciple among the essayists, just as others now working in fields that have attracted some of the best of the most recent generation of historians will lament the absence of essays in demography or the history of the loyalists. We can only reply that each of these possibilities was weighed, that a perceptive reader will find most of these themes or positions reflected in these pages, and that any volume attempting to assess the American Revolution that did not include essays on the themes finally chosen would be equally or perhaps more open to criticism. We are proud to publish the work of these eight historians and do so with the hope that our sights have been set high enough for others to wish to emulate and surpass their accomplishment.

ESSAYS
ON THE
American Revolution

The Central Themes

OF THE

American Revolution

An Interpretation

by

BERNARD BAILYN

The American Revolution not only created the American political nation but molded permanent characteristics of the culture that would develop within it. The Revolution is an event, consequently, whose meaning cannot be confined to the past. Whether we recognize it or not, the sense we make of the history of our national origins helps to define for us, as it has for generations before us, the values, purposes, and acceptable characteristics of our political institutions and cultural life.

To allow, therefore, the bicentennial celebration to degenerate into the hucksterism and confusion that threaten to overwhelm it would be a national humiliation. For when all the medallions have been struck, the pageantry performed, the commercial gimmicks exploited, and the market-tested historical hackwork published, there still remain the questions of what, in the context of the knowledge now available, the event was all about and what bearing it should have on our lives—questions that will surely be answered in some way or other, but not necessarily by those who are informed enough to distinguish fantasy from reality, partisan arguments from historical fact. A great many books have been published on the Revolution in the past fifty years, and a veritable library of documents has been unearthed. But none of this spontaneously generates understanding. What—that makes any difference—does this mass of information tell us that an earlier generation did not know? Where does our knowledge fall away, and myth and wish fulfillment take over? Can we at least identify some of the misunderstandings and distorting presumptions that beset this segment of American history?

If the essays in this book do no more than clarify the boundaries of our knowledge and isolate some of the more paralyzing tangles in our thinking, they will justify themselves as a contribution to the bicentennial events. I trust they will do much more. My own aim in what follows is simply to state in the most general terms my personal understanding of the major themes of the history of the Revolution and to clear up, if I can, confusions that have arisen since these themes were first suggested.

I

To grasp the full importance of the central theme that emerges from the recent writings one must step back a full generation and note the striking incoherence that lay at the heart of the imposing interpretation, or bundle of interpretations, that then prevailed. On the one hand there was a general agreement on the importance of what was called "the natural rights philosophy," perhaps most memorably summarized in Carl Becker's chapter of that title in his book *The Declaration of Independence*, and of the force of British constitutional ideas, described by Charles H. McIlwain and Randolph G. Adams. Almost all writers who attempted general assessments of the origins and meaning of the Revolution found it necessary somewhere in their accounts to attribute an elemental power to these abstract ideas of Locke and the great Contintental reformers and to the principles of British constitutionalism that embodied the precepts of natural law. Somehow, through a process that was never explained, the formal legal precedents, some of them extraordinarily abstruse, and the abstractions propounded in the texts of the *philosophes* were transformed into political and psychological imperatives when certain actions were taken by the English government, and the result was resistance and revolution. The first state governments were presumably constructed in conformity with these beliefs and principles, though in the only work then available that attempted to analyze those new constitutions, Allan Nevins's *The American States During and After the Revolution, 1775–1789* (1924), it was impossible to discover the precise relationship between these overarching ideas and the constitutions that were actually written. In some sense too the Federal Constitution embodied these principles and beliefs, though the best descriptions then available of what had actually happened failed to establish with any precision the connections between these ideas and the decisions reached by the Convention.

There were some writers who *were* concerned with the problem of how ideas and beliefs relate to what men do, but their presumptions were such that, instead of solving the problem realistically, in the end they simply destroyed it, and with it the possibility of understanding why there was a Revolution. For these writers the primary forces at work were social and economic: *they* really determined the outcome of events, though adroit politicians had used the famous ideas of the time to agitate an otherwise inert public opinion. Thus in 1923 Arthur M. Schlesinger, Sr., by then the target of McIlwain's sharp criticism, criticized a book of C. H. Van Tyne's on the causes of the Revolution by deploring his lack of emphasis on the truly important things—trade, currency, the impact of new commercial regulations—and above all his lack of recognition of the role of propaganda in the Revolutionary movement. By propaganda, Schlesinger explained, he meant not "the constitutional grievances recited in state papers and the more serious pamphlets"; that sort of thing, he said, should only be touched on "lightly," for, as he had already explained, "the popular view of the Revolution as a great forensic controversy over abstract governmental rights will not bear close scrutiny."

It was a mistake to believe "that pamphlets were more potent in shaping colonial opinion than the newspapers." Pamphlets contained sustained arguments, appeals to reason, logic, principles, and intellectual coherence, while what really mattered were "the appeals to passion and prejudice to be found in broadsides, bits of popular doggerel, patriotic songs, caricatures, newspapers, slogans, emblems, etc."[1]

Now what is centrally important in this is not the surface contradiction between, on the one hand, a belief in the force of abstruse points of constitutional law and of natural-rights principles and, on the other, the systematic exclusion of ideas and beliefs from an effective role in affairs except as propagandistic weapons. More important are the differing presumptions upon which the two viewpoints rested. The students of constitutional law and Enlightenment ideas assumed that the force of beliefs and ideas is somehow related to their cogency, to the quality of the argumentation that supported them, or to the universality of their appeal. The other writers made the quite opposite assumption that, because they could not see how abstract ideas, reason, belief, indeed the whole realm of intellection and conviction, could constitute motives, such elements could not in themselves influence events at all and therefore in themselves could explain nothing about what actually happened and why. Ultimately they assumed, though they did not discuss the point, that there is only self-interest, and self-interest in turn is shaped by the social and economic forces that determine the external character of people's lives.

All of this—which first became clear in a few key books that appeared almost simultaneously fifty years ago[2]—is worth recalling because it provides the proper perspective within which to understand the central themes of recent writings on the origins

1. *American Historical Review*, XXVIII (1922–1923), 328; *New Viewpoints in American History* (New York, 1922), 179.

2. Besides Schlesinger's *New Viewpoints*, chap. 7, and Becker's *Declaration of Independence*, both published in 1922, Charles H. McIlwain, *The American Revolution: A Constitutional Interpretation* (New York, 1923) and Randolph G. Adams, *Political Ideas of the American Revolution* (Durham, N.C., 1922).

and meaning of the Revolution. For we have come to understand the errors of both of these approaches of the 1920s, which
have shaped all subsequent writing on the subject until our
own time, and thereby found the way forward, I believe, to a
more satisfactory view of the Revolution and of its bearing on
the subsequent course of American history.

We know now that Enlightenment ideas, while they form
the deep background and give a general coloration to the
liberal beliefs of the time, were not the ideas that directly
shaped Americans' responses to particular events or guided the
specific reforms they undertook, nor were they perceived in the
American colonies in quite the same way they were perceived
elsewhere. And we know too that the abstruse points of constitutional law that so engaged the mind of John Adams and
the other high-level polemicists did not determine the outcome
one way or another; they did not in themselves compel allegiance to the American cause or lead people to rebel against
the constituted authorities. In the foreground of people's minds
was a whole world of more immediate, more commonplace, and
more compelling ideas, and they related to behavior in a way
the writers of the twenties could not have conceived.

These ideas, compelling because they were part of an elaborate map of social reality, part of a pattern that made life
comprehensible, have a long derivation, and though drawn in-
directly from the whole of European political culture, they are
directly the products of a series of creative moments in British
political and cultural life. The starting point was the struggle
between king and Commons in the early seventeenth century,
which secured the rule of law and the principle of the consent
of the governed expressed through representative institutions
as necessities for legitimate governance. But though these principles remained fundamental in the pattern of British liberal
thought and though the seventeenth-century ideas of consent
and of parliamentary privilege were drawn on repeatedly in
the eighteenth century by colonial assemblies seeking the legislative autonomy of the House of Commons, it is wrong to think
of these early seventeenth-century ideas as the effective doctrines of eighteenth-century American politics or of the Ameri-

can Revolution. These ideas were overlaid with an array of new conceptions and concerns later in the seventeenth century, in the score of years surrounding the Exclusion Crisis, 1679 to 1681, that gave them much of what to the eighteenth century was their modern tone and that transformed them, in the context of the 1770s, into precepts of rebellion. These few years of desperate struggle over the effort to exclude the future James II from the succession to the throne saw not merely the drafting of Locke's two treatises on government, which to later generations would appear to summarize the whole of English liberal thought before Bentham and Mill, but also the forging of clusters of much more specific ideas on the nature of political freedom and on its social preconditions, illustrated by a fresh view of English history proving the ancient lineage of the liberal state and by a vivid portrayal of the destructive political effect of corruption. And everywhere in this late seventeenth-century world of ideas there was fear—fear that a free condition of life was a precarious thing, ever beset by power-hungry, corrupt enemies who would destroy it.

[Almost—but not quite—all of the ideas and beliefs that shaped the American Revolutionary mind can be found in the voluminous writings of the Exclusion Crisis and in the literature of the Glorious Revolution that in effect brought that upheaval to a peaceful conclusion] There remains still another decisive moment in the shaping of the Revolutionary mind. The terms of settlement of the Glorious Revolution, based on a broad consensus in English public life, forced the extremists of left and right to the margins of English politics, where they remained, after the rocketing instability of the reigns of William III and Anne, to form the shrill and articulate opposition to the government of that fantastically successful political operator, Robert Walpole. It was here, in the writings of the early eighteenth-century opposition of both left and right—the left carrying forward with embellishments most of the radical notions of the seventeenth century, the right nourishing a nostalgia for a half-mythical rural world of stable hierarchical relations, but the two converging from these opposite poles to blast the bloated Leviathan of government they saw developing before them—it was in this populist cry against what appeared to be a swelling financial-governmental complex fat with corruption, complaisant and power-engrossing—in this shrill alarm of alienated intellectuals, outraged moralists, and frustrated politicians, that English liberal thought took on the forms that would most specifically determine the outbreak and character of the American Revolution and that thereafter in vital respects would shape the course of American history.

[These notions, ultimately derived, as I have suggested, from the early seventeenth century, fundamentally redeveloped in the Exclusion Crisis, but now in the early eighteenth century given definitive shape by the political opposition, had great power; they carried great conviction; and they fitted neatly the peculiar circumstances of American political life.] Bearing into the new, modern age of Walpole the traditional anti-statist convictions of seventeenth-century liberalism, the opposition's program was yet distinct in its insistence that all power—royal or plebiscitarian, autocratic or democratic—was evil: necessary, no doubt, for ordered life, but evil nevertheless in the threat it would always pose to the progress of liberty. The opposition's claims were distinct too in their insistence that the primary wielders of power must be kept apart, sealed off from collusive contact with each other in institutions defined by the principles of "mixed" government. And they were distinct, finally, in their heightened emphasis on the dangers of corruption—the corruption of massed wealth, the corruption of luxury, the corruption of indolence and moral obtuseness, all of which threatened to destroy the free British constitution.

To Americans in distant provinces, faced with local governments that seemed at times to violate the basic precepts of political freedom; ultimately governed not by visible human beings they could acknowledge as natural leaders but by an unseen, capricious, unmanageable, but fortunately quite benignly neglectful sovereign; and bred into an intensely Protestant culture whose deep-lying moralism was repeatedly stirred by waves of evangelical fervor—to such people, all of this made the most profound kind of sense, and it shaped the colonists' political awareness in a hundred different ways. Repeatedly through the middle years of the eighteenth century factional leaders responded to local crises by invoking these ideas—not testing their limits or probing their implications, not even applying them systematically, and with little sense that they might serve one segment of political society more than another, but drawing on them almost casually, and repeatedly, when it seemed appropriate in attacking the power of the state. Then, in the 1760s and 1770s, when the colonists believed themselves faced, not as heretofore with local threats generated by the ambitions of inherently unstable factions, but with an organized pan-Atlantic effort of highly placed autocrats to profit by reducing the free way of life the colonists had known —a "design" set on foot by manipulators of the colossus "at home"—they were led by the force of these ideas, now integrated as they had not been before and powerfully reinforced by Continental writings on the laws of nature and of nations and by the latest formulations of the English radicals, into resistance and revolution.

The noble ideas of the Enlightenment and the abstracted details of constitutional law were everywhere present in the responses of the colonists, but they do not form the immediate, instrumental grasp of their minds. They do not explain the triggering of the insurrection. That is explicable only in terms of that elaborate pattern of middle-level beliefs and ideas that formed for these colonial Britishers the map of social and political reality—a map, originally formed within early seventeenth-century English libertarianism, fundamentally reshaped during and just after the Exclusion Crisis, modernized for the eighteenth century by the political opposition, the alienated intelligentsia, and the vigilant moralists of Walpole's time, and diffused by an intricate process of cultural dissemination throughout the political culture of the American colonies.

But how, precisely, did these notions relate to political behavior?

How facile and how unreal were our predecessors' unexamined assumptions either, on the one hand, that formal discourse and articulated belief bear directly on political processes or, on the other hand, that ideas are only epiphenomenal, superstructural, not the shapers of events but their rationalizations, and effectual only when wielded by propagandists whose professions are different from their true intent and whose aim is to manipulate the minds and so direct the actions of ignorant and suggestible masses. Both views are wrong, both lead to hopeless confusion in interpreting an event like the Revolution. But both are resolvable into the concept of "ideology," which draws formal discourse into those "maps of problematic social reality," those shifting patterns of values, attitudes, hopes, fears, and opinions through which people perceive the world and by which they are led to impose themselves upon it. Formal discourse—the contents of the innumerable essays, sermons, pamphlets, and state papers of the Revolutionary period—is indeed powerful in politics and profoundly significant as historical documentation, but not because in some simple sense it constitutes motives or is a form of weaponry. Formal discourse becomes politically powerful when it becomes ideology: when it articulates and fuses into effective formulations opinions and attitudes that are otherwise too scattered and vague to be acted upon; when it mobilizes a general mood, "a set of disconnected, unrealized private emotions," into "a public possession, a social fact"; when it crystallizes otherwise inchoate social and political discontent and thereby shapes what is otherwise instinctive and directs it to attainable goals; when it clarifies, symbolizes, and elevates to structured consciousness the mingled urges that stir within us.[3] But its power is not autonomous. [It can only formulate, reshape, and direct forward moods, attitudes, ideas, and aspirations that in some form, however crude or incomplete, already exist.]

It is in these terms that ideas—not the disembodied abstractions of the *philosophes* or the formal arguments of the constitutional lawyers, but the complex and integrated set of values, beliefs, attitudes, and responses that had evolved through a century and a half of Anglo-American history and that achieved a new level of coherence and force in the polemics that followed the Stamp Act—may be understood to have lain

3. Clifford Geertz, "Ideology as a Cultural System," in David E. Apter, ed., *Ideology and Discontent* (Glencoe, Ill., 1964), 64, 72.

at the heart of the Revolutionary outbreak and to have shaped its outcome and consequences. The colonists—habituated to respond vigorously to acts of arbitrary rule; convinced that the existence of liberty was precarious even in the loosely governed provinces of the British-American world and ever beset by its enemies; more uncertain than ever of what the intricate shufflings in the distant corridors of power in England portended; and ever fearful that England's growing corruption would destroy its capacity to resist the aggressions of ruthless power seekers—saw behind the actions of the English ministry that threw off the delicate balance of Anglo-American politics and that threatened to impose arbitrary power in America not merely misgovernment and not merely insensitivity to the reality of life in the British overseas provinces but a deliberate design to destroy the constitutional safeguards of liberty, which only concerted resistance—violent resistance if necessary—could effectively oppose. Within the ideological context of the time and in communities whose overall political structure was fragile and prone to conflict and breakdown and in which direct, "mob" action against obnoxious authorities was familiar, forceful resistance became for many psychologically imperative, as did the generation-long effort that followed to build still stronger bastions against the inevitable aggressions of power.

The outbreak of the Revolution was not the result of social discontent, or of economic disturbances, or of rising misery, or of those mysterious social strains that seem to beguile the imaginations of historians straining to find peculiar predispositions to upheaval. Nor was there a transformation of mob behavior or of the lives of the "inarticulate" in the pre-Revolutionary years that accounts for the disruption of Anglo-American politics. The rebellion took place in a basically prosperous if temporarily disordered economy and in communities whose effective social distances (despite the successful revival of a few commercialized "feudal" proprietorships) remained narrow enough and whose mobility, however marginally it may have slowed from earlier days, was still high enough to absorb most group discontents. Nor was it the consequence simply of the maturing of the economy and the desires of

American businessmen for greater economic autonomy, or of the inevitable growth of infant institutions and communities to the point where challenges to the parental authority became inescapable: neither economies nor institutions nor communities are doomed to grow through phases of oedipal conflict. There was good sense in the expectation occasionally heard in the eighteenth century that American institutions in a century's time would gradually grow apart from England's as they matured, peacefully attenuating until the connection became mere friendly cooperation. [American resistance in the 1760s and 1770s was a response to acts of power deemed arbitrary, degrading, and uncontrollable—a response, in itself objectively reasonable, that was inflamed to the point of explosion by ideological currents generating fears everywhere in America that irresponsible and self-seeking adventurers—what the twentieth century would call political gangsters—had gained the power of the English government and were turning first, for reasons that were variously explained, to that Rhineland of their aggressions, the colonies.]

Inflamed sensibilities—exaggerated distrust and fear—surrounded the hard core of the Anglo-American conflict and gave it distinctive shape. These perceptions and anxieties made accommodation at first difficult and then impossible. By 1773 there was a widespread suspicion, primarily in New England but elsewhere as well, that the source of the conflict could be traced to actions taken by Gov. Thomas Hutchinson of Massachusetts and a few of his colleagues in office. This long-respected scion of four generations of enterprising New England leaders, it was believed, had deliberately misinformed the British ministry on the intentions and opinions of the colonists in order to advance his personal interests with the venal gang in Whitehall. Conversely, Hutchinson himself and most of the ministry believed that a clique of ruthless colonial demagogues headquartered in Boston was deliberately misinforming the American populace on the ministry's intentions in order to advance their own interests. Perhaps only Benjamin Franklin, who loved England, though somewhat despairingly, and who yet knew himself to be the embodiment to all the world of the hopes and possibilities of America, fully understood not only the substantive issues on both sides of the controversy but also the haze of misunderstandings that surrounded it. Believing— since he was no ideologue himself—that given sufficient time America's natural wealth and power would make its claims to British rights irresistible, he attempted, in one of the most revealing and consequential episodes of the early 1770s, to head off the approaching struggle by manipulating popular fears for what he took to be the general good. By arranging for the circulation of certain of Hutchinson's private letters of the late 1760s, he publicly documented the general suspicions of the governor's "deliberate misrepresentations" and, in thus pinning the blame for the conflict on Hutchinson, sought to exonerate the ministry and gain time for fresh approaches to reconciliation. But though Franklin's calculations were in this as in everything careful and sharp, he failed, in his happy expatriation in England, to gauge correctly the intensity of the political and moral passions of the majority of his country- men. The publication of Hutchinson's letters, bound, in the circumstance, to be considered incriminating, far from easing the conflict, in fact intensified it, for the "revelation" gave visible, human, and dramatic form to what previously had only been general, vague, and disputable surmises; it "proved" to an outraged public that purpose, not ignorance, neglect, or miscalculation, lay behind the actions of the British govern- ment and that reconciliation was therefore unlikely. Only Franklin, characteristically, landed on his feet: while the pub- lication of Hutchinson's letters destroyed the Massachusetts governor and intensified the growing conflict, it helped trans- form the hitherto ambiguous Pennsylvanian into a popular Revolutionary hero.

All of which, as an explanation of the primary cause of the Revolution, is no more "intellectual" or "idealist" or "neo- whig" than locating the origins of World War II in the fear and hatred of Nazism. It does not minimize the long-term background of the conflict but presumes it; it does not drain the Revolution of its internal social struggles, its sectional divisions, and its violence; it does not minimize the social and political changes that the Revolution created; it does not deny —indeed it alone explains—the upsurge of reformist zeal that is so central a part of the Revolution; nor does it rob the military struggle of its importance. It merely explains why at a particular time the colonists rebelled and establishes the point of departure for the constructive efforts that followed.

II

Such, in my view at least, is the central theme of the origins of the Revolution. But this is, of course, only a beginning of an understanding of the meaning of the Revolution as a whole and of its role in shaping the course of American history. Yet seeing the origins of the Revolution this way makes it possible to approach that ultimate stage of maturity in historical interpretation where partisanship is left behind, where the historian can find an equal humanity in all the participants, the winners and the losers, where he can embrace the whole of the event, see it from all sides, mark out the latent limitations within which all the actors were obliged to act, and trace the influence of the event until it fades indistinguishably into the flow of history that succeeds it. It makes it possible, I believe, to understand the loyalists.

For a century and a half after the Revolution the loyalists' story was the subject of the fiercest and blindest partisanship that can be found anywhere in American historiography. The earliest patriotic chroniclers of the Revolution saw the loyalists as the worst of all enemies: traitors, betrayers of their own people and homeland. Just as they portrayed the Founding Fathers as flawless paragons commanding the almost universal allegiance of the population, so they saw the loyalists—those they could not simply ignore—as craven sycophants of a vicious oligarchy, parasites of the worst corruptions of the ancien régime, and they simply blasted them into oblivion. Conversely, Tory historians in England, followed in a modified way in our own time by certain of the more scholarly "imperialist" historians, saw the loyalists much as the loyalists saw themselves, as sensible embodiments of law and order and of a benign rule against which a deluded and hysterical mass, led by demagogues, threw themselves in a frenzy. In very recent years, it is true, the polemics have subsided, and the writing on the loyalists is more informative than it has ever been before, but this more objective writing is largely descriptive, often enumerative if not quantitative in its approach, and it fails to grasp the central interpretative problem that is posed by the lives of the loyalists. For if we are now able to see the peculiar patterns of fears, beliefs, attitudes, perceptions, and aspirations that underlay the Revolutionary movement, we have not yet made clear why any sensible and well-informed person could possibly have opposed the Revolution. And until that is done, until, that is, we also look deliberately from the point of view of the losers at what only later would appear to have been the progressive development, we will not understand what that development was all about; we will not understand the human reality against which the victors struggled, and hence we will not have the story whole or entirely comprehensible.

There are no obvious external characteristics of the loyalist group, aside from the natural fact that it contained many crown officeholders: a multitude of individual circumstances shaped the decisions that were made to remain loyal to England. Nor are the inner characteristics of this large group obvious. The loyalists were neither especially corrupt nor especially stupid nor especially closed to the possibilities of the future. Many of them, aside from the one point in their politics, are indistinguishable from the many obscure "patriots" whose involvement with events was superficial and who simply drifted marginally one way instead of the other in response to immediate pressures. Yet within the loyalist group as a whole, and particularly within its leadership, there appears to have been an essential if rather elusive characteristic, or set of characteristics, that is distinctive and that, properly understood, illuminates the affirmative side of the Revolutionary movement that the loyalists resisted at such great cost.

Committed to the moral as well as the political integrity of the Anglo-American system as it existed, the loyalists were insensitive to the moral basis of the protests that arose against it. Habituated for the most part to seek gains through an intricate and closely calibrated world of patronage and status, they did not respond to the aroused moral passion and the meliorative, optimistic, and idealist impulses that gripped the Revolutionaries' minds and that led them to condemn as corrupt and oppressive the whole system by which their world was governed. They did not sense the constrictions of the existing order, often because they lived so deeply within it, or the frustration it engendered in those who failed to gain the privileges it could bestow. They could find only persistent irrationality in the arguments of the discontented and hence wrote off all of their efforts as politically pathological. And in a limited sense they were right. For the Revolutionary leaders, in their effort somehow to control a world whose political logic was a product of the system it explained, groped for conceptions that could not exist within the received framework of political ideas. They drew on convictions that ran deeper than logic and mobilized sources of political and social energy that burst the boundaries of received political and social wisdom. All of this is reflected in the loyalists' hopeless efforts to come to terms with the developing Revolution. They were outplayed, overtaken, by-passed.

Loyal officials who had risen within the narrow and complex passages of the old political system could not govern a morally aroused populace; they could not assimilate these new forces into the old world they knew so well. Thus Thomas Hutchinson, in refusing to approve a bill of 1771 prohibiting the slave trade in Massachusetts, said he could not believe that the motives of the supporters of the bill were what they said they were, namely, "a scruple . . . of the lawfulness in a merely moral respect of so great a restraint of liberty"; after all, he wrote, technically in the eyes of Massachusetts law slaves were no worse off than servants bound "for a term of years exceeding the ordinary term of human life": they could not lawfully be executed by their masters, and it was even conceivable—though he admitted the point had never been determined—that they might own property.[4]

Failing to carry the new, ideologically explosive politics with them by arguments and tactics that were familiar to them, failing often even to comprehend the nature of the forces that opposed them, and lacking both the means and the desire to control the turbulent communities by brute power, the loyalist leaders were forced to become devious simply to survive. Inevitably they appeared hypocritical, ultimately conspiratorial, though in fact most of them were neither. As the pressure mounted, their responses narrowed. Their ideas became progressively more rigid, their imagination more limited, until in the end they could only plead for civil order as an absolute end in itself, which not only ignored the sources of the conflict but appeared unavoidably to be self-serving.

There is no better testimony to the newness of the forces that were shaping the Revolutionary movement than the failure of the loyalists to control them.

III

Some such understanding of the loyalists must have a place in a general history of the Revolution consistent with what we now know of its origins. A further and perhaps more difficult challenge lies in interpreting within the same general theme the years that followed Independence and that culminate in the permanent construction of the national government. For the developments of those years are of a different order from those of the years that preceded Independence. The central and unifying themes shift; the approach that allowed one to understand the main events of the earlier years no longer serves for the later: a different kind of analysis and a different focus of attention are required.

The dominant fact of the earlier years had been the intensification of the ideological passions first ignited by the Stamp Act crisis and their final bursting into open insurrection. There-

4. Hutchinson to Lord Hillsborough, Boston, May 1, 1771, C.O. 5/768/195, Public Record Office; George H. Moore, *Notes on the History of Slavery in Massachusetts* (New York, 1866), 131–132.

after the ideas, fears, and hopes that had first become decisive in the attacks on the British government were turned to positive uses in the framing of the first state constitutions, in the transforming of regressive social institutions that had been casually accepted in the ancien régime, and in directing Americans' efforts to new goals altogether: in education, in law, in religion, and in the distribution of land. But the Revolutionary spirit was changing as the original élan slowly filtered through the ordinary activities of life. The initial outburst, in which in some degree the majority of the colonists shared, could not be sustained, nor could the agreement on essentials that had brought together quite disparate groups. Passions cooled as ordinary life reasserted itself and cultural, sectional, and social differences, some of them newly created by the war and the displacement of the loyalists, became important. In the 1780s and 1790s the essential themes of American history became immensely more complicated than they had been in the years before 1776, and they cannot be understood in essentially ideological terms. The creation of the American republic in the period between 1776 and the end of Washington's administration is not a story primarily of developments in the inner lives of people's minds, beliefs, and sensibilities, nor is it simply the working out of the ideas and aims that had earlier accounted for the break with England. It is the product of a complicated interplay between the maturing of Revolutionary ideas and ideals and the involvements of everyday life—in politics, in business, and in the whole range of social activities.

A single characteristic of this later Revolutionary period predominates. Despite depressions, doubts, and fears for the future and despite the universal easing of ideological fervor, the general mood remained high through all of these years. There was a freshness and boldness in the tone of the eighties, a continuing belief that the world was still open, that young, energetic, daring, hopeful, imaginative men had taken charge and were drawing their power directly from the soil of the society they ruled and not from a distant, capricious, unmanageable sovereign. It was not simply that new forms of government were being devised. A new civilization, it was felt, a civilization whose origins could now be seen to have lain in the earliest years of settlement, was being created, free from the weight of the past, free from the corruption and inflexibility of the tangled old-regime whose toils had so encumbered Americans in the late colonial period. Some sense of this had existed before Independence, but unevenly, polemically, and without a generalized sanction. On a few rare occasions writers and preachers like Jonathan Mayhew had sketched a vision of future American grandeur; a sense of American separateness had begun to be felt and expressed and had been reinforced now and then from abroad; and in Congregational circles the sense of special mission that had gripped the minds of the Puritan settlers had in modified form persisted. But these had been scattered responses and expressions, constrained within the limits of a provincial culture that, like Scotland's, had centered in the distant and ancient complexity of London.

If the colonists in the 1760s had been a "youthful" people, their mood had surely belied it. Nothing so clearly documents the transforming effect of the Revolution as the elevation of spirit, the sense of enterprise and experimentation, that suddenly emerged with Independence and that may be found in every sphere of life in the earliest years of the new Republic. This expectant stretching and spirited, hopeful striving can be found in all the activities of men: in the brilliantly imaginative provisions made for opening up new lands in the West and for settling new governments within them—provisions that erased in one bold, cleansing stroke the whole sordid, corrupt, and ineffective mess that the English government had made of that problem; in the surge of people westward, hopefully risking security for new and quite unknown possibilities; in the vast outburst of commercial enterprise, spilling out into the once-restricted markets of the West Indies and Spanish America, out to the continent of Europe, to Alaska, to Russia, and even to China; in experimental finance and path-breaking forms of banking; in bold if not always successful diplomacy; and above all in continuing experiments in government ranging from the recasting of public institutions and of the forms for recruiting leaders to the separation of church and state, federal relations among states, and a new concept of citizenship. Far from the 1780s being a conservative or "counterrevolutionary" period that culminated in a Thermidor at Philadelphia and far from that decade being dominated by self-searching despair for the future of republican hopes, those years witnessed a vast release of American energies that swept forward into every corner of life. But in no simple way. The pattern is a complex one, in which ideological impulses move through the ordinary affairs of life, shape them, and are themselves reshaped by the pressures they meet.

In no area were these pressures more complex than in social organization. The background had been notably complex. For a century and a half conditions of life in these frontier communities had weakened the whole range of social reinforcements of traditional order; yet, with complicated variations, a quasi-traditional order had existed, as had traditional beliefs and expectations, most forcefully the sense that a proper social organization was hierarchical, with more or less clearly articulated levels of superiority and inferiority, respected both in principle and practice. The Revolution made changes in all of this, but not gross changes and not even immediately visible changes. There was no "leveling" of the social order and no outright destruction of familiar social institutions. "Democracy," in its modern form, was not created, in fact or theory, though the essential groundwork was laid. While the war, like so many wars before and since, transformed the economy and sped up mobility in significant ways, and while the displacement of the loyalists and the confiscation of much of their property created room at the top and sources of profit that had not existed before, no sweeping egalitarianism—in status, in wealth, or in power—was imposed. Newcomers to position and influence arrived more quickly and rose higher than they could have done earlier, but social distances remained much as before: narrow perhaps and rather easily bridgeable by European standards, but in local terms highly visible and palpably restrictive. And while the creation of new governments multiplied the available public offices and new men were everywhere seen in seats of power, and while the people as a whole were constitutionally involved in the processes of government as never before, socio-political elites whose origins went back a century persisted, apparently unaffected, in local communities, north and south.

And yet—everything was changing. The pressure of culturally sanctioned expectations had shifted to emphasize the status of the individual as against the community and the integrity of his rights as against those of the state. The quasi-traditional society of the colonial period was not immediately destroyed, but the erosions that circumstance had made were not only multiplied, deepened, and broadened but ideologically reinforced as they had never been before. The effect upon a released society, developing economically, demographically, and institutionally at a fantastic rate, was transforming. The process of America's swift emergence as a distinctive society in the early nineteenth century we have scarcely begun to understand, but it is at least clear that the society Tocqueville found in America was the product, not of a sudden brutal Revolutionary wrench, but of the gradually evolving interplay between a libertarian ideology and the circumstances of life in a wildly expanding frontier world.

The Convention at Philadelphia was a product of the same subtle interplay. The document it produced was neither a repudiation of '76, nor an instrument devised to protect aristocracies threatened in the states, nor the mark of a slaveholders' plot. It is a second-generation expression of the original ideological impulses of the Revolution applied to the everyday, practical problems of the 1780s. Young men, almost none of whom had played a major role in the struggle that had led to Independence, began with—took for granted—what their predecessors had finally achieved and proceeded far beyond them, in circumstances that no one had foreseen. The old ideas and attitudes are there, but now they are diffused, changed, viewed from different angles, and applied to new problems. The fear of power is there, but so too is the inescapable need to create a government potentially more powerful than any yet known—a government complete with its own independent treasury based on the right to tax, a government equipped with all the apparatus of coercion that had proved so fearful a bane to the subjects of despotic regimes. New safeguards must be built; new possibilities explored in the balance of freedom and power. Consent of the governed and the idea of the actual representation of people are there as fundamental principles of government, but so too is the belief that the subjects of this government were not only people but states as well, whose sovereignty must both be preserved and dissolved in this newer and greater creation. The very concept of sovereignty must therefore be probed, and provision now deliberately made for just that inconceivable monster in politics—*imperium in imperio,* states within a state—that right-minded, liberal men had refused to consider barely a decade before. New, awkward, strange political, economic, and constitutional urgencies are everywhere there, impelling forward to an unknown terrain minds formed in an earlier world. The results were daring, too daring and too threatening for some, but they gave workable and hopeful solutions to inescapable problems, solutions devised by young minds using old notions in new experimental ways. In this sense the Constitution of 1787 was the prototypical creation of the age: hopeful, boldly experimental, realistic, and faithful to the urges that had led to Revolution.

IV

Such a view of the central themes of the Revolution—neither whig nor tory, idealist nor materialist, liberal nor conservative: a view that might best perhaps be called anthropological—helps one go beyond the immediate events of the Revolution itself and assess the most general meaning of the event in the broad sweep of eighteenth-century history and to isolate its impact on the overall course of American history.

There had been nothing inevitable in the outbreak of revolution. Deep flows of potentially revolutionary beliefs and apprehensions had moved through the delicate structure of mid-eighteenth-century American politics—as they had through the more deeply stable politics of England—but there had been no necessity for them to break through the channels of civility; the "dysfunctions" that may have existed could have continued to function "dysfunctionally" for ages untold. Even when an explosion was generally expected, some knew ways to avoid it. Burke knew the way; so too, at least in the earlier years of crisis, did the preeminent victim of the Revolution, Thomas Hutchinson. But they, and others like them, lacked the power, and those who had the power lacked the wisdom and the concern to avoid the confrontation. What was inevitable—what no one could have restrained—was America's emergence into the modern world as a liberal, more or less democratic, and capitalist society. That would have happened in any case. But that this emergence took place as it did—that it was impelled forward by a peculiar ideological explosion generated within a society less traditional than any then known—this crucial fact has colored the whole of our subsequent history, and not only our own, but the world's.

How different elsewhere the process of modernization has been, and how important the differences are! In France too political modernization came through an eighteenth-century revolution, but there the prevailing ideas were radically egalitarian, directed to the destruction of a resistant, highly stratified social order dominated by a deeply entrenched, parasitic nobility and capable of implementation only through a powerful, revolutionary state. The French Revolution created a new state system more elaborate and more effective than the one it had overthrown, a state justified both by the dominant theories of revolution and by the undoubted fact that only such a power could dislodge the privileged world of the French ancien régime. In Germany two generations later an attempted liberal revolution failed altogether: its leaders could not break through the corporatist barriers that protected the urban workers or animate a sunken, conservative peasantry by appeals to laissez-faire. Traditionalism thereafter deepened in Germany and produced in the end a dynamic industrial regime politically so paternalistic and socially so regressive that it constituted a threat to liberalism everywhere.

But it is the contrast with England that is ultimately most

revealing. For England's was the parent political culture, and there too, as in America, well before the end of the eighteenth century, social and economic changes had eroded the traditional order and laid the groundwork for a modern liberal state. But the state that in fact resulted in nineteenth-century England was profoundly different from the American state; the two societies differed as much in politics as in social organization. The constitutional starting point had been the same: a balance of socio-constitutional forces in a theoretically "mixed" monarchical state. But England's political modernization, which eliminated the crown and the House of Lords as effective political forces and elevated a slowly democratized and increasingly representative House of Commons to absolute power, moved gradually, through decades of change. Its creators were the most pragmatic and the least theoretical of politicians; they were more Tory than Whig, and their goal was stability through socio-economic upheavals and war. Burke's and the Rockinghams' "economical reform" and Pitt's fiscal reorganization were pragmatic responses to political pressures and the urgencies of war; they served no systematic effort to recast politics or the structure of the state. But they began the destruction of the system of "influence" through which the government of England for so long had been managed. And that was the merest beginning. Multiplying through the reigns of three weak and feckless kings, consolidated by threats from abroad and stresses at home, increments of change in England added bit by bit to the transforming of the eighteenth-century constitution. By the time of Peel's ministry of 1841 much was formally the same, but the essential structure had been rebuilt. All the powers of the state—executive, legislative, and administrative—had become concentrated in the majority leadership of the House of Commons, which was increasingly responsive to a broadening political world. The modern constitution, politics, and state—Bagehot's "cabinet government" supplemented by universal suffrage, national political parties, and an independent civil service—had evolved slowly and had gradually reshaped for modern use the system that Walpole had built. Somewhere deep within it there lay scattered elements of the configuration of ideas, fears, beliefs, and attitudes that had so engrossed the thoughts and so fired the imagination of opposition groups in eighteenth-century England and America; but they were now antique fragments, recognizable only by experts, cemented haphazardly into the new radicalism of Bentham, the Chartists, and Mill.

In America, however, this earlier opposition ideology survived intact and fundamentally shaped the emerging state. The modernization of American politics and government during and after the Revolution took the form of a sudden, radical realization of the program that had first been fully set forth by the opposition intelligentsia—the political moralists, the uncompromising republicans, the coffeehouse journalists, and the nostalgic Tories—in the reign of George the First. Where the English opposition, forcing its way against a complacent social and political order, had only striven and dreamed, Americans, driven by the same aspirations but living in a society in many ways modern, and now released politically, could suddenly act. Where the English opposition had vainly agitated for partial reforms in the fierce debates that had raged over the duration of Parliaments, over restraints on the press, over standing armies, and over the force of wealth and patronage in corrupting the guardians of popular rights, American leaders moved swiftly and with little social disruption to implement systematically the outermost possibilities of the whole range of radically libertarian ideas. In the process they not only built permanently into the modern American state system the specific constitutional and political reforms that had been so passionately and so vainly sought for so long in opposition circles, but also infused into American political culture two inner drives, two central spirits, that would distinguish it ever after.

They are the major themes of eighteenth-century radical libertarianism brought to realization here. The first is the belief that power is evil, a necessity perhaps but an evil necessity; that it is infinitely corrupting; and that it must be controlled, limited, restricted in every way compatible with a minimum of civil order. Written constitutions; the separation of powers; bills of rights; limitations on executives, on legislatures, and courts; restrictions on the right to coerce and to wage war—all express the profound distrust of power that lies at the ideological heart of the American Revolution and that has remained with us as a permanent legacy ever after. While in England the use of power became more concentrated in the passage to the modern state, and while in France and Germany it became more highly structured and more efficient, in America it became more diffused, more scattered, more open to suspicion, less likely ever to acquire a stable, unchallenged role in the conduct of public life.

The distrust of power, generated deep within the ideological origins of the Revolution, runs through the entire course of American history and is as potent an element in our national life today, when the instruments of power are so fearfully effective and the actuality of the state so overwhelming and inescapable, as it was two hundred years ago.

Equally a part of our contemporary struggles is the second great theme that derives from the sources of Revolutionary ideology: the belief that through the ages it had been privilege —artificial, man-made and man-secured privilege, ascribed to some and denied to others mainly at birth—that, more than anything else except the misuse of power, had crushed men's hopes for fulfillment. Not all of the early eighteenth-century English opposition had been gripped by this belief. All elements had been concerned with corruption and with power, but this broad populist animus had drawn together quite different groups that shared only their common hatred of the Leviathan State and their fear of the swollen politico-financial powers that, they believed, had created it. Some had been liberal—believers, that is, in the Jeffersonian ideal of the atomic individual and of a free community of independent yeomen freeholders; but some had been reactionary, or at least, like Bolingbroke, romantically nostalgic: they had sought not a broadening of the individual's self-determination but a return to a lost society of articulated statuses and elaborated hierarchies in which privilege counted for more rather than for less than it did in the modernizing world of eighteenth-century England. Americans had almost never shared these latter views, even in the proprietary and plantation colonies where the social reality might have seemed most congruous; and when the Revolution moved from the negative, critical phase of the years before Independence to the constructive era that followed, this reactionary strand of thought was simply ignored, to be taken up only occasionally thereafter by men who scarcely knew the context from which it was derived; and the radical-libertarian impulse swept forward.

The dominant belief struck at the heart of the privileged world. Everywhere in America the principle prevailed that in a free community the purpose of institutions is to liberate men, not to confine them, and to give them the substance and the spirit to stand firm before the forces that would restrict them. To see in the Founders' failure to destroy chattel slavery the opposite belief, or some self-delusive hypocrisy that somehow condemns as false the liberal character of the Revolution—to see in the Declaration of Independence a statement of principles that was meant to apply only to whites and that was ignored even by its author in its application to slavery, and to believe that the purpose of the Constitution was to sustain aristocracy and perpetuate black bondage—is, I believe, to fundamentally misread the history of the time.

To condemn the founders of the Republic for having tolerated and perpetuated a society that rested on slavery is to expect them to have been able to transcend altogether the limitations of their own age. The eighteenth century was a brutal age. Human relations in British society were savage in a hundred different ways. In the placid countryside and sleepy market towns of eighteenth-century England, J. H. Plumb writes,

the starving poor were run down by the yeomanry, herded into jails, strung up on gibbets, transported to the colonies. No one cared. This was a part of life like the seasons, like the deep-drinking, meat-stuffing orgies of the good times and bumper harvests. The wheel turned, some were crushed, some favoured. Life was cheap enough. Boys were urged to fight. Dogs baited bulls and bears. Cocks slaughtered each other for trivial wagers. . . . Death came so easily. A stolen penknife and a boy of ten was strung up at Norwich; a handkerchief, taken secretly by a girl of fourteen, brought her the noose. Every six weeks London gave itself to a raucous fete as men

and women were dragged to Tyburn to meet their end at the hang-
man's hands. The same violence, the same cruelty, the same wild
aggressive spirit infused all ranks of society. . . . Young aristocrats
—the Macaronis—fantastically and extravagantly dressed, rip-roared
through the town, tipping up night watchmen, beating up innocent
men and women. Jails and workhouses resembled concentration
camps; starvation and cruelty killed the sick, the poor and the
guilty. . . . Vile slums in the overcrowded towns bred violent epi-
demics; typhoid, cholera, smallpox ravaged the land.[5]

Chattel slavery was brutal and degrading, but as far as the
colonists knew, slavery in one form or another had always
existed, and if it was brutal and degrading, so too was much
else of ordinary life at the lower levels of society. Only gradually were men coming to see that this was a *peculiarly* degrading and a *uniquely* brutalizing institution, and to this
dawning awareness the Revolution made a major contribution. To note only that certain leaders of the Revolution continued to enjoy the profits of so savage an institution and in
their reforms failed to obliterate it inverts the proportions of
the story. What is significant in the historical context of the
time is not that the liberty-loving Revolutionaries allowed slavery to survive, but that they—even those who profited directly
from the institution—went so far in condemning it, confining
it, and setting in motion the forces that would ultimately destroy it. For they were practical and moderate men, though
idealistic and hopeful of human progress. Their mingling of
the ideal and the real, their reluctance to allow either element
to absorb the other altogether, their refusal, in a word, to
allow the Revolutionary movement to slide off into fanaticism,
is one of the Revolution's most important features. And of this,
as of so much else, Jefferson is the supreme exemplar: in him
a ruthless practicality mingled so incongruously with a sublime
idealism that his personality seemed to his enemies, as it has
seemed to modern historians concentrating on his "darker side,"
to have been grossly lacking in integrity. All of the Founders
hoped to create a free society in America; not all of them could,
or would, recognize, as Jefferson did, that this could only end

5. J. H. Plumb, *Men and Centuries* (Boston, 1963), 9–10.

in the destruction of chattel slavery. And those who recognized this and who strove to break the hold of this vicious institution so long before its condemnation became a common moral stance acted within a system of priorities that limited what they could achieve.

The highest priority was reserved for whatever tended to guarantee the survival of the republican nation itself, for in its continuing existence lay all hopes for the future. Most of the Revolutionary leaders hated slavery—not one of them ever publicly endorsed it—but they valued the preservation of the Union more. A successful and liberty-loving republic might someday destroy the slavery that it had been obliged to tolerate at the start; a weak and fragmented nation would never be able to do so. The haters of slavery were also limited in what they could accomplish by their respect for property, which like personal liberty was also part of the liberal state they sought to create. And they were, finally, fearful of the unforeseeable consequences in race relations that would result if the slaves—to the colonists still mysteriously alien, politically backward, and at least latently hostile people—were suddenly set free. It took a vast leap of the imagination in the eighteenth century to consider integrating into the political community the existing slave population, whose very "nature" was the subject of puzzled inquiry and who had hitherto been politically nonexistent. But despite all of this, from the very earliest days of the Revolutionary movement the agonizing contradiction between chattel slavery and the freedom of a liberal state was seen, and the hope was formed that somehow, someday, the abhorrent practice of owning men would be destroyed. In the year of Jefferson's death slavery still existed, but it was "a crippled, restricted, peculiar institution," destroyed in the North, forbidden in the Northwest, compressed deeper and deeper—and more and more explosively—into the South. If the Free Soilers of the 1850s, like the Republican platform writers of 1860, exaggerated the Founders' political commitment to the outright abolition of slavery, they correctly sensed the antislavery temper of the Revolutionary age. The ideological continuity between Jefferson and Lincoln is direct; however much their approach to the question of race may have differed, both deeply believed that slavery was "wrong and ought to be restricted"; both groped for ways of advancing that restriction; neither would destroy the Union to effect it.[6]

The Founding Fathers were mortals, not gods; they could not overcome their own limitations and the complexities of life that kept them from realizing their ideals. But the destruction of privilege and the creation of a political system that demanded of its leaders the responsible and humane use of power were their highest aspirations. To note that the struggle to achieve these goals is still part of our lives—that it is indeed the very essence of the politics of our time—is only to say that the American Revolution, a unique product of the eighteenth century, is still in process, in this bicentennial age. It will continue to be, so long as men seek to create a just and free society.

6. William W. Freehling, "The Founding Fathers and Slavery," *AHR*, LXXVII (1972), 91. (Mr. Freehling's formulation in general seems to me excellent, and I have followed it closely in this paragraph.) Major L. Wilson, "The Free Soil Concept of Progress and the Irrepressible Conflict," *American Quarterly*, XXII (1970), 769–790.

2

An Uneasy Connection

An Analysis of the Preconditions of the American Revolution

by

JACK P. GREENE

I

To a question about "the temper of America towards Great-Britain before the year 1763," Benjamin Franklin, in his famous "examination" before the House of Commons during the debates over the repeal of the Stamp Act in early 1766, replied that it was the "best in the world." The colonies, he said,

submitted willingly to the government of the Crown, and paid, in all their courts, obedience to acts of parliament. Numerous as the people are in the several old provinces, they cost you nothing in forts, citadels, garrisons or armies, to keep them in subjection. They were governed by this country at the expense only of a little pen, ink, and paper. They were led by a thread. They had not only a respect, but an affection, for Great Britain, for its laws, its customs and manners, and even a fondness for its fashions, that greatly increased the commerce. Natives of Britain were always treated with particular regard; to be an Old-England man was, of itself, a character of some respect, and gave a kind of rank among us.[1]

1. "Examination of Benjamin Franklin in the House of Commons," Feb. 13, 1766, in Jack P. Greene, ed., *Colonies to Nation: 1763–1789* (New York, 1967), 73.

That Franklin was correct in this assessment was widely sec-
onded by his contemporaries and has been the considered judgment of the most sophisticated students of the problem over
the past quarter of a century.[2]

So persuaded have modern historians been that the relationship between Britain and the colonies prior to the Stamp Act
crisis was basically satisfactory to both parties that they have,
with very few exceptions, organized their continuing search for
an adequate explanation of the American Revolution around
a single, overriding question: why in less than a dozen years
after 1763 the colonists became so estranged from Britain as
to take up arms against her and, a little more than a year later,
to declare for independence. The focus of their inquiries has
thus been primarily upon the colonial response to the pre-
Revolutionary controversy and upon the many medium-range
issues and conditions that contributed to the creation of a revolutionary situation in the colonies between 1764 and 1774 and
the short-run developments that touched off armed conflict in
1775 and led to the colonial decision to seek independence in
1776.

[A result of this preoccupation with the immediate origins of
the Revolution has been the neglect of two other, interrelated
questions also raised by Franklin's remarks: first, whether the
relationship between Britain and the colonies actually was so
satisfactory prior to 1763, and, second, if the existing imperial
system worked as well for Britain as Franklin contended, why
the British government would ever undertake—much less per-
sist in—measures that would in any way impair such an obviously beneficial arrangement.] Of course, neither of these
questions is new. They were widely canvassed by men on both
sides of the Atlantic in the 1760s and 1770s, and they provided
a focus for most of the early students of the causes of the Revolution from George Bancroft to Charles M. Andrews.[3] But no

2. See the discussion in Jack P. Greene, "The Flight from Determinism:
A Review of Recent Literature on the Coming of the American Revolution,"
South Atlantic Quarterly, LXI (1962), 235–239, and *The Reappraisal of
the American Revolution in Recent Historical Literature* (Washington,
D.C., 1967), 32–52.

3. See Greene, *Reappraisal of the American Revolution*, 1–7.

recent historian has dealt with both of these questions systematically or attempted to relate them either to each other or to the question of the impact of post-1763 developments upon the "tempers" of Britons and Americans towards each other.[4] This essay seeks, through a reconsideration of these questions, to provide a comprehensive discussion of the preconditions—the long-term, underlying causes—of the Revolution.[5] Such a discussion is a prerequisite both for a clearer understanding of colonial and British behavior after 1763 and for the eventual achievement of a more satisfactory conceptual framework for analyzing the causal pattern of the American Revolution.

II

When one looks closely at the relationship between Britain and the colonies during the century from 1660 to 1760, one dis-

4. Two important exceptions are Gordon S. Wood, "Rhetoric and Reality in the American Revolution," *William and Mary Quarterly*, 3d Ser., XXIII (1966), 3–32, and Bernard Bailyn, *The Origins of American Politics* (New York, 1968). Both consider the question of what in colonial social and political life (and, in Bailyn's case, the imperial-colonial relationship as well) made it unstable and hence, by implication, prone to revolution.

5. Limitations of space have prevented me from including any consideration of the many manifestations of social strain that a number of earlier and many recent writers have tried to link causally with the Revolution. I have excluded them partly because the links so far suggested have not been successfully established and partly because most of the manifestations of social strain and/or tensions thus far cited seem to me to be no more than the normal concomitants of the rapid social changes taking place in the colonies during the mid-18th century. I believe that, like all important conditions and developments that occur contemporaneously with great political events, these evidences of strain had a bearing upon—and even some degree of causal importance for—the Revolution. But none of them can as yet be assigned a major causal role in the Revolution, which, on the basis of what we now know, must continue to be regarded primarily as a political crisis within the British imperial system rather than a social crisis within the American colonies. This is not to say that the social life of the colonies is not worth far more attention. On the contrary, I regard the rapid social changes taking place in the colonies and the extraordinary demographic, economic, and territorial growth with which they were associated as far more central to an understanding of 18th-century American development than the Revolution itself. For an elaboration of this view and a lengthy discussion of the literature on the "social origins" of the Revolution, see my essay "The Social Origins of the American Revolution: An Interpretation," *Political Science Quarterly*, LXXXVII (1972), forthcoming.

covers, as Charles M. Andrews argued so brilliantly almost a half century ago in *The Colonial Background of the American Revolution*,[6] that it was in many respects an uneasy connection —and one that was becoming considerably more so through the middle decades of the eighteenth century as a result of several important structural changes taking place in both the colonies and Britain. Throughout these decades, contemporaries on both sides of the Atlantic conventionally described the imperial-colonial relationship in terms of the familiar parent-child metaphor with Britain as the mother country and the colonies as its infant offspring. The clear implication of this usage was, of course, that the colonies had by no means yet reached a state of competency. [As is well known, however, by the middle of the eighteenth century in most of the colonies, the colonists themselves were already handling a substantial portion of their internal affairs with an impressive and even a relatively quiet efficiency: to an extraordinary degree, the several colonies had become what Edward Shils has referred to as "pockets of approximate independence" within the transatlantic imperial polity.[7] In all save the newest colonies of Georgia and Nova Scotia, they possessed by 1750 virtually all of the conditions necessary for self-governing states.]

[The first of these conditions was the emergence of stable, coherent, effective, and acknowledged local political and social elites.] We do not know nearly enough about the nature, structure, and functioning of these elites. But it is certainly clear from what we already know that their size, cohesion, self-confidence, sense of group identity, openness, and authority over the public varied considerably from one colony to another according to their antiquity, experience, and effectiveness and according to the political and socio-structural characteristics of their particular society. At one end of the spectrum were the relatively cohesive, self-conscious, and unified gentry groups of Virginia and South Carolina; at the other were the more fissured elites of Pennsylvania, New York, Rhode Island, and

6. (New Haven, 1924), esp. 3–118.
7. Edward Shils, "Centre and Periphery," in *The Logic of Personal Knowledge: Essays Presented to Michael Polanyi* (Glencoe, Ill., 1961), 125.

Massachusetts. In reference to the point at hand, however, the degree of cohesion and sense of group identity matter less than the degree of visibility and public authority, and as the societies of the colonies had become more clearly differentiated during the early eighteenth century, the local ruling elites had come to be more clearly defined and their right to authority more and more widely acknowledged. By the middle of the century, there existed in virtually every colony authoritative ruling groups with great social and economic power, extensive political experience, confidence in their capacity to govern, and broad public support. Indeed, the direction of colonial political life throughout the middle of the eighteenth century was probably toward more and more public deference to these ruling elites; certainly, their willingness to mobilize various groups of marginal members of political society in the protests against the Stamp Act as well as at later stages of the pre-Revolutionary conflict strongly suggests not a fear of such groups but a confidence in their ability to control them. The relatively small incidence of excessive and independent behavior by those groups in turn suggests that the confidence of the elite was not misplaced.[8]

A second and complementary condition was the development of local centers and institutions of acknowledged and functioning authority within the colonies, that is, centers and institutions in which authority was concentrated and from which it was dispersed outward through a settled network of local urban administrative centers and institutions to the outermost perimeters of colonial society. Whether merely small administrative centers such as Annapolis or Williamsburg or large, central trading places such as Philadelphia, Boston, New York, and Charleston, the colonial capitals supplied the colonists with

8. There is no comprehensive study of elite development in the 18th-century colonies. On the relationship of the elite to other elements in colonial society, see Pauline Maier, "The Charleston Mob and the Evolution of Popular Politics in Revolutionary South Carolina, 1765–1784," *Perspectives in American History*, IV (1970), 173–196, and "Popular Uprisings and Civil Authority in Eighteenth-Century America," *WMQ*, 3d Ser., XXVII (1970), 3–35.

internal foci to which they customarily looked for political leadership and models for social behavior.[9]

Perhaps even more important was the emergence of a set of viable governing institutions both at the local level in the towns and the counties and, especially significant, at the colony level in the form of the elected lower houses of assembly. More than any other political institution in the colonies, the lower houses were endowed with charismatic authority both because, as the representatives of the colonists, they were thought to hold in trusteeship all of the sacred rights and privileges of the public and to be the sole giver of internal public law and because of their presumed—and actively cultivated—equivalence to the British Parliament, that emporium of British freedom and embodiment of all that was most sacred to Englishmen everywhere. As powerful, independent, self-confident institutions—in most colonies, the primary vehicles through which the local elite exerted its leadership and expressed its aspirations —with vigorous traditions of opposing all attempts by external authorities to encroach upon their own or their constituents' rights and with the general confidence of the public, the lower houses were potentially effective mechanisms for crystallizing and expressing grievances against Great Britain.[10] Together with the elites who spoke through them, the local centers and institutions, particularly the lower houses, in each colony thus provided authoritative symbols for the colony at large and thereby served as a preexisting local alternative to imperial authority.

A third and closely related condition was the development of remarkably elastic political systems, not so elastic by any

9. On this point, see Carl Bridenbaugh, *Cities in Revolt: Urban Life in America, 1743–1776* (New York, 1955).

10. Jack P. Greene, *The Quest for Power: The Lower Houses of Assembly in the Southern Royal Colonies, 1689–1776* (Chapel Hill, 1963), and "Political Mimesis: A Consideration of the Historical Roots of Legislative Behavior in the British Colonies in the Eighteenth Century," *American Historical Review*, LXXV (1969–1970), 337–360. In my usage of the word charisma, I have followed Edward Shils, "The Concentration and Dispersion of Charisma: Their Bearing on Economic Policy in Underdeveloped Countries," *World Politics*, XI (1958), 1–19.

means as the political system of the United States during the middle decades of the nineteenth century, but probably much more elastic than any contemporary Western political system. They were elastic in two senses. First, they were inclusivist rather than exclusivist. For analytic purposes, one may divide the potential participants in the political process, that is, the free adult male population, into three categories: the elite, including both colony-wide and local officeholders; a broader "politically relevant strata or mobilized population" that participated with some regularity in the political process; and a passive or underlying population that took little part in the political system, in some cases because they were legally excluded by racial or property qualifications and in others because they had no interest in doing so.[11] Available evidence seems to suggest that by contemporary standards the first two groups were relatively large and the third group relatively small. The elite seems to have extended rather far down into the wealth structure and to have taken in as much as 3 percent to 5 percent of the free adult males, while the second category may have included as many as 60 percent to 90 percent of the same group. This wide diffusion of offices and extensive participation in the political process meant that colonial Americans— leaders and followers alike—had very wide training in politics and self-government and were thoroughly socialized to an ongoing and tested political system.[12]

A second sense in which the political systems of the colonies were elastic was in their capacity to permit the resolution of internal conflict. Indeed, they were early forced to develop that capacity. The expansive character of American life pre-

11. These definitions are derived from Karl Deutsch, *The Nerves of Government, Models of Political Communication and Control* (New York, 1963), 40.

12. The literature on the franchise is discussed in Jack P. Greene, "Changing Interpretations of Early American Politics," in Ray A. Billington, ed., *The Reinterpretation of Early American History: Essays in Honor of John Edwin Pomfret* (San Marino, Calif., 1966), 156–159. See also Richard L. Bushman, *From Puritan to Yankee: Character and the Social Order in Connecticut, 1690–1765* (Cambridge, Mass., 1967), the single best study of the process of political inclusion.

vented any group from obtaining a long-standing monopoly of political power, economic opportunity, or social status; new groups were constantly springing up demanding parity with the old. They could not always achieve their demands peacefully, and the still unwritten history of collective violence in early America may very well show that the incidence of violent—and illegitimate—opposition was rising rather than falling during the eighteenth century. But my impression is just the opposite, that opposition demands were increasingly being channeled through the normal processes of government and that the capacity of the political systems of the colonies to absorb new and diverse groups was steadily expanding during the middle of the century as a result of severe pressures created by a combination of rapid demographic and economic growth and increasing social, cultural, and religious diversity.[13]

[The rising competence of the colonies in nonpolitical or semipolitical spheres during the eighteenth century was a fourth condition that had prepared them for self-government. This competence was made possible by the dramatic enlargement of internal and external trade, travel, and migration; the increasing availability of knowledge through a broad spectrum of educational, cultural, social, economic, and religious institutions and through a rising number of books, magazines, and newspapers of colonial, British, and European origin accessible to the colonists; the development of more efficient means and networks of communication within and among the colonies and between the colonies and Great Britain; and the emergence of relatively large numbers of men with the technical skills, especially in law, trade, and finance, requisite for the successful functioning of an autonomous society] These developments not only provided the colonists with some of the technical wherewithal—for example, lawyers and newspapers—that turned out to be of crucial importance in resisting Britain and creating a new nation; they also helped to free the colonies from total dependence upon Britain for certain kinds of essential skills, to raise levels of literacy and educa-

13. For a case study, see Bushman, *Puritan to Yankee*.

tion within the colonies, to liberate them from their former isolation and rusticity, to widen their "range of perception and imagination," and to create a potential for cooperation, for overcoming the "inherent localism" and traditional disunity they had stubbornly and perpetually manifested throughout most of their existence.[14]

[A fifth and final condition was the tremendous increase in the size and wealth of the colonies in terms of the number of people, the amount of productive land, labor, and skills, and the extent of settled territory] The wealth of the colonies had become sufficient to give them a potential for economic and military resistance, while the sheer vastness of all of the continental colonies, taken together, constituted a formidable obstacle to suppressing any large-scale or broadly diffused movement of resistance. Indeed, this condition may well have been the most important of all, because it is the only one of the five not shared to a large degree by the British West Indian colonies, which did not revolt.

It is thus clear in retrospect that the colonies had achieved a high degree of competency by the 1750s and 1760s. Far "removed from the sources of metropolitan authority," they had early been transformed by the very exigencies of life in America from passive "recipients of tradition and objects of authority into independent, differentiated, initiating" social and political entities that put a high premium upon resourcefulness, self-control, and the ability to act successfully and confidently in an uncertain environment that frequently threw them back upon their own devices. [By 1760 the colonies were thus not only able to meet most of the objective conditions necessary for self-government but even had to a significant degree been governing themselves, maintaining internal civil order, prospering, and building an ever more complex and closely integrated society for at least three-quarters of a century and in some cases much longer. Equally important, such a large measure of

14. Lawrence A. Cremin, *American Education: The Colonial Experience 1607–1783* (New York, 1970), esp. 416–417, 520, 549–550, 556, 567; Shils, "Concentration and Dispersion of Charisma," *World Politics*, XI (1958), 19.

de facto autonomy at every level and in all sectors of colonial society—with all of the responsibilities it required—had prepared them psychologically for self-government and independence.[15]

[The corollary of this impressive increase in colonial competency was the continued weakness of British power in the colonies. The bureaucratic structures organized, for the most part during the Restoration, to supervise and maintain control over the colonies had never been adequate for the tasks they were assigned.] As Andrews was fond of pointing out, there was no central governing agency within Britain with effective authority to deal quickly and efficiently with colonial matters until 1768, on the very eve of the Revolution. The Board of Trade, which had primary responsibility for the colonies after 1696, had only advisory powers, and its history is essentially one of failure to obtain the ministerial and parliamentary support necessary for its many and repeated attempts to establish a more elaborate and effective system of colonial administration. Moreover, its staff was so small and the number of separate colonies with which it had to deal so great that it could not possibly keep abreast of the rapidly fluctuating political and economic circumstances of every colony. This situation was exacerbated by the absence of any efficient means of communication between Britain and the colonies—a regular system of packet boats was not established until 1755—and by the seeming inability of the Board to force its representatives in the colonies to supply it with up-to-date information. Finally, like all of the agencies within the British government that had any colonial responsibilities, the Board was invariably more responsive to the demands of powerful interest groups within Britain than it was to those of the colonists. [The result, therefore, was an administrative structure in Britain that for most of its existence had insufficient influence or power either to obtain support for its policies at home or to enforce them in the colonies, a structure that was both poorly informed about what was happen-

15. Cremin, *American Education*, 556, 568; Shils, "Concentration and Dispersion of Charisma," *World Politics*, XI (1958), 19.

ing in the colonies and only minimally responsive to colonial demands.[16]

Within the colonies the situation was little, if any, better. Imperial administrative machinery was insufficient for the enforcement of imperial policy, and authorities in Britain had no effective controls over the machinery that did exist. The governors, the primary representatives of the imperial government in the colonies, had almost no coercive resources at their command. Prior to the introduction of large numbers of British troops at the beginning of the French and Indian War in the mid-1750s, there was no more than a handful of regular troops in any colony on more than a temporary basis, and governors had few other dependable resources with which they could put down opposition to imperial policies, whether it came from the elected representative assemblies, the press, local governing institutions, or some segment of the public at large. Theoretically great, even their control over judicial machinery was, in most cases, highly tenuous. Of course, most governors did have some utilitarian resources in the form of crown or proprietary lands or access to other special privileges or concessions that could be used to build up a solid base of support for their administration. But few had much patronage—in the Anglo-American political world of the eighteenth century, the most important utilitarian resource of all—at their disposal. Imperial authorities never sought to strengthen the ties between Britain and the colonies by systematically admitting "the leading members of the provincial aristocracies" into the metropolitan political establishment. Increasingly, in fact, they even excluded such men from the few royal offices available in the colonies, which, especially after 1720, were usually filled by the ministry at home with needy place seekers. After 1740, even the largely honorific seats on the governors' advisory councils, which had in earlier times usually been reserved for wealthy and well-

16. See Andrews, *Colonial Background*; "The American Revolution: An Interpretation," *AHR*, XXXI (1925–1926), 219–232; and *The Colonial Period of American History* (New Haven, 1934–1938), IV; and Michael Kammen, *Empire and Interest: The American Colonies and the Politics of Mercantilism* (Philadelphia, 1970), 1–94.

affected colonists, came more and more to be filled in the same way.[17]

With little prospect for solid backing from home, only a rudimentary bureaucracy on which they could count for assistance (and over which they frequently had little control), and little patronage through which they might have gained the support of strategically placed members of local elites, governors frequently allied themselves with the dominant political groups within the colonies and did little more than keep up the appearance of adherence to the policies of the home government. Far from being able to co-opt the provincial elites by binding them to the imperial order in the colonies with strong ties of interest and obligation, the governors were, rather, co-opted by those elites; and the local standing and influence of governors, which in many cases was by no means inconsiderable, came to depend at least as much upon local connections as upon their formal position as representatives of the imperial government. Gubernatorial influence was thus highly personal and did not automatically extend beyond an individual governor to his successor, much less to the imperial government in Britain. Whatever power Britain had over the colonies by the mid-eighteenth century derived not from its monopoly of force, not from its efficiency and responsiveness, and not from a systematically cultivated network of interests and political obligations.[18]

The counterpoint of this continuing weakness of British power in the colonies was the dramatic increase in the importance of the colonies to Britain's economy during the first seven decades of the eighteenth century. The population of the continental colonies soared from 257,060 in 1700 to 635,083 in 1730 and 1,593,625 in 1760. The average decennial rate of increase was nearly 36 percent. As the population increased, the colonies not only supplied Britain at extremely favorable rates with a growing variety of raw materials, many of which were

17. See Bailyn, *Origins of American Politics*, 66–80; Ronald Syme, *Colonial Elites: Rome, Spain and the Americas* (London, 1958); and Jack P. Greene, *Great Britain and the American Colonies, 1606–1763* (New York, 1970), xxv-xlv. The quotation is from Syme, *Colonial Elites*, 3.

18. Syme, *Colonial Elites*; Greene, *Great Britain and the American Colonies*, xxv–xlv.

subsequently reexported at a considerable profit to British middlemen, but also provided a growing stimulus to British manufacturers by taking an ever-rising amount of British finished products. Indeed, during the eighteenth century, the colonial trade became "the most rapidly growing section"—and accounted for a significant proportion of the total volume—of British overseas trade. Imports from the colonies (including the West Indies) accounted for 20 percent of the total volume of English imports in 1700–1701 and 36 percent in 1772–1773, while exports to the colonies rose from 10 percent of the total volume of English exports during the former year to 37 percent during the latter. In real figures, imports from the continental colonies increased very sharply in every decade from an annual average value of £265,480 in 1701–1710 to £667,135 in 1731–1740 and £1,042,619 in 1761–1770, an overall growth of 165 percent. During the same period, exports to the colonies rose over twice as fast, increasing at an overall rate of almost 400 percent from an annual average value of £267,302 in 1701–1710 to £646,192 in 1731–1740 and £1,797,922 in 1761–1770.[19] The colonial trade thus constituted a large and critical segment of the British economy and was becoming more important every decade. It is conventional to think in terms of the colonies' dependence upon Britain, but it is also very important to keep in mind that in the economic sphere Britain was becoming increasingly dependent on the colonies. To a considerable degree, the growing awareness of how much the economic well-being of Britain actually did depend upon the colonies, one strongly suspects, accounts for Parliament's willingness to contribute substantial sums toward the expenses of settling Georgia beginning in the 1730s and Nova Scotia starting in 1749 and to make such enormous outlays of money and men in defense of them during the Seven Years' War. Such profitable possessions

19. Phyllis Deane and W. A. Cole, *British Economic Growth 1688–1959: Trends and Structure* (Cambridge, Mass., 1962), 34, 86; the population figures and the statistics for imports and exports to Britain are computed from the tables "Estimated Population of the American Colonies" and "Value of Exports to and Imports from England, by American Colonies: 1697 to 1776," *Historical Statistics of the United States, Colonial Times to 1957* (Washington, D.C., 1960), Ser. Z, 756, 757.

could never be permitted to fall into the hands of Britain's Continental rivals.

III

In itself, no one of these structural features—not the growing competence of the colonies, the continued weakness of British power in the colonies, or the increasing importance of the colonies to Britain's economy—was productive of sufficient strain to make the possibility of revolution very great; in combination, however, they contributed to the development of two fundamental discrepancies within the imperial-colonial relationship, discrepancies that made the potential for dysfunction within the empire extremely high. The first was the obvious discrepancy between theory and fact, between what imperial authorities thought the colonies should be and what they actually were. The increasing competency of the colonies during the eighteenth century obviously called for some adjustment in imperial behavior and attitudes towards the colonies, and such an adjustment appeared to have been made during the long ministry of Sir Robert Walpole from 1721 to 1742. Under Walpole, an informal accommodation between imperial authorities and the colonies had been achieved that permitted the colonies a generous amount of de facto self-government and economic freedom. Coming after more than sixty years of wrangling between imperial authorities, who, beginning with the Restoration, had repeatedly sought to bring the colonies under tighter control, and colonists, who insisted upon retaining a large measure of autonomy, this accommodation represented something of a return to the old contractual relationship between mother country and colonies that had obtained during the first half century of English colonization, a relationship that had permitted the colonists the widest possible latitude to pursue their own objectives with a minimum of reciprocal obligations to the imperial government at home.[20] But the accommodation was entirely pragmatic: it required no intellectual adjustment on the part of the authorities in Britain. On the contrary, by

20. On this point, see the introduction to Greene, *Great Britain and the American Colonies.*

helping to forestall any explicit colonial challenges to traditional imperial notions about the colonies, it actually reinforced them. Equally important, by contributing to keep imperial-colonial relations relatively placid, it also helped to foster the dangerous illusion within the British political nation that imperial authorities actually did have the colonies firmly in hand —or at least that they could bring them under strict control if it ever became necessary to do so.

There were, of course, still other foundations for this illusion. The one seemingly substantial basis for it was the remarkable success of the navigation system that had been worked out largely between 1651 and 1705. This system was an application to the colonial sphere of that general cluster of social and economic attitudes that Adam Smith subsequently designated mercantilism. Fundamentally, these attitudes represented an attempt to impose some order upon and to achieve some control over the enormous economic and social energy unleashed by the expansion of market opportunities in the sixteenth and seventeenth centuries. Like most other expressions of mercantilism, however, the navigation system was never completely effective: from the enactment of its first provisions right up to the American Revolution, the constant lament of those charged with its enforcement was that it was being frequently and flagrantly violated by self-serving and unpatriotic colonials. But we must emphasize not only how often or under what conditions it was violated but also, given the difficulties of and the inadequate means available for enforcement, how extraordinarily well the navigation system succeeded in turning the economic energies of the colonists into channels that were at once profitable to both mother country and colonies.

By and large, this success was attributable far less to imperial coercion than to colonial compliance. Students of the navigation system have traditionally concerned themselves with the question of how much the navigation system cost the colonists.[21]

21. See Lawrence A. Harper, "The Effects of the Navigation Acts on the Thirteen Colonies," in Richard B. Morris, ed., *The Era of the American Revolution: Studies Inscribed to Evarts Boutell Greene* (New York, 1939), and "Mercantilism and the American Revolution," *Canadian Historical*

Far more deserving of emphasis is the very great extent to which they had been able to prosper under that system and, by the early decades of the eighteenth century, had actually developed a strong stake in maintaining their connections with it.[22] This is not to say, of course, that there were not significant pockets of dissatisfaction with the system from time to time and place to place within the colonies during the eighteenth century, or that some specific aspects of the system, most notably the Molasses Act of 1733, would not have created major colonial discontent had they been enforced, or that the system was not more profitable for Britain than it was for the colonies. [It is to say that the extent of colonial compliance suggests, not total satisfaction with, but a very high degree of accommodation to the system and that, however voluntary and selective in character that compliance may have been, it provided, along with the concomitant absence of much manifest colonial opposition to the system as a whole, the principal support for the imperial illusion of control over the colonies.]

[A far more compelling foundation for this illusion was the overpowering conviction—the deeply rooted and pervasive belief—of the inherent superiority of Britain, of its political institutions and its culture.] The belief did not apply only to Britain's standing vis-à-vis the colonies. Following the Glorious Revolution, it was widely believed within the British political nation that the British constitution as it had been restored by the Revolutionary Settlement represented the ultimate political achievement of all time, permitting the enjoyment of so many liberties and at the same time preserving a high degree of political order. "Pride in the liberty-preserving constitution of Britain was universal," extending to all groups both in and

---

Review, XXIII (1942), 29–34; Curtis P. Nettels, "British Mercantilism and the Economic Development of the Thirteen Colonies," *Journal of Economic History,* XII (1952), 105–114; and Robert Paul Thomas, "A Quantitative Approach to the Study of the Effects of British Imperial Policy upon Colonial Welfare: Some Preliminary Findings," *Jour. Econ. Hist.,* XXV (1965), 615–638.

22. This point of view is an extension of the argument in Oliver M. Dickerson, *The Navigation Acts and the American Revolution* (Philadelphia, 1951), 3–158.

out of power, and this pride was matched by an almost equally pervasive reverence for the king, Lords, and Commons assembled in Parliament, which was at once the chief guardian of the constitution and its omnipotent interpreter. By its mere possession of the vast authority of so extraordinary a constitution, Parliament seemed to embody all that was most sacred to Englishmen everywhere—in the colonies as well as in Britain—and to command the unqualified respect and obedience of all who came under its sway. The power of Parliament knew no geographical bounds within the British dominions: it was limited only by its own obligation not to violate the essential principles of the constitution, an obligation that it alone had the capacity and the authority to judge.[23]

Nor were Britain's superiority and glory limited to the political realm. The prose and poetry of Addison, Defoe, Gay, Pope, Steele, Swift, and a host of lesser writers during the first half of the eighteenth century were widely heralded as evidence that Britain had achieved its "Augustan Age" in literature. And, despite a number of temporary setbacks, the economic picture, especially as measured by a rising volume of foreign trade and a quickening pace in domestic economic activity, seemed to be especially bright, so bright, in fact, that it was thought in Britain and feared on the Continent that Britain would eventually outstrip all of its traditional Continental rivals in wealth and power.[24]

Not everyone, of course, viewed the situation in Hanoverian Britain with approval. Implicit in the comparison of contemporary Britain with Augustan Rome was a "historically derived fatalism," a prediction that, like the Rome of Augustus, the Britain of George I and George II would sooner or later degenerate from its epitome of virtue and freedom into a corrupt

23. Bernard Bailyn, *The Ideological Origins of the American Revolution* (Cambridge, Mass., 1967), 45–46; Jack P. Greene, "The Plunge of Lemmings: A Consideration of Recent Writings on British Politics and the American Revolution," *So. Atlan. Qtly.*, LXVII (1968), 141–175.

24. See James William Johnson, *The Formation of English Neo-Classical Thought* (Princeton, 1967); Deane and Cole, *British Economic Growth*, 41–97.

state of vice and slavery. The shrill prophecy of a wide spectrum of opposition writers, many of whom were the very men whose writings seemed to earn for British literature the appellation Augustan, during Walpole's ministry was that this decline would come sooner rather than later. But, although the manner of Walpole's achievement only intensified the worries of his opponents, his extraordinary success in achieving political stability without manifestly destroying any of the essentials of the constitution undermined much of the credibility of opposition claims, while the great British military and naval victories during the Seven Years' War brought Britain territory and power unequaled, it was said, since the glorious days of Rome. Despite the obviously disquieting implications of the parallel between Rome and Britain, Britain's greatest days, the Cassandras to the contrary notwithstanding, still seemed—throughout the middle decades of the eighteenth century—to lie in the future rather than in the present.[25]

In the face of such achievements, such evident national superiority in politics, literature, economic development, and war, who could doubt that Britain was in every respect superior to its colonies overseas, those distant and culturally backward refuges for the deviants, the outcasts, and the unsuccessful of Britain and Europe? As imperial usage of the parent-child metaphor so clearly revealed, the colonies were by definition thought to be subordinate and dependent, bound by their position within the imperial family order to yield obedience to their mother country and unable, like children, either to control their own passions—were they not forever squabbling among themselves?—or to protect themselves from external aggression. [Given the pervasiveness of such attitudes, any acknowledgment of colonial competency on the part of British authorities was virtually impossible, for competency carried with it the hint of an equivalence between the colonies and Britain.] In view of

25. See Isaac Kramnick, *Bolingbroke and His Circle: The Politics of Nostalgia in the Age of Walpole* (Cambridge, Mass., 1968); J. H. Plumb, *The Origins of Political Stability: England 1676–1725* (Boston, 1967), esp. 160–189; and James William Johnson, "The Meaning of 'Augustan'," *Journal of the History of Ideas*, XIX (1958), 521.

the intensity and extensity of British convictions of superiority, such a hint would have been a patent and disturbing violation of the national self-image.[26]

[The second discrepancy within the imperial-colonial relationship was between two divergent conceptions of what the relationship actually was.] This discrepancy may be discussed in terms of a question raised by much of the previous discussion: if British coercive power over the colonies was so weak and colonial competence so high, what was it that continued to bind the colonies to Britain? Part of the answer, as we have already suggested, is to be found in the very real utilitarian benefits they derived from the connection. Despite the limitations imposed upon them by the navigation system, perhaps in part because of them, the colonies had prospered during the first half of the eighteenth century and had a strong vested interest in maintaining their economic ties with Britain. Far more important than these utilitarian benefits, however, were, as Franklin underscored in his *Examination*, the vital and deeply rooted customary bonds of allegiance and affection that tied the colonies very tightly to their parent state, ties whose strength had increased enormously through the middle decades of the eighteenth century as a result of the growing involvement of the colonies with Britain, the emergence of colonial elites intent upon reproducing in the colonies a society that resembled that of Britain as closely as possible, and the increasing Anglicization of colonial life in both form and substance.

These bonds had powerful symbolic and psychological roots. For the colonists, Britain was the central source of not only political and cultural but moral authority: it was at once the repository of the sacred "order of symbols, of values and beliefs," which were thought to give structure and legitimation to the lives of all Englishmen in Britain and the colonies and the site of the institutions charged with the exemplification and protection of that order. This "sacred order" at the very center

26. There is no satisfactory treatment of this subject, but see the suggestive analysis in Richard Koebner, *Empire* (Cambridge, Mass., 1961), 77–237, where the author explores at length some of the implications of the contrasting meanings attached to the term *empire* in Britain and the colonies during the 18th century.

of British life provided a "standard by which [all] existing authority" and the actions of all authoritative institutions could be judged, defined the qualities necessary for those individuals who exercised authority, and specified the proper relationship of citizens to authority and authority to citizens. For colonists on the outermost peripheries of the British polity, the need to identify with—to have some direct link to—this sacred order, the yearning for incorporation into a central system of values and institutions that transcended and gave more general meaning to their own peripheral and particular existence, was overpowering. Their very distance from the center, their acute sense of being so far removed from the "vital zone" of authority in Britain, and the intensities of local pressures toward the development of autochthonous—and hence unlegitimated—values, habits of actions, and institutions combined to make the colonists unusually dependent upon Britain for evaluative standards and models of behavior. So much weight did the authority of the metropolis carry in the colonies that, as Franklin also suggested in his *Examination*, those individuals in the colonies who were or were thought to be "closely and positively" connected through institutional or personal ties to Britain automatically enjoyed a "special status." Moreover, as the colonies came more and more into the ambit of British life during the eighteenth century and came to feel considerably closer to the center of authority, the "locus of the sacred," the extent of their dependence increased because their closer proximity to the center made them feel their remoteness from it and their position as outsiders far more compellingly than did their forebears.[27]

Britain also served the colonies as a source of pride and self-

27. Shils, "Centre and Periphery," in *Logic of Personal Knowledge*, 117–124; Edward A. Tiryakian, "A Model of Societal Change and Its Lead Indicators," in Samuel Z. Klausner, ed., *The Study of Total Societies* (New York, 1967), 82; Chalmers Johnson, *Revolutionary Change* (Boston, 1966), 12; Fred Weinstein and Gerald M. Platt, *The Wish to be Free: Society, Psyche, and Value Change* (Berkeley and Los Angeles, 1969), 5–6; Jack P. Greene, "Search for Identity: An Interpretation of the Meaning of Selected Patterns of Social Response in Eighteenth-Century America," *Journal of Social History*, III (1970), 189–220; and "Examination of Franklin," in Greene, ed., *Colonies to Nation*, 73.

esteem as well as of moral authority. To have a share, if often largely only a peripheral share, in the achievements of Britain during the eighteenth century—in the internal civil achievements following the Glorious Revolution and the external economic and military achievements represented by the enormous expansion of foreign trade and the overwhelming victory over the French and Spanish in the Seven Years' War—was an exhilarating experience that operated to heighten British patriotism in the colonies and to strengthen still further the psychological bonds between them and Britain.[28] Thus, whatever the weaknesses of British coercive power and whatever the objectionable conditions attached to the utilitarian benefits offered the colonies by the connection with Britain, Britain had enormously powerful normative resources with which to bind the colonies to it.

But these resources were not, of course, so powerful as to be able to bind the colonies to Britain under any conditions. Strong as it was, the colonial attachment to Britain, it is now abundantly clear, was conditional. If it was true, as John Dickinson later remarked, that the "Dependence" of the colonists could not "be retained but by preserving their affections," it was also true, as he so strongly emphasized, that "their affections" could not "be preserved, but by treating them in such a manner, as they think consistent with Freedom and Justice."[29] If to British authorities the parent-child metaphor meant that the colonies were to be dependent and subordinate, to the colonists it meant that Britain was to be nurturant and protective— not primarily in the limited sense that the British government was expected to provide bounties and other specific economic encouragements to the colonists or to protect them against attack by rival European powers. Such benefits, especially the promise of defense, certainly continued to be important to the colonies at least until after the British victories in North America and the West Indies during the Seven Years' War. Far

28. On the increasing British patriotism, see Max Savelle, *Seeds of Liberty: The Genesis of the American Mind* (Seattle, 1965), 553–583.

29. Dickinson to William Pitt, Dec. 21, 1765, in Edmund S. Morgan, ed., *Prologue to Revolution: Sources and Documents on the Stamp Act Crisis, 1764–1766* (Chapel Hill, 1959), 119.

more important, however, was the nurturance and protection expected by the colonists in a much larger sense: the sense in which they expected Britain to provide a favorable political and economic climate in which they could pursue with a minimum amount of anxiety their own, specifically colonial and individual, ends, while it also continued to provide a praiseworthy example by which they could measure their own achievements.

To provide such a standard of measurement British authorities had to behave toward the colonies in accordance with certain deep-seated and pervasive beliefs about the limits of legitimate political action that had become integral and sacred components of colonial political culture as it had gradually taken shape during the first century and a half of settlement. Traceable primarily to the social and political thought of the civic humanists of the Italian Renaissance and secondarily to native English sources including the writings of common lawyers such as Sir Edward Coke or the religious literature generated by the English Reformation, these beliefs and the system of social and political perceptions they composed had been transmitted to the colonies largely through the rich social and political literature that poured forth from English presses after 1640. Perhaps because they were so far removed from the center of power within the empire, the colonists, as Bernard Bailyn has demonstrated, seem to have found the literature of opposition, the writings of those resident Britons who were also on the outside, especially attractive. But it is probably somewhat misleading to draw too sharp a distinction between opposition and "mainstream" thought, and it is possible to argue that in its essentials opposition thought was, at least after the Glorious Revolution, to a large extent really only a more pure, intense, and uncompromising version of the same central ideas that animated mainstream thought. To be sure, there were very important differences in emphases and bitter disagreements over the meaning and tendency of particular political and social developments, emphases and disagreements that were carried over to and reproduced in the colonies as they were or were not appropriate to specific local conditions. But there was a hard core of unchallenged beliefs that was common to all major variants of Anglo-American political and social thought and formed the central premises for an emerging colonial perceptual system; and, in all probability, that they were unchallenged—that there simply were no competing ideas about any of these fundamental postulates of social and political life—is what primarily accounts both for their almost universal acceptance among the colonists and for their enormous determinative power in shaping the colonists' interpretations of political actions and social behavior.

This hard core of belief, this social and political perceptual system, has been so fully described by Bernard Bailyn, Caroline Robbins, Isaac Kramnick, and J. G. A. Pocock that it requires only a brief summary here.[30] Proceeding from the assumptions that all men were by nature imperfect creatures who could not withstand the temptations of power and luxury and that power and luxury were corrupting and aggressive forces whose natural victims were liberty and virtue, this system of ideas stressed the omnipresent dangers to society and the polity from corruption by luxury and power, respectively. It emphasized the necessity for virtue, personal independence, disinterestedness, and devotion to the public welfare by rulers and the importance of a balanced government by which the various constituent components of the polity would keep a constant check upon one another as the only device by which liberty could be preserved and the polity prevented from degenerating into some vicious species of tyranny. Because all societies were thought to be highly susceptible to internal decay through moral corruption, any seeming rise in the incidence of hedonistic behavior, any sign of increasing luxury or vice, was a source of grave concern, a harbinger of certain decline and extinction; because the ideal was for the polity to remain in a perpetual and unchanging

30. Bailyn, *Ideological Origins*, 1–159, and *Origins of American Politics*, 14–58; Caroline Robbins, *The Eighteenth-Century Commonwealthman: Studies in the Transmission, Development, and Circumstances of English Liberal Thought from the Restoration of Charles II until the War with the Thirteen Colonies* (Cambridge, Mass., 1959); Kramnick, *Bolingbroke and His Circle*; and J. G. A. Pocock, "Civic Humanism and Its Role in Anglo-American Thought" and "Machiavelli, Harrington, and English Political Ideologies in the Eighteenth Century," in *Politics, Language and Time: Essays on Political Thought and History* (New York, 1971), 80–147.

state of equilibrium, virtually all change was by definition malignant and had to be resisted. This system of ideas thus taught people to explain any deviation from the existing political situation, especially those that seemed somehow to be inimical to one's fundamental interests or to the manifest principles of the constitution, as the probable result of a conspiracy of corrupt men in power to subvert liberty in behalf of their own selfish designs.

Plausible enough to people out of power in Britain itself, such an explanation was extraordinarily persuasive to the inhabitants of distant colonies who were not only far removed from the point at which decisions were made but did not participate to any significant degree in the system that made them. The simple fact of distance between Britain and the colonies thus created an underlying propensity towards distortion within the imperial-colonial relationship that made it absolutely crucial that British authorities always act in accord with the traditional imperatives of Anglo-American political culture in their relations with the colonies.[31] If Britain had a nurturant obligation to help the colonies become and remain British (in the sense of encouraging them to abide by those imperatives), British authorities first had to make certain that they kept themselves so.

But the voluntary attachment of the colonies to Britain depended upon something far more fundamental than the careful observation by British authorities of these traditional imperatives: it depended as well upon their willingness not to violate a basic substructure of expectations among the colonists that those imperatives were thought to protect. For the colonists, this substructure, which had gradually taken shape over the first 150 years of colonization, had come to constitute a kind of sacred, if not entirely explicit, moral order, the preservation of which was felt to be absolutely essential to the continuation of a just—and, therefore, acceptable—relationship between Britain and the colonies. The most obvious and explicit element in this substructure of expectations was that the imperial government

31. Of course, distance also made colonial behavior equally liable to distortion by imperial authorities.

would not in any way violate the sanctity of the elected lower houses of assembly and other institutions and symbols of self-government and authority in each colony, institutions and symbols that, as we remarked earlier, had come to assume such extensive authority within the colonies that they, rather than Parliament, had long since come to be regarded by the colonists as the most immediate and primary guardians of their rights and property.[32]

A second and extremely elusive component of this substructure of implicit operating assumptions was the expectation that the imperial government would place as few impediments as possible in the way of the colonists' free pursuit of their own social and economic interests. Indeed, when one looks closely at so many aspects of colonial political behavior—at the selective nature of colonial compliance with the navigation acts; the kinds of situations that produced collective violence; the specific content of political disputes, both internal and external; the character of most legislation; and the unapologetically self-interested behavior of so many individuals—when one studies all of these aspects of colonial political life he comes away with a strong impression that there was a very sharp disjuncture between the ways men talked about political society and sought to legitimate political activity, on the one hand, and the ways they assumed political society would—and ought to—work, on the other. For what emerges from an examination of colonial political behavior is an implicit conception of political society that is much less concerned with the primacy of the general welfare or the other classic imperatives of Anglo-American political culture than with the protection and facilitation of group interests and individual enterprise. What the actions of the colonists seemed to assume, in fact, is that political society was a human device not only, in the conventional sense, for the maintenance of orderly relations among the men who composed it and for the protection of its members from their own and others' human frailties but also, and probably consider-

---

32. See Greene, *Quest for Power*, and "Political Mimesis," *AHR*, LXXV (1969–1970), 337–360.

ably more important, for the protection of the individual's property in his land, goods, and person, in which one's property in person included the right of striving, of pursuing (as well as protecting) one's interests, of seeking to alter one's place on the scale of economic well-being, social status, or political power.

The critical point about such a conception is that it assigns to political society no more authority over the individual and to the individual no more obligation to political society than is absolutely necessary to make sure that others have the same freedom as he has. Political society is, thus, still regulative and negative as it had been in more traditional conceptions; but it is also facilitative and positive in that it encourages—at the very least, by not in any way inhibiting—the individual to preoccupy himself with his own goals without forcing him to be much concerned with the social well-being of the community as a whole. The presumed tendency of individuals who live in a political society operating on such assumptions is for them to subordinate the welfare of the community to the pursuit of self-interest or at least to exaggerate the normal tendency for individuals to define the welfare of the community in terms of their own interests.[33]

This is not to suggest that colonial behavior was free from the usual imperatives of the traditional status or organic conception of political society, imperatives that placed very heavy emphasis upon the obligations of citizens to put the welfare of the community as a whole before any personal considerations. On the contrary, in the colonies, as in every other contemporary Western society, such imperatives dominated explicit thinking about social and political relations. As was the case in Britain and elsewhere, however, the power of such ideas derived primarily out of men's needs to legitimate their actions—to themselves as well as to others—by conceiving of and presenting them in certain time-honored and publicly sanctioned forms and out

33. In this discussion, I have drawn heavily on the ideas of C. B. Macpherson, *The Political Theory of Possessive Individualism* (Oxford, 1962), esp. 263–271.

of the absence of a more accurately descriptive and publicly acceptable alternative terminology. The traditional imperatives were, in any case, often not descriptive of behavior or of the conception of political society implicit in that behavior.[34]

In terms of the present discussion, however, the important points are that, however much—or little—restraint these traditional imperatives may have imposed upon the colonists' behavior within their own societies, they exercised virtually none upon their behavior within the larger political society of the empire as a whole and that there was a deeply ingrained tendency within colonial society to judge the appropriateness of any political measure, especially those originating with the imperial government, in terms of how it did or did not facilitate the pursuit of group and individual interests within the colonies. To whatever degree they disapproved of self-oriented behavior in a specifically colonial context, they found it fully acceptable in the larger arena of imperial affairs. For one thing, of course, what seemed to imperial officials to be patently self-interested behavior by colonists might very well have been in the best general interests of a particular colony and therefore have appeared to the colonists as a selfless example of community-mindedness. But more important, the wide latitude in the pursuit of their own colonial and individual ends enjoyed by the colonists during their first century and a half and especially during and immediately after Walpole's tenure conditioned them to think of their connection with Britain as an instru-

34. The extent to which the traditional imperatives were so descriptive varied enormously from one colony to another, and they everywhere existed in a state of tension with the more individualistic sense of political society I have been describing. The strength of community sentiment as revealed by the extent to which the traditional imperatives had been internalized may furnish one means for classifying the divergent political societies of the colonies and pinpointing the differences among them. We might, for instance, attempt to arrange colonial societies along a spectrum running from more to less community orientation, and such a device might enable us to identify more clearly shifts in the nature and orientation of political life within those societies. By taking an awareness of this tension into the study of other aspects of colonial social development, perhaps especially into the study of law and justice, one might also be able to identify more clearly those aspects of colonial life that contributed to make this individualistic conception of political society so powerful.

mentality through which they might profitably seek those ends.[35]

A third, related, and even more elusive component of this implicit structure of expectations was the assumption that the imperial government would not interfere with the capacity of the colonists as individuals to maintain their personal autonomy. One possible approach to this subject—and, given the present state of analysis, any approach must necessarily be highly tentative and speculative—is through a consideration of the possible social and psychological meaning, on both the cultural and personal levels, of the colonists' heavy emphasis upon virtue and independence as the central mandates of individual behavior. In the conventional usage of the day, *virtue* meant the voluntary observance of the recognized standards of right conduct, while *independence* implied exemption from all external control or support. Of course, these two mandates were integral parts of the British, as well as the colonial, value system and were given especially great stress by the "country" opposition both during Walpole's ministry and earlier.[36] But they may have been given a greater emphasis in the colonies, for, whereas in Britain they served an essentially defensive purpose (that is, in a psychological sense, as ego protective), in the colonies their function was both defensive and adaptive.[37] From the very first days of settlement, the challenges of the American environment had put a high value upon initiative and self-control. Wilderness conditions and later the lack of many of the traditional restraints and supportive social institutions that the colonists had had in England had early forced

35. See, for example, the claim of the New York General Assembly in Oct. 1764 in its petition against the Grenville program that "a Freedom to drive all kinds of Traffick in a Subordination to, and not inconsistent with, the *British* Trade; and an Exemption from all Duties in such a Course of Commerce, is humbly claimed by the Colonies, as the most essential of all the Rights to which they are intitled, as Colonists from, and connected, in the common Bond of Liberty, with the uninslaved Sons of *Great-Britain*," in Morgan, ed., *Prologue to Revolution*, 11–12.

36. See Pocock, "Machiavelli, Harrington, and English Political Ideologies in the Eighteenth Century," in *Politics, Language and Time*, 104–147.

37. This distinction between *defensive* and *adaptive* is implied in Weinstein and Platt, *Wish to be Free*, 7–19.

men to rely heavily upon their own resources.[38] Mastery of environment, in other words, had to an unusual degree required mastery of self, and full mastery of self in turn required that a man have both virtue—freedom from one's own passions —and independence—freedom from the passions and/or control of others. In the colonies, therefore, the extent of a man's personal autonomy was thus the measure both of his virtue and independence and, more important, of his capacity to maintain self-control and to manipulate—or adapt to—his environment: that is, to act as every man was supposed to act in that society. As such, personal autonomy was absolutely crucial to the maintenance of a man's self-esteem, for any threat to his autonomy from either internal or external sources was also a threat to his ability to function effectively in his environment and, therefore, by definition degrading and corrosive of his self-esteem. For maintaining their own self-control, for preserving their own virtue, the colonists were entirely responsible as individuals, though their deep dependence upon Britain for normative standards and their excessive fears of hedonistic behavior clearly did not bespeak complete confidence in their abilities for doing so.[39] With regard to maintaining their independence—their ability to act without external controls— on the other hand, the colonists shared responsibility with British authorities, and there was always a possibility that those authorities might impose restraints that by striking at the colonists' autonomy as individuals would threaten their ego capacities (as defined by their ability to control themselves and manipulate their environment) and thereby call forth large-scale personal anxiety, guilt, shame, and feelings of inadequacy that could only be overcome by a *manly* resistance to those restraints. The implicit expectation of the colonists was thus that the British government would continue to provide a stable external background that would not call into question their accustomed autonomy, their ability—so crucial to their self-esteem and their continuing capacity to function as successful

38. On this point, see Cremin, *American Education, passim.*
39. See Greene, "Search for Identity," *Jour. Soc. Hist.,* III (1970), 189–220.

individuals in colonial society—to act in accordance with the mandates of virtue and independence.[40]

The voluntary attachment of the colonists to Britain thus depended, we can now see, to a large extent upon a set of implicit expectations about imperial behavior towards the colonies, expectations that proceeded from the assumptions that it was the moral obligation of the *mother* country to provide nurturance and protection for the colonies. What nurturance and protection had come to mean for the colonists—the specific central components of the mother country's moral obligations to them—were: first, that the imperial government would not undermine in any serious way the colonists' self-esteem as defined by their capacity as individuals to act effectively (that is, with a high degree of autonomy) in the colonial environment; second, that it would interfere as little as possible with their ability to pursue whatever purposeful activity seemed to them to be in their best interests; third, that it would respect the sanctity of the local self-governing institutions on which they depended for the immediate protection of the property, in person as well as in goods, they had acquired as a result of that activity; and, fourth, that in its dealings with the colonies it would continue to manifest respect for all of those central imperatives of Anglo-American political culture that were thought by Englishmen everywhere to be essential for the preservation of liberty and property.

This cluster of implicit expectations on the part of the colonists suggested a conception of the imperial-colonial connection that was fundamentally different from that held by imperial authorities. The divergency is most clearly revealed in the different meanings attached to the parent-child metaphor in Britain and in the colonies, in the explicit British emphasis upon the disciplinary implications of the metaphor and the colonial stress upon the nurturant and facilitative. The British

40. On these points, see the New York Petition to the House of Commons, Oct. 18, 1764, in Morgan, ed., *Prologue to Revolution*, 13. In putting together this discussion I have drawn heavily on conversations with Fred Weinstein.

emphasis implied a relationship of perpetual dependency of the colonies upon the mother country, while the colonial suggested an eventual equivalence. This continuing discrepancy between competing and potentially conflicting ideas about the character of the imperial-colonial relationship was, of course, closely connected to the discrepancy discussed earlier between imperial theory and colonial reality. During the century from 1660 to 1760, the colonies had acquired an increasing competency as a result of certain fundamental and irreversible structural changes in virtually every sphere of colonial life, changes that brought about a significant decrease in the degree of the colonists' actual dependence upon—and, correspondingly, obligations to—Britain. Though the perpetuation of the market structures that had been worked out within the empire during the seventeenth and early eighteenth centuries was, from the colonists' point of view, highly desirable and though the colonists continued to rely heavily upon Britain for various normative resources, the one essential need the colonists had for Britain by 1750 was protection against Britain's powerful European rivals, France and Spain; and this decrease in colonial dependence and decline in colonial obligations rendered traditional imperial theories about what the colonies should be largely inappropriate to existing conditions in the colonies.

The existence of these two related and overlapping discrepancies, the one between imperial theory and colonial reality and the other between imperial and colonial ideas about the nature of the imperial-colonial connection, was thus the essential precondition that gave the British Empire a latent potential for revolution through the middle decades of the eighteenth century. I say *latent* potential because these discrepancies had first to be clearly defined and their implications fully explored before they could actually become sufficiently dysfunctional to cause the disruption or disintegration of the empire. Indeed, the irony is that, so long as they were only dimly perceived and not explicitly confronted, these discrepancies actually functioned as an essential—probably *the* essential—component of stability with the empire, because they permitted the colonists to exercise a considerable amount of autonomy without requiring imperial officials explicitly to abandon their traditional notions about the character of the empire. So long as the imperial government did not attempt to remove these discrepancies by enforcing those notions or acting in a sustained or systematic way upon them, the potential for any large-scale revolt by the colonies was not extremely high.[41]

This is not to say, of course, that these discrepancies were not in themselves productive of considerable strain and anxiety on both sides of the Atlantic. The intermittent attempts by imperial authorities to establish closer supervision over the colonies, attempts that dated back to 1660 and even earlier, had given rise to frequent and repeated demands by colonists for some explicit arrangement that would have provided them with considerable autonomy in both the political and economic realms and afforded them full protection against the awesome might of the imperial government. For the British, there was always the fear that these irrepressible and undisciplined little "commonwealths" in America would sooner or later acquire the wherewithal to become "independent" of their "Mother Kingdom."[42] These fears were fed not merely by the facts of colonial behavior but by the very logic of the parent-child metaphor, for that logic suggested that the colonies, like children, would eventually reach their maturity and become independent. The metaphor, the very terms in which the imperial-colonial connection was perceived and discussed, thus encouraged fears of colonial independence in Britain and, in all probability, unconscious wishes for independence in the colonies.[43]

Although there is no doubt that these anxieties helped to

41. For a fuller discussion of these points, see Greene, *Great Britain and the American Colonies*, xxxi–xlvii.

42. See *ibid.*, xxxi–xlvii, 267–271.

43. Suggestions of such fantasies are in Benjamin Franklin, "Observations Concerning the Increase of Mankind, Peopling of Countries, etc." 1751, in Leonard W. Labaree, ed., *The Papers of Benjamin Franklin*, IV (New Haven, 1961), 227–234; and Lewis Evans, "A Brief Account of Pennsylvania in a Letter to Richard Peters, Esq., in Answer to Some Queries of a Gentleman in Europe, 1753," MS, Historical Society of Pennsylvania, Philadelphia. On the possible presence and meaning of such fantasies in similar situations, see Weinstein and Platt, *Wish to be Free*, 35.

generate a latent distrust between the colonies and Britain, neither that distrust nor the fears that lay behind and supported it could become an active cause of disruption between Britain and the colonies so long as the delicate and uneasy accommodation that had been worked out under Walpole continued to obtain. That it would not obtain was by no means predictable. The accommodation had, in the first place, been based upon the pragmatic, if only half-conscious, recognition that a union of entities with differing interests and goals could most easily be maintained by muting, by not calling attention to, the differences; and, given the overall economic success of the empire under Walpole, only the most compelling reasons could have been expected to produce a change in tactics by his successors. Perhaps even more important than Walpole's sense that accommodation rather than confrontation was the best strategy to preserve the colonists' attachment to Britain was the fact that, at the same time the tensions created by the two fundamental discrepancies in the imperial-colonial relationship may have been encouraging the development of suppressed fantasies of independence among the colonists, they were also operating to reinforce a powerful yearning for dependence, a yearning rooted in the psychological dependence of the colonists upon Britain for their normative standards and their strong and habitual ties of allegiance and affection. That dependence and those ties were so strong as to prevent the colonists from ever permitting whatever unconscious fantasies they may have had about equivalence and independence from becoming conscious, codified wishes.[44] The British Empire in the 1740s and 1750s thus manifested a classic crisis of authority between parents and children with all of the potential conflicts such a crisis implies. But it was still a latent crisis.

Given the potential for dysfunction produced by these two discrepancies in the imperial-colonial relationship, there was a strong possibility that some serious, if probably inadvertent, transgression of the existing moral order as it was conceived by one party or the other would shatter it beyond repair. But the important point is that such a transgression was necessary be-

44. Weinstein and Platt, *Wish to be Free*, 34–35.

fore any of the preconditions we have been describing could become causes of revolution or imperial disintegration. Some structural conditions had pointed the colonists toward equivalence and independence and, in doing so, had undermined the traditional bonds between Britain and the colonies and made the relationship relatively fragile. But these preconditions did no more than make the creation of a dysfunctional situation possible. Whether or not and when such a situation would be created would be determined by other kinds of intervening causes.

IV

What began the process by which the old British Empire acquired for the first time a marked susceptibility to disintegration or revolution, what, in fact, was the salient precondition of the American Revolution, was the decision by colonial authorities in Britain to abandon Walpole's policy of accommodation and to attempt to bring the colonies under much more rigid controls.[45] This decision was taken, not abruptly in 1763, as has traditionally been supposed, and not even in 1759, as Bernhard Knollenberg has recently argued, but gradually in the decade beginning in 1748.[46] Neither this general decision nor the many specific policy decisions of which it was composed constituted any sharp ideological break with the past. On the contrary, they merely represented another attempt to implement the traditional goals of English colonial policy as they had been worked out following the Restoration, to act in accord with the guiding assumptions behind the British conception of the meaning of the parent-child metaphor. But the situation differed markedly from the one that had obtained during the Restoration or in the decades immediately following the Glorious Revolution, the two periods during which similarly

45. The remarks in this section are based upon extensive research into the Colonial Office Papers and other relevant private and public records on British colonial policy from 1745 to 1759. This research was conducted in the summer of 1963 and intermittently thereafter. Precise citations will only be provided for quotations. Portions of this section are adapted from the introduction to my *Great Britain and the American Colonies*, xli–xlv.

46. See Bernhard Knollenberg, *Origin of the American Revolution: 1759–1766* (New York, 1960).

systematic attempts had been made. The differences arose out of the conjoint facts that the colonies were infinitely more competent and correspondingly less dependent upon Britain, as we explained earlier, and that the attempt followed a long period of over a quarter of a century during which the imperial government appeared to have abandoned most of the goals it suddenly once again seemed bent upon achieving. Thus, whatever ideological continuity there may have been between post-1748 and pre-1748 policy, there was a radical discontinuity in both the tactics of imperial policy and in the quality of imperial-colonial relations.

The explanation for this fundamental change in the tone and direction of British policy towards the colonies is to be found in three separate conditions, one long-run and two short-run. The long-run condition, which, in all probability, was by far the most important, was the extraordinary territorial, demographic, and economic growth of the colonies discussed earlier. At least since the 1690s, British officials had intermittently expressed the fear that the colonies might one day seek to throw off their dependency on Britain, set up their own manufactures, and become economic rivals rather than subordinate and complementary partners with Britain, goals, they implied, that were probably the secret ambition of many colonials. By lending increasing plausibility to this fear at the same time that it raised the importance of the colonies to the British economy to a point at which the maintenance of control over the colonies seemed to be absolutely crucial to the continued prosperity and power of the British nation, the phenomenal growth of the colonies seems to have been an ever-growing source of anxiety within the British political nation throughout the middle decades of the eighteenth century. Indeed, in all probability, there was a direct correlation between the increasing economic and strategic worth of the colonies to Britain and the amount of anxiety—much of it still existing only on a semiconscious and implicit level—among British officials over the possible loss of imperial control over the colonies. The extent to which such anxiety actually impinged upon British consciousness and underlay the redirection of British policy towards the colonies may be gauged by a significant rise in the frequency and urgency of explicit expressions of fears of colonial independence within imperial circles during the late 1740s and the 1750s. Much later, during the Stamp Act crisis, an anonymous American writer protested "the *jealous* and baseless supposition, formed on the other side of the water, that the colonists want only a favorable opportunity of setting up for themselves. This charge against us hath for many years been kept a going in *Britain*, with such diligence and management," he complained, "that the minds of the people there are almost universally embittered against us."[47] Though this writer did not even sense the deep-seated anxiety that underlay these charges, he was correct in his perception that they were everywhere manifest: in official position papers prepared by the Board of Trade, in correspondence between imperial officials and royal governors, in speeches in the House of Commons, and in a proliferating number of tracts —both published and unpublished—on the state of the colonies and the need for reforms in their administration.

If the rapid growth of the colonies with the consequent increase in their value to Britain was the single most important precondition behind the shift in British policy beginning in the late 1740s, there were two short-run conditions that, in combination, accounted for its timing. The first was the end of the era of internal domestic political instability in Britain that had begun in 1739 and was intensified by the vigorous competition for power through the mid-1740s following the fall of Sir Robert Walpole in 1742. Having already won the confidence of George II and wooed many opposition leaders to the side of the government, Henry Pelham finally managed to restore "peace to the body politic" and establish his regime on "a sound parliamentary basis" as a result of the government's overwhelming victory in the elections of 1747. "For the next seven years . . . the stability characteristic of Walpole's ministry at its zenith was again the salient feature of English government," and this freedom from domestic distractions along with the conclusion of the War of the Austrian Succession in 1748

47. "A Letter from a Plain Yeoman," May 11, 1765, in Morgan, ed., *Prologue to Revolution*, 73.

meant that British political leaders were freer than at any time since the mid-1730s to devote significant attention to the colonies.[48]

An even more important short-run condition that helped to determine the timing of this shift in policy and that itself contributed to intensify the growing anxiety and heightened sense of urgency that lay behind it was the simultaneous eruption of a series of severe political and social disturbances in many of the colonies. During the late 1740s and early 1750s, there were so many problems of such vast proportions in so many colonies that the empire seemed to authorities at a distance in London to be on the verge of disintegration. Violent factional disputes had thrown New Jersey into civil war, put an end to all legislative activity in New Hampshire and North Carolina, and seriously weakened the position of the royal administration in Jamaica, Bermuda, and New York. From New York, South Carolina, New Jersey, Bermuda, Jamaica, North Carolina, and New Hampshire—from all of the royal colonies except Massachusetts, Virginia, Barbados, and the Leeward Islands—governors complained that they were powerless to carry out imperial directions against the opposition of local interests and the exorbitant power of the local lower houses of assembly. From Bermuda there came reports that the status of the king's governor had sunk so low that one member of the assembly had even offered a reward for his assassination. So desperate was the situation throughout all the colonies that it became exceedingly difficult for imperial authorities to maintain their illusion of control over them.

The conjunction between the growing realization in Britain of the value of the colonies and the corresponding fear of the long-term implications of their rapid expansion, on the one hand, and the reestablishment of domestic political stability in Britain and the shattering of the imperial illusion of control, on the other, are thus the main reasons for the redirection of British policy beginning in the late 1740s. The Board of Trade had responded to the urgency of the situation as early as 1745

48. John B. Owen, *The Rise of the Pelhams* (London, 1957), 316–320.

by showing signs of a vigor it had not demonstrated since the earlier decades of the century, but it was not until 1748, when Lord Monson, the president of the Board, died and the War of the Austrian Succession was concluded, that the systematic attention called for by the situation was actually given to colonial affairs. When the duke of Newcastle proposed to replace the casual Monson with his brother-in-law, the duke of Leeds, who wanted "some office which required little attendance and less application," the duke of Bedford, then in charge of the colonies as secretary of state for the Southern Department, reminded Newcastle in a piece of classic understatement that it would have been "Highly improper, considering the present Situation of things, to have a nonefficient Man at the head of that Board."[49] What was needed, Bedford implied, and what they obtained in the person of George Dunk, earl of Halifax, was a man of energy and ambition who would give to colonial problems the attention they required.

Under the guidance of Halifax, who continued in office until 1761, the Board of Trade systematically set about the task of shoring up imperial authority in the colonies. It presided over a major effort to strengthen the defenses of the British colonies against French Canada by turning Nova Scotia, hitherto only a nominal British colony inhabited almost entirely by neutral and even hostile French, into a full-fledged British colony. Much more important, it prepared a series of long reports on the difficulties in most of the major trouble spots in the colonies, and the recommendations in these reports clearly revealed that, despite the long era of accommodation and easy administration since the advent of Walpole, the members of the Board and other colonial officials had not altered their long-standing conceptions about the proper relationship between the mother country and the colonies and that they were intent upon enforcing the traditional, but hitherto largely unachieved, goals of British colonial policy. Except for the Nova Scotia enterprise, which received strong backing from the administration

49. As quoted by Oliver M. Dickerson, *American Colonial Government 1696–1765* (Cleveland, 1912), 39.

and large sums of money from Parliament, none of the Board's recommendations received the necessary support from the administration, though colonial affairs did receive far more attention from the Privy Council and administration than they had in the past few decades.[50] However desperate the situation in the colonies might appear to those best informed about it, existing procedures were too cumbersome and the preoccupation with domestic matters too great to permit effective action on most colonial problems. In part to remedy this situation, Halifax pushed very hard to have himself appointed a separate secretary of state with broad jurisdiction and full responsibility for the colonies. Although he failed in this effort because of the opposition of George II and the two older secretaries of state, he did succeed in securing enlarged powers for the Board of Trade in April 1752.

Armed with its new powers, the Board embarked upon an even more vigorous campaign to bring the colonies under closer imperial control. It established a packet-boat system to provide more regular communications with the colonies, urged each of the royal governors to secure a comprehensive revisal of the laws of his colony and to send home copies of all public papers promptly, revived ancient demands for settling a permanent revenue in those colonies that had not already voted one, insisted upon the inclusion of suspending clauses in an ever-wider variety of colonial laws, vigorously denounced any efforts by the colonial lower houses that seemed in any way to threaten the prerogative of the crown, issued a number of restrictive royal instructions, and enjoined the governors "strictly to adhere to your instructions and not to deviate from them in any point but upon evident necessity justified by the particular Circumstances of the case."[51]

Although the Board of Trade's programs were greeted in many places with enthusiasm by royal officeholders and others

50. John W. Wilkes, *A Whig in Power: The Political Career of Henry Pelham* (Evanston, Ill., 1964), 200–205.

51. Board of Trade to governors, June 3, 1752, C.O. 324/5/318–323, Public Record Office.

who had long been alarmed by the imbalance of the colonial
constitutions in favor of the representative assemblies, they
were, in general, adamantly opposed by the lower houses and
other powerful local interest groups, whose members considered
them a violation of the traditional relationship between mother
country and colonies as it had gradually been worked out over
the previous century and, in many instances, an attack upon the
established constitutions of the colonies. Even with its enlarged
authority and its new assertiveness, the Board could not effectively meet such opposition. The Board could and did intimidate the governors into a strict observance of their instructions,
but that only reduced their room for maneuver when they
needed all the latitude possible to accomplish the impossible
tasks assigned to them. Thus, the Board succeeded in its objectives only in New Hampshire, where Gov. Benning Wentworth had put together a powerful political combination that
monopolized all political power and stifled opposition, and in
the new civil governments in Nova Scotia and Georgia, where
the Board took extraordinary pains "to check all Irregulari-
ties and unnecessary Deviations from the Constitution of the
Mother Country in their Infancy."[52] By the time the outbreak
of the Seven Years' War forced it to suspend its reform activities in 1756, the Board had realized that its general campaign
was a failure. Especially in the older colonies on the continent,
imperial control was not much greater in 1756 than it had been
eight years earlier. Unable to accomplish its objectives with the
prerogative powers at its command, the Board increasingly had
been driven to threaten the intervention of Parliament, and in
1757, the House of Commons actually did intervene for the
first time in the domestic affairs of a colony when it censured the
Jamaica Assembly for making extravagant constitutional claims
while resisting instructions from the Board.

Collectively, the efforts of Halifax and his colleagues between
1748 and 1756 represented a major reversal in the tone and
quality of imperial behavior toward the colonies. The full

52. [John Pownall], "General Propositions . . . ," Shelburne Papers, LXI,
559–566, William L. Clements Library, Ann Arbor, Mich.

magnitude and nature of the change can perhaps only be fully illustrated by a detailed study of imperial-colonial relations during these years. But its general character and thrust are patently clear: it amounted to a shift on the part of imperial authorities from a posture toward the colonies that was essentially permissive to one that was basically restrictive, from a traditional reliance upon normative and affectual resources for the maintenance of British control over the colonies to a dependence upon coercion. These years witnessed the revival or development and the attempted imposition of a whole series of specific policies that violated or threatened to violate in one way or another fundamental aspects of the implicit structure of colonial expectations about the nature of the imperial-colonial relationship and the proper modes of imperial behavior towards the colonies. The vast majority of those policies that colonials found so objectionable between 1759 and 1776 were, in fact, either worked out or proposed in one form or another during these years, and attempts were actually made to implement many of them.

Although the program of reform between 1748 and 1756 engendered among the colonists considerable individual, group, and local dissatisfaction with specific aspects of imperial behavior, it obviously did not create a general malaise that brought the colonists to the brink of rebellion or otherwise create a significant predisposition towards revolution on the part of the colonists. The impact of most of its particular components was too local to invite a general or collective opposition, and the program as a whole was sufficiently scattered and contingent as to conceal from those not at or near the center of colonial administration, as well as from most subsequent historians, its full depth and general character. The result was that most of the program could be interpreted by the colonists as simply additional episodes in the continuing efforts of the imperial administration, "except in some short and shining Periods, to establish," in John Dickinson's words, "a Prerogative in America quite different from that in Great Britain." Such efforts and the "invidious Distinction" they sought to create between Englishmen in the colonies and those at home had always been a source of "Uneasiness" among the colonists. But they could scarcely be regarded as new and may even have come to seem less threatening than they had been fifty or a hundred years earlier when the colonists had had less experience in coping with them.[53]

In terms of the causal significance of this change in posture and policy for the American Revolution, the fact that it yielded only minimal results is certainly equally as important as the fact that it was undertaken in the first place and much more important than the isolated and transitory pockets of discontent it created among the colonists. For the abject failure of most of the components of this early effort at reform served both to heighten imperial fears that the colonies would sooner or later get completely out of hand and to increase—almost to the point of obsession—imperial determination to secure tighter control over the colonies and to channel the colonists' expansive energies into forms of endeavors more acceptable to Britain. More specifically, this general lack of success had two results of momentous implications for the future. First, it helped to persuade many powerful figures in the British political nation that the successful exertion of British control over the colonies would require much more than the kinds of ad hoc and piecemeal solutions that had been attempted between 1748 and 1756. The widespread sentiment for a more comprehensive and sweeping program of reform was manifest in a number of new proposals by imperial officials and would-be imperial statesmen alike during and just after the war for, in the words of Malachy Postlethwayt in 1757, "a strict and speedy inquiry [by Parliament] . . . to remedy [colonial] disorders before they grow too obstinate, and to put the government and trade of all our colonies into so good and sound a state, that every one may have its due share of nutriment, and thereby be the better fitted and disposed for the uses and benefit of the whole body politic, *especially of Great-Britain, their head, mother, and*

53. Dickinson to Pitt, Dec. 21, 1765, in Morgan, ed., *Prologue to Revolution*, 120; Greene, "Political Mimesis," *AHR*, LXXV (1969–1970), 337–360.

protectress." [54] The second result, as Postlethwayt's statement suggests, was to convince imperial officials that any such reconstruction would have to be undertaken by Parliament, because "no other Authority than that of the British Parliament," as a writer later suggested in 1763, would "be regarded in the colonys or be able to awe them into acquiescence." [55]

v

It is thus primarily because of the conclusions drawn from the experience by the British political nation, rather than because of the many specific local and largely unconnected grievances they created among the colonists, that the reforms of the years 1748 to 1756 and the fundamental redirection of British policy that they represented must be given a central place in the causal pattern of the Revolution. This is not to suggest that a revolution was logically inevitable after 1748 or 1756 or that under different conditions imperial officials might not have subsequently changed their posture and policies toward the colonies. It is to say that the experience of imperial officials with the reform program between 1748 and 1756 made a severe disruption within the empire highly probable and that the empirical conditions that obtained thereafter only served to confirm the conclusions already drawn from the earlier experience and to keep imperial officials firmly on a reformist course.

Although the Seven Years' War forced the temporary abandonment of the reform program, the war experience only intensified the impulses that had lain behind it, as the weakness of British authority over the colonies was more fully exposed than ever before. Throughout the war, aggressive lower houses openly used the government's need for defense funds to pry still more authority away from the governors; many colonial traders flagrantly violated the navigation acts, in many cases with the implicit connivance of the colonial governments and even of imperial customs officials; and many of the colonial

54. Postlethwayt, *The Universal Dictionary of Trade and Commerce* ([London], 1757), I, 373. I have supplied the italics.

55. "Hints Respecting the Civil Establishment in Our American Colonies," [1763], Shelburne Papers, LXIX, 508, Clements Lib.

legislatures failed to comply with imperial requisitions for men and money for the war effort—even with the promise of reimbursement by Parliament.[56] The war experience thus reinforced preexisting imperial fears of loss of control over and potential rivalry from the colonies, deepened their suspicions that the colonists harbored secret desires for independence, and intensified their determination for reform. As soon as the British and colonial armies had defeated the French in Canada in 1759 and 1760 and colonial support for the war effort was no longer vital, imperial authorities, as Bernhard Knollenberg has shown in such rich detail, undertook a variety of new restrictive measures to bolster imperial authority over the colonies.[57] But Knollenberg was incorrect in thinking that the impulse behind these measures was new. The shift from a permissive to a restrictive policy, from the traditional reliance upon the colonists' affections and allegiance to Britain to a dependence upon coercion to keep the colonies bound closely to Britain, had already occurred during the critical years from 1748 to 1756. The new measures of 1759 to 1764 were merely a renewal and an extension of the earlier reform program.

But they were an extension within a significantly different— and far more fragile—context. The war had been a liberating and (psychologically) reinforcing experience for the colonists. That so much of the war was fought on American soil and that the British government made such an enormous effort to defend the colonies contributed to an expanded sense of colonial self-importance. Moreover, the colonists' own substantial contribution to the war effort functioned not only to raise their self-esteem as individuals but to give them as collective groups a sense of having a closer and more integral relationship to the central institutional and value systems in Britain. The war thereby produced a surge of British patriotism among the colonists and, as Richard Koebner has implied, created among them heightened expectations for a larger role within the empire,

56. See Thomas C. Barrow, *Trade and Empire: The British Customs Service in Colonial America 1660-1775* (Cambridge, Mass., 1967), 134-185, and Lawrence H. Gipson, *The British Empire before the American Revolution* (Caldwell, Idaho, and New York, 1936-1969), VI-VIII.

57. Knollenberg, *Origins of the American Revolution.*

a role that would raise the status of the colonies from dependence upon to at least a near equivalence with the mother country.[58] By contrast, the war left many members of the British political nation with feelings of bitterness and resentment towards the colonists and a determination to restore them to a proper state of dependence. Having incurred an enormous debt and a heavy tax burden in defense of the colonies and having had exaggerated reports of American opulence and the low level of taxation in the colonies,[59] they regarded colonial failures to comply with royal requisitions and other examples of resistance to or violations of imperial regulations as evidences of extreme ingratitude that could not go unremarked, lest such excessive behavior rob Britain of the large investment it had made in protecting and securing the colonies.

If the experience of the war caused the expectations of men on opposite sides of the Atlantic about the relationship between Britain and the colonies in the postwar world to veer off in such different directions, the war itself altered the very structure of that relationship. As Lawrence H. Gipson has argued, the expulsion of the French and Spanish from eastern North America removed the need for the last absolutely essential nurturing element the British had to offer the mainland colonies —protection against the French and Spanish—and thereby presumably removed a major, if by no means the most powerful, remaining block that had helped to keep whatever fantasies the colonists may have had about equivalence and independence in an unconscious and unarticulated state.[60] What has not been so clearly perceived, and what would seem to have been far more important, is that by destroying their rivals and thus making it less necessary to pacify the colonies, the British vic-

58. Koebner, *Empire*, 105–165.

59. See *The Power and Grandeur of Great-Britain Founded on the Liberty of the Colonies* (Philadelphia, 1768), 7. That the tax burden of the colonies may not have been so low, especially in terms of available liquid resources, has recently been suggested by Marvin L. Michael Kay in a case study of North Carolina: "The Payment of Provincial and Local Taxes in North Carolina, 1748–1771," *WMQ*, 3d Ser., XXVI (1969), 218–240.

60. Lawrence H. Gipson, "The American Revolution as an Aftermath of the Great War for Empire, 1754–1763," *Political Science Quarterly*, LXV (1950), 86–104.

tory left imperial authorities with a much freer hand to go ahead with their program of colonial reform. Moreover, for the first time during and after the war, the British had significant coercive resources in the colonies in the form of a large number of royal troops. By giving them an excessive confidence in their ability to suppress potential colonial opposition, the presence of these troops may well have made imperial officials less cautious in dealing with the colonies than they had been a decade earlier.

In combination, the psychological consequences and structural changes produced by the war made the relationship between Britain and the colonies much more volatile than it had been before the war. The colonists now had heightened expectations about their position in the empire and less need for Britain's protection, while British officials were bitter about colonial behavior during the war, more determined than ever to bring the colonies under closer control, persuaded that they would have to use the authority of Parliament to do so, and possessed of an army to back them up if it should be needed. Given this set of converging conditions, it was highly predictable that British officials in the 1760s would take some action, probably even by bringing parliamentary authority to bear upon the colonies in new, unaccustomed, and hence, for the colonists, illegitimate ways, that could be interpreted by the colonists as a fundamental violation of the existing relationship between them and Great Britain.

The Grenville program, of course, did precisely that. The Sugar Act and the associated reforms in the navigation system immediately followed by the Stamp Act seemed to the colonists to be an intolerable breach of traditional relationships within the empire, a sharp and deadly assault upon some of the most sacred components of the customary moral order as the colonists had come to perceive it. This program, along with the severe crisis produced by the Stamp Act, did in fact alter the quality and character of imperial-colonial relations profoundly.

The first of the imperial reform measures to affect equally all of the colonies at once, the Stamp Act forced the colonists to identify more fully than ever before some of the major ambiguities and sources of strain within the imperial-colonial connection and even to restructure their perceptions of that relationship as it had existed in the past. From the new perspective supplied by the Grenville program, they began to redefine their situation in a way that permitted them to interpret as grievances things that had previously gone unremarked and to regard components of the earlier ad hoc imperial reform program as part of a comprehensive assault upon the existing moral order that had been in progress for some time.[61] This new perspective not only made the colonists hypersensitive to any subsequent violations of that moral order but also, as Bernard Bailyn has shown so clearly, created a strong predisposition to distort as violations a variety of imperial behaviors that were not in fact violations with the result that, although the colonists actually misinterpreted such behaviors, they became grievances anyway because they were regarded as such.[62] Moreover, because the Stamp Act could be interpreted as at least a partial withdrawal of affection by the parent state, it permitted the colonists to raise to the level of consciousness and internalize whatever preexisting hostile wishes they may have had toward Britain and thereby to legitimate aggressive actions against the imperial government.

For the British political nation, on the other hand, the intensity of colonial opposition during the Stamp Act crisis only confirmed their long-standing suspicions that the colonists wanted nothing more than "to throw off all dependance and subjection."[63] How else could a community that was committed to the beliefs that Parliament was omnipotent and sovereignty indivisible interpret such an outrageous challenge to parliamentary authority? The consequences of such a development were almost too abhorrent to contemplate. The separation of the colonies would inevitably mean, many people

61. On how the Stamp Act crisis reshaped the colonists' perception of the past, see Christopher Gadsden's remarks in a letter to ————, Dec. 2, 1765, in Richard Walsh, ed., *The Writings of Christopher Gadsden* (Columbia, S.C., 1966), 67.

62. Bailyn, *Ideological Origins*, 55–159.

63. Anti-Sejanus to *London Chronicle*, Nov. 28–30, 1765, in Morgan, ed., *Prologue to Revolution*, 100.

thought, that Britain would "dwindle and decline every day in our trade, whilst they thrive and prosper exceedingly" so that Britons would "run away as fast as they can from this country to that, and Old England" would "become a poor, deserted, deplorable kingdom," reduced to impotence and robbed of its power by children of its own nurture.[64] Clearly, imperial authorities had been right in the impulse that had animated them since 1748: the colonies had to be brought under tighter control.

Over the past decade, it has become modish to dismiss colonial fears of conspiracy as they developed between 1763 and 1776 as simple paranoia arising out of a particular culturally conditioned mind set. But insofar as it implies that there was no real substance to these fears, such an interpretation is seriously deficient. Clearly, the kind of conspiracy many colonists thought existed did not: there was no secret combination of power-hungry ministers seeking to destroy liberty in America. Since 1748, however, there had been an unmistakable and continuing effort by imperial authorities to bring the colonies under tighter regulation, an effort to implement—by various forms of coercion, if necessary—an older conception of what the colonies ought to be at a point when the colonies no longer needed the kind of resources the British could offer in return for colonial acceptance of that conception. Given the colonists' customary expectations about the nature of the imperial-colonial relationship, this effort, and its many specific components, seemed to the colonists—and *was in fact*—a fundamental attack upon the extant moral order within the empire as they conceived of that order. In view of the "utter neglect paid by the State or nation of Great Britain to these Settlements," of the relative laxity of imperial controls prior to 1748, Britain's subsequent efforts at reform, at the assertion of "an absolute Dominion over the Colonies," could only be interpreted by many colonists as oppressive and self-serving, as undeniable

64. "John Ploughshare" to *London Chronicle*, Feb. 20, 1766, and Anti-Sejanus to *London Chronicle*, Jan. 23, 1766, *ibid.*, 103, 131. On the importance of the beliefs in the omnipotence of Parliament and the indivisibility of sovereignty in shaping British behavior between 1765 and 1776, see Greene, "Plunge of Lemmings," *So. Atlan. Qtly.*, LXVII (1968), 141–175.

evidence that Britain had never had much genuine affection for or interest in the colonies "until they grew into maturity and opulence," whereupon they finally attracted "not her love, but her avarice, and in consequence the imposition of her Maternal Authority."[65] In this situation, the parent-child metaphor, "so long applyed to Great Britain and her Colonys," came to be seen by the colonists in the years after 1765, not as a reference of affection, but as a degrading and absurdly inappropriate symbol of subjection.[66]

VI

The assumption behind this essay has been that any satisfactory analysis of the causes of the American Revolution has to consider not only the nature and content of colonial opposition to Britain after 1763 but also the long-term conditions that made the imperial-colonial relationship, however satisfactory it may have seemed on the surface, so fragile; and we must also consider when and why British authorities altered their traditional posture towards the colonies. What I have tried to suggest is that the change in posture began in the late 1740s and that the explanation for it is to be found primarily in the dramatic rise of the economic importance of the colonies to Britain and the attendant fears within the British political nation that the colonies would shake off their dependence and leave Britain to sink slowly back into its former undifferentiated state among the nations of western Europe. Fed by developments in the 1750s and 1760s, these fears underlay British behavior throughout the years of controversy from 1763 to 1776. Ironically, as so often happens in the affairs of men, the measures taken by imperial authorities to prevent these fears from coming true helped to bring about the very thing they most wished to prevent.

65. The quotations are from [Edward Long], "Tract against Taxing the Colonies," [*ca.* 1769], Long Papers, Additional Manuscripts 22680, fols. 18–22, British Museum.
66. George Mason to the Committee of London Merchants, June 6, 1766, in Morgan, ed., *Prologue to Revolution*, 158–159.

3

Violence

AND THE

American Revolution

by

RICHARD MAXWELL BROWN*

As Americans we approach the great Revolutionary bicentennial with a solemnity arising not merely from national pride
but from a genuine conviction that the American Revolution
was one of the most progressive events in the history of the human race. We are mindful that the American Revolution and
the Founding Fathers have been an inspiration for liberty-
loving people all over the world. To the extent that democratic
government has flourished in the world since 1776 much, very
much, is due to the American Revolution. The main historical
significance of the American Revolution to all peoples of the
world as well as ourselves has been a positive one. Studying the

* For critical readings of the original version of this essay I wish to
thank Professors William W. Abbot, Winthrop D. Jordan, and Richard
D. Brown. Although I have profited much from their comments, they
would not necessarily agree with the interpretations presented in this revised version of the essay. In fact, in a lengthy commentary Professor Abbot
strongly—and ably—rejected the original version, and I expect that he
would dissent from the current one. I am grateful, too, for the perceptive
and rigorous editing of this essay by Stephen G. Kurtz and James H. Hutson.
Any errors that might occur are, of course, entirely my own.

American Revolution from the perspective of its significant contribution to the history of American and world progress has been the preoccupation of many American historians.

It would be an oversimplified and unsophisticated view of the historical process, however, that saw an event as large and as complex as the American Revolution as having only one dimension. There is another side of the story, for the Revolution has not been an unmixed good in its nature or impact—something true of most great historical events. The Revolution has also made a contribution to the demonic side of our national history, for its origin was violent and the concept of popular sovereignty lent itself frequently to majoritarian tyranny. Long ago Herbert Butterfield reminded us that "from the work of any historian who has concentrated his researches upon any change or transition, there emerges a truth of history which seems to combine the truth of philosophy. It is nothing less than the whole of the past, with its complexity of movement, its entanglement of issues, and its intricate interactions, which produced the whole of the complex present."[1] Violence is a part of the "complex present" of American life today, just as it was a notable part of the Revolutionary era.

American violence owes much to the dead weight of unsolved problems hanging over from the past. The negative features of American history—abysmal relations between whites and peoples of other color and the brutal and brutalizing processes by which the frontier was extended and our economy industrialized—have long been known to us as violent chapters in the story of our development, but it has been difficult for us to accept that the most noble event in our history, the Revolution, was entwined with a civil violence that was often ignoble. Among the intellectual bequests of the American Revolution has been the example that violence in a good cause pays, a lesson that has been well learned by Americans. In our enthusiasm we have found many good causes, and in emulation of the Revolutionary example we have turned frequently to violence in pursuit of them.

1. Herbert Butterfield, *The Whig Interpretation of History* (London, 1931), 19.

An inheritance of violence is revealed when we examine closely the colonial tradition of insurgency that preceded the Revolution—the riot as an instrument of revolutionary direct action honed by repeated use in the colonies and Britain, the historical and communal matrix of patriotic violence in the Revolutionary cockpit, Boston, the techniques and the intellectual basis of majoritarian violence as they were perfected during the Revolutionary era, and, finally, specific examples of the way in which the symbols of the Revolution have been employed in subsequent violent group action by Americans.

I

The era of the American Revolution was marked by a series of violent outbreaks in town and countryside. A sequence of urban violence runs from the Stamp Act riots in 1765 through the Sons of Liberty violence, the Boston Massacre, the burning of the *Gaspee*, and the Boston Tea Party to the incident that triggered the Revolutionary War—the fighting at Lexington and Concord. Side by side with the urban violence of the 1760s and 1770s were outbursts of violence in rural America: the Paxton Boys uprising in Pennsylvania and the Regulator movements in North and South Carolina,[2] the development of the so-called "cracker" as a violent southern prototype on the colonial frontier,[3] the rise of lynch law in Virginia,[4] and bloody wars with Indians.[5] The 1760s and 1770s—along with the 1670s

2. Brooke Hindle, "The March of the Paxton Boys," *William and Mary Quarterly*, 3d Ser., III (1946), 461–486; James H. Hutson, *Pennsylvania Politics, 1746–1770: The Movement for Royal Government and Its Consequences* (Princeton, 1972), 84*ff*; John S. Bassett, "The Regulators of North Carolina (1765–1771)," American Historical Association, *Annual Report for the Year 1894* (Washington, D.C., 1895), 141–212; Richard Maxwell Brown, *The South Carolina Regulators* (Cambridge, Mass., 1963).

3. Brown, *South Carolina Regulators*, 184.

4. James E. Cutler, *Lynch-Law: An Investigation into the History of Lynching in the United States* (New York, 1905), 24–30.

5. Pontiac's Rebellion (1763), Lord Dunmore's War against the Shawnees (1775), and Indian wars connected with the Revolutionary War (1776–1782) are briefly treated in Ray Allen Billington, *Westward Expansion: A History of the American Frontier*, 3d ed. (New York, 1967), 137–139, 165–168, 175–191. For the Cherokee War in South Carolina (1760–1761) see Brown, *South Carolina Regulators*, 1–12. In the comment cited above Professor Abbot

and 1680s, the 1830s through the 1850s, the 1870s through the 1890s, and the 1960s—have been among the peak periods of violence in American history. While it is clear that the urban violence of the 1760s and 1770s merged directly into the Revolutionary War, the connection between the rural violence of the period and the Revolution was more indirect. Incidents of rural tumult were not usually connected with the controversy between England and the colonies, yet rural violence was obviously significant. Like outbreaks in the cities, rural turbulence added to the violent ambience of the period and helped to predispose and prepare Americans for the forceful overthrow of British authority.

Why was the era of the 1760s and 1770s such a violent period? Why did the colonists react so violently to British policy? Although violence was not the cause of the American Revolution,[6] two historical factors contributed to the Americans' violent mode of opposing British policy in the 1760s and 1770s: one was the colonial tradition of insurgency that reached back into the seventeenth century, and the other was the habitual use of the riot as a purposive weapon of protest and dissent in both Great Britain and America during the preceding two centuries.

---

correctly called attention to the impact of "organized warfare" and "the colonists' ancient sport of killing French and Indians." The absence of a substantial scholarly study linking our heritage of military warfare with our history of domestic violence is a notable lacuna in our literature on American violence; important as it is, it is beyond the scope of this essay. In my article "Historical Patterns of Violence in America" in Hugh Davis Graham and Ted R. Gurr, eds., *The History of Violence in America* (New York, 1969), 66–67, I briefly noted "Indian Wars" as being among the major contributors to the history of American violence and emphasized that from 1607 to the final massacre at Wounded Knee in 1890 white warfare with Indians "has done much to shape our proclivity to violence." Scholarship on the warfare of the colonists with the French and the Indians is bountiful. Aside from Francis Parkman's classic volumes and those of the late Lawrence H. Gipson, I have space only to cite Howard H. Peckham, *The Colonial Wars, 1689–1762* (Chicago, 1964), for a pointed general treatment, and Douglas E. Leach, *Flintlock and Tomahawk: New England in King Philip's War* (New York, 1966), which skillfully delineates the typically brutalizing effects of that late 17th-century Indian war on the white colonists.

6. For the problem of American Revolutionary causation see the essays in this book by Bernard Bailyn, Jack P. Greene, Rowland Berthoff and John M. Murrin, and Edmund S. Morgan.

In the period from 1645 to 1760 there were eighteen insurgent movements directed by white Americans toward the overthrow of colonial governments. Among these eighteen insurrections were five major ones: Bacon's Rebellion in Virginia (1676–1677) and Leisler's Rebellion in New York (1689), the overthrow of Gov. Edmund Andros in Massachusetts (1689), Coode's Rebellion in Maryland (1689), and the overturn of the proprietary government in South Carolina (1719).[7] Medium-grade uprisings were the Ingle-Claiborne insurrection in Maryland (1645–1646), Fendall's first rebellion in Maryland (1660), the New Jersey antiquitrent uprising (1672), Culpeper's Rebellion in North Carolina (1677–1678), the overthrow of Gov. Seth Sothel in North Carolina (1689), the ouster of Gov. John Colleton in South Carolina (1690), and Cary's rebellion in North Carolina (1709–1711).[8] Finally, there were such minor insurgencies as the Davyes-Pate uprising in Maryland (1676), the second Fendall rebellion in Maryland (1680–1681), Gove's insurrection in New Hampshire (1682–1683), the Essex County uprising in Massachusetts (1687), the rebellion against Gov. Andrew Hamilton in New Jersey (1699), and Hambright's march on the Pennsylvania government in 1755.[9] Only six of these uprisings were violent, and only one—Bacon's Rebellion in Virginia—produced major violence. More typical of these eighteen colo-

7. Wilcomb E. Washburn, *The Governor and the Rebel: A History of Bacon's Rebellion in Virginia* (Chapel Hill, 1957); Jerome R. Reich, *Leisler's Rebellion: A Study of Democracy in New York, 1664–1720* (Chicago, 1953); William H. Whitmore, ed., *The Andros Tracts* (Boston, 1868), I, 11–12, and *passim*; Michael G. Hall, Lawrence H. Leder, and Michael G. Kammen, eds., *The Glorious Revolution in America: Documents on the Colonial Crisis* (Chapel Hill, 1964), 9–79, 143–211; M. Eugene Sirmans, *Colonial South Carolina: A Political History, 1663–1763* (Chapel Hill, 1966), 126–128.

8. Wesley Frank Craven, *The Southern Colonies in the Seventeenth Century* (Baton Rouge, 1949), 233–234, 297–299; Richard P. McCormick, *New Jersey from Colony to State, 1609–1789* (Princeton, 1964), 26–27; Craven, *Southern Colonies*, 409–410; Samuel A'Court Ashe, *History of North Carolina* (Greensboro, N.C., 1908–1925), I, 160–178; Sirmans, *Colonial South Carolina*, 47–48.

9. Craven, *Southern Colonies*, 411, 412; Everett S. Stackpole, *History of New Hampshire* (New York, 1916), I, 133–136; Thomas F. Waters, *Ipswich in the Massachusetts Bay Colony* (Ipswich, Mass., 1905), I, 238–267; Edwin P. Tanner, *The Province of New Jersey: 1664–1738* (New York, 1908), 95–96; Hutson, *Pennsylvania Politics*, 25–26.

nial upheavals were the seven armed uprisings unaccompanied by violence and the five nonviolent uprisings that employed neither force nor the explicit threat of force.[10]

While bloodshed was not a predominant characteristic of these eighteen colonial uprisings, they were notable examples of pervasive antiauthoritarianism in colonial America that came to the surface on occasion and that in the Revolutionary period would flare into violent rebellion. Despite the relative lack of violence the colonial insurgencies were far from ineffective: six were successful, six gained temporary success before ultimately failing, and only six were outright failures.[11] Furthermore the insurrections were widespread. Nine of the thirteen colonies were affected, and five of the most important colonies —Massachusetts, New York, Pennsylvania, Virginia, and South Carolina—had insurgencies. Aside from the wide geographical distribution of the uprisings, several had a deep impact upon the history of colonial America. Bacon's Rebellion in Virginia and Leisler's Rebellion in New York were among the most important events in the history of early America, for each grew out of deep-seated tensions and each had a long-lasting effect on the subsequent history of their colonies. Three other rebellions—the overthrow of Governor Andros in Massachusetts, Coode's Rebellion in Maryland, and the shattering of the proprietary regime in South Carolina—also permanently altered the course of history in their colonies.

It is noteworthy that these insurgencies were concentrated in the last three decades of the seventeenth century. Thirteen of the eighteen uprisings took place from 1670 to 1700, among

10. The six violent rebellions were Ingle-Claiborne, Gove's, anti-Hamilton, Cary's, South Carolina antiproprietary, and Bacon's. The seven nonviolent armed uprisings were Culpeper's, Leisler's, Coode's, anti-Andros, anti-Sothel, anti-Colleton, and Hambright's. The five nonforceful uprisings were Fendall's first and second, New Jersey antiquitrent, Davyes-Pate, and Essex County.

11. The six successful insurgencies were Culpeper's, anti-Andros, Coode's, anti-Colleton, anti-Sothel, and South Carolina antiproprietary. The six temporarily successful rebellions were Ingle-Claiborne, Fendall's first, New Jersey antiquitrent, Bacon's, Leisler's, and Cary's. The six failed rebellions were Davyes-Pate, Fendall's second, Gove's, Essex County, anti-Hamilton, and Hambright's.

them the crucial Bacon's, Culpeper's, Leisler's, anti-Andros, and Coode's rebellions.[12] Historians have noted the turbulent character of late seventeenth-century colonial America, and one, Clarence L. Ver Steeg, has interpreted the late seventeenth and and early eighteenth century as a time of "transition" when "English colonies became American provinces," a period of marked social instability causing "a serious strain upon people and institutions."[13] In view of the ubiquity of insurgent activity it would be no great exaggeration to call the years 1670 to 1700 the first American revolutionary period.

There were also six black insurrectionary plots or uprisings in colonial America before 1760. Slave uprising plots were uncovered and broken in New Jersey in 1734, in Maryland in the late 1730s, and in South Carolina in 1740.[14] The three black uprisings that did occur were far more violent than most of the white uprisings. Violent black upheavals occurred in New York City in 1712 and 1741 and in South Carolina (the Stono insurrection) in 1739.[15] All six of the black plots or uprisings came during a period, 1712 to 1741, when, with one exception, white insurrections had run their course.[16] All of the black plots or uprisings failed, and none had the impact upon their colonies that Bacon's or Leisler's rebellions, for example, had on theirs. But the violence of the three black insurrections that actually occurred (along with the brutality with which they were sup-

12. The other uprisings that took place in the period from 1670 to 1700 were Gove's, New Jersey antiquitrent, Davyes-Pate, Fendall's second, Essex County, anti-Sothel, anti-Colleton, and anti-Hamilton.

13. Clarence L. Ver Steeg, *The Formative Years, 1607–1763* (New York, 1964), chap. 6, quoting from 129, 149. Four uprisings occurred in 1689: anti-Sothel in North Carolina, Coode's in Maryland, Leisler's in New York, and anti-Andros in Massachusetts. These rebellions were all connected with the Glorious Revolution in England, which seemed to elicit the outbreaks in America, although the latter sprang from deep-seated, indigenous American grievances. See Hall, Leder, and Kammen, eds., *Glorious Revolution in America.*

14. Winthrop D. Jordan, *White over Black: The Development of American Attitudes Toward the Negro, 1550–1812* (Chapel Hill, 1968), 114, 121.

15. *Ibid.*, 116–121. See also Daniel Horsmanden, *The New York Conspiracy* (1810), ed. Thomas J. Davis (Boston, 1971), with Davis's perceptive introduction, vii–xxv.

16. The exception was the overthrow of the proprietary government in South Carolina in 1719.

pressed) points to a significant degree of psychic tension between whites and blacks in colonial America. As in the case of the white rebellions it is possible to connect the black uprisings with a major trend in American colonial history. Winthrop D. Jordan has seen these black disturbances "which affected many colonies around 1740" as "suggestive of widespread heightening of diffuse social tensions throughout the colonies" and has noted that "the disturbances coincided with the Great Awakening of religious excitement."[17] Although white people looked with horror and morbid fascination upon the idea of black rebellion, the black uprisings may have served to keep the idea of insurrection in the background of white consciousness long after the main period of colonial insurgency had come to an end.

Supplementing the colonial tradition of insurgency was a background of noninsurrectionary riotous activity that preceded the Revolutionary period for more than a century and in effect came to a peak in it. One of the settled convictions of recent scholarship on the eighteenth century in Great Britain and America is that the riot was a purposive instrument of social, economic, and political protest action. George Rudé, the leading historian of early modern riots in England and France, has done much to discredit the belief, going back to Gustave Le Bon, that the riotous mob is mainly a psychological phenomenon inchoate in purpose, uncontrolled in action, and not subject to analysis in terms of any sort of rational behavior.[18] In this country a similar view of the riot as a purposive agent of group action has been the theme of Arthur M. Schlesinger, Sr., Edmund S. and Helen M. Morgan, Lloyd I. Rudolph, Bernard Bailyn, Gordon S. Wood, William Ander Smith, Jesse Lemisch, G. B. Warden, and Pauline Maier.[19]

17. Jordan, *White over Black*, 120.

18. George Rudé, *The Crowd in History: A Study of Popular Disturbances in France and England, 1730–1848* (New York 1964); Gustave Le Bon, *The Crowd: A Study of the Popular Mind* (New York, 1896).

19. Arthur M. Schlesinger, Sr., "Political Mobs and the American Revolution, 1765–1776," American Philosophical Society, *Proceedings*, LXXIX (1955), 244–250; Edmund S. and Helen M. Morgan, *The Stamp Act Crisis: Prologue to Revolution*, rev. ed. (New York, 1963); Lloyd I. Rudolph, "The

Writing recently of the directed and semilegitimate character of eighteenth-century American rioters, Pauline Maier has
noted that "not all eighteenth-century mobs simply defied the
law: some used extralegal means to implement official demands
to enforce laws not otherwise enforceable, others in effect
extended the law in urgent situations beyond technical limits.
Since leading eighteenth-century Americans had known many
occasions on which mobs took on the defense of public welfare,
which was, after all, the stated purpose of government, they
were less likely to deny popular upheavals all legitimacy than
are modern leaders. While not advocating popular uprisings,
they could still grant such incidents an established and necessary role in free societies, one that made them an integral and
even respected element of the political order."[20] Similarly William Ander Smith has pointed to an eighteenth-century "mob
tradition, which served Englishmen and Scots as an extralegal

Eighteenth-Century Mob in America and Europe," *American Quarterly*,
XI (1959), 447–469; Bernard Bailyn, ed., *Pamphlets of the American Revolution, 1750–1776* (Cambridge, Mass., 1965), I, 581–584; Gordon S. Wood,
"A Note on Mobs in the American Revolution," *WMQ*, 3d Ser., XXIII
(1966), 635–642; Jesse Lemisch, "Jack Tar in the Streets: Merchant Seamen
in the Politics of Revolutionary America," *ibid.*, 3d Ser., XXV (1968), 371–
407; William Ander Smith, "Anglo-Colonial Society and the Mob: 1740–
1775" (Ph.D. diss., Claremont Graduate School, 1965); G. B. Warden,
Boston: 1689–1776 (Boston, 1970); Pauline Maier, "Popular Uprisings and
Civil Authority in Eighteenth-Century America," *WMQ*, 3d Ser., XXVII
(1970), 3–35. All of these scholars reject the dominant view of a generation
ago (e.g., Philip G. Davidson, *Propaganda and the American Revolution,
1763–1783* [Chapel Hill, 1941]) that 18th-century mobs in Revolutionary
America were not purposively pursuing their own aims but were manipu-
lated by the propaganda of calculating leaders such as Samuel Adams. The
older mob-manipulation viewpoint has been held in recent years by Clifford
K. Shipton in biographical sketches of Harvard alumni (Samuel Adams,
James Bowdoin, and others who took part in the patriotic movement) in
Shipton's volumes of *Sibley's Harvard Graduates: Biographical Sketches of
Those Who Attended Harvard College* . . . (Cambridge and Boston,
1933–), IX–XV, and in Hiller B. Zobel, *The Boston Massacre* (New York,
1970) . Lengthy critiques of Zobel's book have been published by Jesse Lem-
isch in the *Harvard Law Review*, LXXXIV (1970), 485–504, and by Pauline
Maier in *The Journal of Interdisciplinary History*, II (1971), 119–135.
Rudolph, writing before Rudé's work on European mobs had made its
full impact, attributed purposive action to American mobs while denying
it to those of Europe.

20. Maier, "Popular Uprisings," *WMQ*, 3d Ser., XXVII (1970), 4.

channel by which to make their grievances known and felt by a government which was more concerned with political broker- age and overseas empire than with internal social stresses. Since concern for English rights and liberties was a concept deeply imbedded in the society, it came to be tacitly accepted by that society that mob violence in defense of those rights or in protest against some major grievances was in itself a legitimate, if not a legal right of freeborn English subjects." [21]

Rioting was not merely a colonial phenomenon. Smith has shown that in England from 1740 to 1775 there were 159 riots.[22] In the American colonies from 1641 to 1759 there were at least 40 riots (see Appendix 1). Since the listing in Appendix 1 is by no means definitive, but is a selective list based on secondary sources, and since it lists singly several events that produced more than one riot (e.g., the boundary riots in various colonies), a round number of 75 to 100 riots would not be an excessive estimate of the total number of riots that actually occurred from 1641 to 1759.[23] In the colonies from 1760 to 1775 riot activity surged upward as the Revolutionary crisis mounted. In that six- teen-year period there were at least 44 riots (see Appendix 2).[24]

Furthermore the riots were truly Anglo-American in impact, for riots on one side of the Atlantic were watched closely on the other, given the lag in time for communications to cross the ocean. In 1768 Samuel Adams, Boston's patriot agitator and something of a specialist in regard to group violence, remarked on riot activity in England: "There, we are told, is the Weavers mob, the Seamens Mob, the Taylors mob, the Coal Miners mob . . . and in short it is to be feared the whole Kingdome, always excepting the [King] and the P[arliament], will unite in one

21. Smith, "Anglo-Colonial Society and the Mob," 1.

22. *Ibid.*, 31–32.

23. The listing in Appendix 1 is based almost entirely upon the riots cited in Maier, "Popular Uprisings," *WMQ*, 3d Ser., XXVII (1970), 3–35, and David M. Matteson, "Riots in the United States," MS, David Maydole Matteson Papers, Library of Congress. I am indebted to Prof. Robert V. Bruce for calling Matteson's manuscript to my attention.

24. The number 44 is an understatement for the total of riots in the period from 1760 to 1775. The approach in compiling Appendix 2 was the same as for Appendix 1; it is therefore subject to the same limitations.

general scene of tumult." [25] As in America there were peak years
of riot activity in England: 6 riots in 1740, 13 in the years 1749
to 1753, 31 in 1756 to 1758, and 84 in 1765 to 1770.[26] Of the
159 riots in England from 1740 to 1775 certain types—in response to social and economic dislocations in a rapidly changing
economy—were predominant. There were 96 riots induced by
food shortages and 20 riots stemming from industrial and commercial stresses. Rural riots against land enclosures and turn-
pike management and riots against impressment and other
activities of the military were common.[27]

Amidst the welter of British mob activity in the eighteenth
century there were three riots that were in themselves cause
célèbres and models for the type of controlled urban violence
that the colonists leveled against British policy in the 1760s and
1770s. These three riots were the Bushell (or Glasgow) riot of
1725, the Porteous (or Edinburgh) riot of 1736, and the London
"Jew Bill" turmoil of 1753. In each one of these events (which
were major ones not because of the casualties involved—for
those were light—but because of their notoriety) violence was
used or threatened in order to protest government action in
the same way that during the 1760s and 1770s violence was used
by urban Americans to protest and stymie British policy.

The Bushell riot of 1725 came about when Glasgow citizens
rose violently in protest against a new tax on malt. They destroyed the dwelling of their member of Parliament, Daniel
Campbell (whom they believed to have supported the tax), in
much the same way that forty years later an angry but con-

25. Smith, "Anglo-Colonial Society and the Mob," 68, quoting from
Harry A. Cushing, ed., *The Writings of Samuel Adams* (New York, 1904),
I, 237. For the reporting of British riots in American colonial newspapers
see Smith, 89.

26. Smith, "Anglo-Colonial Society and the Mob," 31–32.

27. *Ibid.* A recent work emphasizing the "stunningly rapid transformation" of the British economy in the mid-18th century and citing relevant
authorities in the literature of economic history is Michael G. Kammen,
*Empire and Interest: The American Colonies and the Politics of Mercan-
tilism* (Philadelphia, 1970), vi, chap. 4. Smith, "Anglo-Colonial Society
and the Mob," sees British mob activity within the context of an economy
of scarcity and American mob activity in the context of an economy of
abundance.

trolled Boston mob wrecked the home of Lt. Gov. Thomas Hutchinson. To quell the violence Captain Bushell was sent to Glasgow where soldiers under his command fired into the mob and killed several citizens. Bushell was tried in court and convicted of murder but was pardoned by the crown. The city was fined by Parliament to pay for the damages to Campbell's house.[28]

The protest against the malt tax faded, but the violence of Captain Bushell's men and his pardon had not been forgotten by Edinburgh citizens when eleven years later in 1736 a similar situation arose. In Edinburgh two smugglers had been captured, tried, and convicted in a very unpopular decision. In a courtroom scuffle one of them escaped. The other, Alexander Wilson, became a hero, and on the day of his scheduled execution Capt. John Porteous was ordered to call the entire city guard to duty to forestall disorder. After the hanging of Wilson the mob began to harass Porteous and his men with the result that the soldiers fired into the crowd, killed six, and wounded eleven. Porteous was tried and convicted of murder. When the queen gave him a six-week stay of execution a mob (fearing that like Captain Bushell earlier Porteous would go free) broke into the jail, took Porteous out, and hanged him. The murder of Porteous was a most orderly, well-controlled mob action comparable later to the well-planned and well-executed Stamp Act riots and Tea Party in Boston. Parliament responded to the disciplined protest of the Edinburgh mob by fining the city £2,000.[29]

The parallels between the Bushell and Porteous riots and the Boston Massacre of 1770 are striking, and the Scottish riots were in the minds of Americans and Englishmen in the 1760s and 1770s as colonial violence spiraled upward. Capt. Thomas Preston, who commanded the British soldiers that fired on Crispus Attucks and the others in the Boston Massacre, had not forgotten the experience of Captain Porteous. His gratitude to John Adams and Josiah Quincy, Jr., who defended him suc-

28. Smith, "Anglo-Colonial Society and the Mob," 92–93, 99.
29. *Ibid.*, 94–99.

cessfully in court, was tempered by his fear (unjustified, as it turned out) that like Porteous he would be killed by a mob when released from jail.[30] In 1774 Lord North and his ministry were specifically guided by the earlier precedents of the Bushell and Porteous riots when confronted with the problem of dealing with the Boston Tea Party. Lord North sponsored the Coercive Acts in conscious emulation of Parliament's action a half century earlier in punishing Glasgow and Edinburgh.[31] Although the Parliament led by Lord North did not fine Boston or Massachusetts, as had been the case with Glasgow and Edinburgh, the principle of municipal and provincial punishment was embodied in two of the Coercive Acts; the Boston Port Act struck a vital blow at the city by closing its port to shipping, and the Massachusetts Government Act chastised the province as a whole by substantially reducing Massachusetts's chartered privileges of self-government.

An even more striking example of the effectiveness of urban mob action in Britain—one that was a portent of similar mob protest in America against the Stamp Act—occurred in London in 1753 in connection with the so-called "Jew Bill." "The Jewish Naturalization Bill of 1753 was an innocuous enough measure," William Ander Smith has written. "It merely provided that Jews wealthy enough to do so could get private naturalization bills for themselves introduced in Parliament, so avoiding anti-semitic slights and insults that were a part of public naturalization at Magistrate's Court." In sponsoring this legislation Henry Pelham and the duke of Newcastle hoped to "provide some token reward to [Jews] like Sampson Gideon, who had aided the government so ably in . . . the time of the Forty-Five Rebellion." But with a parliamentary election coming up, opponents of the Pelhams seized on the Jewish naturalization enactment as a potentially winning issue. With the London lower class being rabidly anti-Semitic and the middle and upper classes "frightened with stories about Jews taking over control of English trade and banking," the populace was soon agitated. As

30. Zobel, *Boston Massacre*, 216, 236, 266.
31. Smith, "Anglo-Colonial Society and the Mob," 91.

turmoil boiled in the streets the cautious Pelhams beat a swift retreat and brought about repeal of the act.[32]

Paralleling and notably similar to the British mob tradition was an indigenous colonial mob tradition that, like the tradition of insurgency, stretched back into the seventeenth century. The forty riots from 1641 to 1759 were characterized by diversity of type and by widespread geographical distribution (see Appendix 1). Economic troubles accounted for eleven riots;[33] intercolonial boundary disputes caused seven;[34] six were political or economic-political;[35] religious and maritime controversies spawned three each;[36] elections, impressment of seamen, and social factors caused two riots each;[37] one riot was a protest against the customs system;[38] and three riots fall under mis-

32. *Ibid.*, 103–108. In an important article, "The Charleston Mob and the Evolution of Popular Politics in Revolutionary South Carolina, 1765–1784," *Perspectives in American History*, IV (1970), 173–198, that further documents the current image of the purposive, controlled character of Revolutionary-era mobs, Pauline Maier concisely notes that "throughout the eighteenth century the mob had played an important role in British politics. It had forced Walpole's abandonment of his excise scheme in 1733, defeated the Jew bill two decades later, caused the repeal of the cider tax in 1766, and again in 1780, the year of the bloody Gordon riots, the mob opposed legislative concessions to Irish Catholics. The Americans understood this process" (p. 181).

33. The 11 economic riots were Virginia tobacco (1682), New Jersey land (1699–1700, 1745–1754), Massachusetts food (1710, 1713), Massachusetts anti-markethouse (1737), Connecticut ship (1724), North Carolina antiquitrent (1737), Pennsylvania fish-dam (1738), New York antirent (1751–1757), and North Carolina land-tax (1759).

34. The seven intercolonial boundary disputes were Rhode Island (1663–1750), Connecticut (1663–1750), Massachusetts (1663–1750), New York-Connecticut (1718), New York-New Jersey (1719–1764), Pennsylvania-Maryland (1721–1737), and New York-Massachusetts (1751–1757).

35. The six political or economic-political riots were Rhode Island (1654–1655), North Carolina Capt. Gibbs (1690), South Carolina (1703), North Carolina (1718), New Hampshire mast-tree (1734), and New Hampshire surveyor of woods (1754).

36. The three religious riots were in Rhode Island (1641), New York (1703–1710), and in Flatbush, N.Y. (1711). The three maritime riots were in New Hampshire (1699), New York (1705), and Portsmouth, N.H. (1757).

37. The two election riots were in Pennsylvania (1742, 1750). The two impressment riots were in New York (1711) and Massachusetts (1747). The two riots caused by social factors were in Pennsylvania (1704) and Connecticut (1722).

38. The customs riot was in Rhode Island (1719).

cellaneous headings.[39] Of the forty riots seven may be seen as being generally anti-British in character.[40] The riots were well distributed among eleven colonies: New York had eight; Massachusetts had seven; New Hampshire and Pennsylvania had five each; Rhode Island, Connecticut, and North Carolina had four each; New Jersey had three; Maryland had two; and Virginia and South Carolina had one each.[41] There was also a fairly even chronological distribution of the riots by decades as follows:[42]

Decade	Riots	Decade	Riots
1640s	1	1700s	8
1650s	2	1710s	12
1660s	3	1720s	7
1670s	3	1730s	10
1680s	4	1740s	7
1690s	6	1750s	12

Three riots may be briefly cited as examples of mob action in the pre-Revolutionary period. First, Virginia was the scene of the tobacco plant cutters' riots of 1682. These riots, originating north of the York River in Gloucester County, arose in response to the Virginia assembly's failure to restrict tobacco cultivation in the face of an economically ruinous oversupply. Seized by deep emotions that were near hysteria, bands of tobacco planters spread into neighboring Middlesex, New Kent, and other counties, systematically cutting down the young, growing plants. Four leaders of the movement were brought to trial, and two of them were executed.[43] This may have been the first example in American history of the technique of dealing, though il-

39. Riots of a miscellaneous nature were in Maryland (1654), Massachusetts (1737), and Brentwoods, N.H. (1757).

40. The seven anti-British riots were in New York City (1711), Rhode Island (1719), New Hampshire (1734), Massachusetts (1747), and New Hampshire (1754 and two in 1757).

41. The colony-by-colony total adds up to 44 rather than 40, because boundary-dispute riots always involved two colonies.

42. The decade-by-decade total is 75 rather than 40, because many of the riots—e.g., the New Jersey land riots—spanned more than one decade.

43. Thomas J. Wertenbaker, *Virginia Under the Stuarts: 1607–1688* (Princeton, 1914), 232–238.

legally, with agricultural distress by destroying surplus crops or products. Crop restriction by the federal government has been familiar in our own time, but sometimes in the past—as in seventeenth-century Virginia—it has been accomplished by extralegal and violent action.[44]

A second example of the colonial riot may be seen in the New Jersey land riots of the 1740s and 1750s. The trouble grew out of an old controversy that had settlers on one side and the East Jersey proprietors on the other. The settlers claimed to hold their land by virtue of the so-called Elizabethtown titles and by purchases from the Indians, while the proprietors denied the validity of such titles. The settlers first rioted against the proprietary land policy in Newark in 1745, but in succeeding years and well into the 1750s the violence spread into the counties of Middlesex, Somerset, Morris, and Hunterdon. The rioters developed a large and powerful organization in northern and western Jersey. "Jails were wrecked," writes Richard P. McCormick, "sheriffs and judicial officers were threatened, and armed bands took vengeance on those who held titles from the proprietors." Law enforcement was powerless, and, states McCormick, "doubtless these lessons" of the efficacy of violent force "were remembered by the patriot leaders two decades later."[45]

Probably the most stunning of the pre-1760 urban American riots was the Boston anti-impressment riot of 1747. America's earliest cities—the bustling colonial ports of Boston, Newport, New York, Philadelphia, Charleston, and Norfolk—had their share of tumult, contributed in large part by the violence-prone, lower-class population attached to the maritime industry—seamen, dock workers, laborers, and artisans. On November 17, 1747, this element of the Boston population—"armed seamen, servants, Negroes, and others"—rioted against an attempt to impress local men for service in the Royal Navy. For three days the rioters dominated the city, forcing the governor to flee to an island in the bay. The freeing of most of the impressed men

44. On a 20th-century violent movement organized to restrict the growth of tobacco, see James O. Nall, *The Tobacco Night Riders of Kentucky and Tennessee: 1905–1909* (Louisville, 1939).

45. McCormick, *New Jersey*, 77–78. See also Gary S. Horowitz, "New Jersey Land Riots, 1745–1755" (Ph.D. diss., Ohio State University, 1966).

amounted to a substantial victory for the rioters.[46] There was no attempt by the rioters to overturn the social and economic structure of Boston, and once the rioters had gained their anti-impressment objective they subsided.

With ample precedent, then, in both British and colonial experience, it is no wonder that the urban patriots of the 1760s and 1770s used the riot as an instrument of resistance to and rebellion against' British policy. In the period from 1760 to 1775 there were at least forty-four riots in the colonies (see Appendix 2). There was a distinct urban tenor to the rioting, for eight of the largest American cities had more than half of the rioting—twenty-eight of forty-four riots. New York City had five; Newport had six; Boston, Norfolk, and Providence had eleven; New London and New Haven had two apiece; and Philadelphia was relatively calm with only two. Rhode Island led all the colonies with thirteen; New York and Massachusetts had seven each; Pennsylvania and Connecticut had four apiece; Virginia had three; North Carolina had two; and New Jersey, Maryland, Georgia, South Carolina, and present Vermont had one each. There were three riots in 1760, none in 1761 and 1762, one in 1763, and from 1764 to 1775 the number of riots annually varied from two to seven with four or five per year being common. The revolutionary character of the times is illustrated by the thirty (of forty-four) riots that were anti-British in one way or another. The thirty anti-British riots included seventeen riots directed against customs enforcement and six in protest over the impressment of Americans for the Royal Navy. The remaining twenty-one riots arose from a variety of causes including politics, economics, morals offenses, Indian relations, religion, and crime.

In resistance to the Stamp Act, Edmund S. Morgan has written, "Boston showed the way."[47] This judgment of Boston's

46. Thomas Hutchinson, *The History of Massachusetts-Bay, from the Charter of King William and Queen Mary, in 1691, Until the Year 1750* (Boston, 1767), 330–333. See also Carl Bridenbaugh, *Cities in Revolt: Urban Life in America, 1743–1776* (New York, 1964), 114–117, and Warden, *Boston*, 135–138.

47. Edmund S. Morgan, *The Birth of the Republic, 1763–89* (Chicago, 1956), 20.

importance may be extended to the remainder of the entire pre-1776 period, for Boston violence was a major feature in the trend to the Revolutionary War. While the Stamp Act riots inaugurated Boston's violent role in the Revolutionary era, there were three other significant Boston riots among the forty-four that occurred in colonial America from 1760 to 1775; the sloop *Liberty* (anticustoms) riot of 1768, the Boston Massacre of 1770, and the Boston Tea Party of 1773. Although many cities experienced violence (especially New York and Newport), the cockpit of urban Revolutionary turbulence was Boston.

Behind the violence in Boston was the city's remarkable patriot infrastructure of the 1760s and 1770s, headed by James Otis, Samuel Adams, and their colleagues. The infrastructure grew out of the convergence of a historical tradition with a contemporary situation. The historical tradition was the Cooke-Caucus heritage of popular politics in Boston, and the contemporary situation was the diversity and complexity of Boston's social, economic, and political life in the 1760s, which formed a fertile seedbed for the growth of the anti-British movement.

Boston's patriot infrastructure of the 1760s was a sophisticated updating of "America's first urban political 'machine,'" whose basis was first laid in late seventeenth-century Boston by Elisha Cooke, Sr. His son, Elisha Cooke, Jr., carried on and perfected the organization to the extent that the historian of the Cooke political tradition, G. B. Warden, has stated that he "contributed more than anyone else to the public life of colonial Boston."[48] In Elisha Cooke, Jr.'s, time the machine expanded its base from its original late seventeenth-century locus among the property holders of the South End to a broader city-wide character. Following the younger Cooke's death in 1737 the machine,

48. Warden, *Boston*, 93. This entire paragraph is based on Warden's valuable book. It has been customary for historians (e.g., John C. Miller, *Sam Adams: Pioneer in Propaganda* [Boston, 1936]) to cite the link between the Cooke tradition and Samuel Adams, but it has remained for Warden to give us—in this long-needed study of the politics of colonial Boston—the first comprehensive treatment of the connection. Warden's Ph.D. dissertation, "Boston Politics, 1692–1765" (Yale University, 1966), is helpful too, for it contains a valuable unpublished analysis of the era of Elisha Cooke, Sr.

or "Caucus" as it came to be known, remained a vital factor in the politics of Boston. It is significant that the father of patriot Samuel Adams was a leading member of the Caucus and that the young Samuel Adams was literally raised in the Cooke-Caucus tradition. Warden has emphasized that the Boston "political alliances" that lasted until 1776 originated in the 1730s, the era of the original Caucus Club that stemmed from the leadership of the two Cookes.

The patriot infrastructure of the 1760s was most intricately connected with Boston's vibrant associational life.[49] First, there were the patriot organizations themselves: the Loyal Nine (which has been portrayed as both the genesis and the executive committee of the Sons of Liberty) and the much broader, more inclusive Sons of Liberty. Then there were the highly political Caucus Clubs: the original Caucus Club, of which Samuel Adams was a leading member, and the three area Caucus Clubs —South End, North End, and Middle—that emerged during the decade of the 1760s. The tireless Sam Adams was a member of all three of the newer Caucus Clubs as well as the old one. The

49. The following sketch of the patriot infrastructure in Boston is based on the standard authorities among which the following have been most helpful: Charles W. Akers, *Called Unto Liberty: A Life of Jonathan Mayhew, 1720–1766* (Cambridge, Mass., 1964); George P. Anderson, "Ebenezer Mackintosh: Stamp Act Rioter and Patriot," Colonial Society of Massachusetts, *Transactions*, XXVI (1927), 15–64, 348–361; Bernard Bailyn, "Religion and Revolution: Three Biographical Studies," *Perspectives*, IV (1970), 85–169; Bridenbaugh, *Cities in Revolt*; Alice M. Baldwin, *The New England Clergy and the American Revolution* (Durham, N.C., 1928); John Cary, *Joseph Warren: Physician, Politician, Patriot* (Urbana, Ill., 1961); Alan and Katherine Day, "Another Look at the Boston 'Caucus,' " *Journal of American Studies*, V (1971), 19–42; Benjamin W. Labaree, *The Boston Tea Party* (New York, 1964); R. S. Longley, "Mob Activities in Revolutionary Massachusetts," *New England Quarterly*, VI (1933), 98–130; Miller, *Sam Adams*; Morgan and Morgan, *Stamp Act Crisis*; Arthur M. Schlesinger, Sr., *Prelude to Independence: The Newspaper War on Britain, 1764–1776* (New York, 1958); John Shy, *Toward Lexington: The Role of the British Army in the Coming of the American Revolution* (Princeton, 1965); Page Smith, *John Adams* (Garden City, N.Y., 1962); Smith, "Anglo-Colonial Society and the Mob"; Warden, *Boston*; Zobel, *Boston Massacre*. Very valuable are Shipton's biographical sketches of the following Harvard graduates (graduating class indicated) in *Sibley's Harvard Graduates*, IX–XV: Samuel Swift '35, Samuel Adams '40, Samuel Cooper '43, James Otis '43, Thomas Cushing '44, James Bowdoin '45, Benjamin Church '54, John Hancock '54, John Avery '59, Joseph Warren '59, and Josiah Quincy, Jr., '63.

political Caucus Clubs were only four among numerous clubs, most of them social or occupational in character. Core patriot leaders were prominent members in many of these clubs, some of which were founded with political purposes in mind or were "politicized" by the activities of the patriot members. A notable example was the Saint Andrew's lodge of the "ancient" order of freemasons, a lodge that was founded in the early 1760s and that quickly came to be in effect a whig political club for rising young Bostonians such as Joseph Warren and Paul Revere. This was in contrast to the established Saint John's lodge of the "modern" order of freemasonry, which tended to include older, wealthier men of conservative political inclinations.[50]

Closely linked to Boston's club life were the taverns where so many of the clubs met. Among the taverns of Boston—which then as now tended to attract clienteles knit together by common political, social, and occupational interests—was the Green Dragon, which was owned by the patriot-dominated Saint Andrew's lodge and which became a favorite meeting place of the Sons of Liberty and whiggish intellectuals. The Salutation Tavern had by custom been a favorite of North End shipyard workers that, while not losing its original patronage, became a premier resort of patriot workingmen. There were other regular meeting places: the Liberty Tree in the South End was a popular rallying ground for outdoor meetings; the counting room of Chase and Speakman's distillery became the secret seat of the Loyal Nine, one of whose members, Thomas Chase, was a partner in the distillery; and above the *Boston Gazette* office was a long room that provided a meeting place and a name for the important Long Room Club, an elite society of sixteen patriots whose membership included James Otis, Sam Adams, Josiah Quincy, Jr., Benjamin Church, William Molineux, and Joseph Warren.

In the realm of communications and propaganda, the infrastructure had its own printing office and paper, the *Boston*

50. James Otis, a member of the Saint John's lodge, is the exception that proves the rule, for Otis, in economic and social status, did conform to the Saint John's type and had joined it before the Saint Andrew's lodge was founded.

Gazette, under the co-editorship and management of Benjamin Edes, a Loyal Nine member, and John Gill. The *Gazette* became the organ for the patriot sentiments of James Otis and Sam Adams (whom Gov. Francis Bernard termed the "principal managers" of the paper) and John Hancock, Joseph Warren, and Josiah Quincy, Jr., among others. Sam Adams regularly composed pieces and corrected the copy of other patriots in the *Gazette* office, and John Adams, who seems always to have been in the thick of the infrastructure though not a manager, recorded a visit to the *Gazette* with Otis, Sam Adams, and Gill, who were "preparing for the next day's newspaper, a curious employment, cooking up paragraphs, articles, occurrences, etc., working the political engine." Aside from the newspaper the *Gazette* printing office was also used for running off and selling handbills, broadsides, and the numerous political pamphlets that so effectively promoted the anti-British cause.[51]

Related to the patriot network were certain churches and ministers: the Reverend Samuel Cooper's Brattle Street Church, the Reverend Jonathan Mayhew's West Church, and the Reverend Charles Chauncy's First Church. With the probable exception of Cooper, whose parishioners included Samuel Adams, John Hancock, and James Bowdoin, these ministers confined their anti-British activities to sermons and publications. Mayhew and Chauncy were members of the patriot elite in Boston but were not apparently included in the inner circle as Cooper may have been. In the avidly attended churches of late colonial Boston the impact of a patriotic sermon could be very great, as Mayhew's anti-Stamp Act delivery of 1765 demonstrated. Another leading minister of Boston, the Reverend Andrew Eliot of the New North Church, was an intellectual exponent of the patriot ideology, though a temporizing personality ultimately prevented him from making the full commitment to the movement that distinguished Cooper, Mayhew, and Chauncy.

Crucial to the patriot cause was the nexus between the infrastructure and the formal political organizations that met in the city—the Boston town meeting, the provincial council, and

51. For example, 4 of the 14 Revolutionary pamphlets reprinted in Bailyn, ed., *Pamphlets*, I, were originally printed in the shop of Edes and Gill.

the provincial assembly. The powerful town meeting named the many municipal officials, determined taxes and assessments, and adopted public service projects that were a rich source of jobs and economic largesse. For years the original Caucus and its allies in the Merchants Club had acted as the unofficial directing body of the town meeting in which Caucus stalwart Sam Adams played a key role. Although the town meeting and its important subsidiary committees were not always under the dominance of Sam Adams in the 1760s and 1770s, they generally were. In the provincial assembly James Otis, John Hancock, and Sam Adams, who as clerk turned a minor office into a powerful one, effectively forwarded the patriot interest. The wealthy and aristocratic merchant James Bowdoin never joined in the operations of the patriot inner circle, but in political and ideological terms he was a committed whig, and as the dominant member of the provincial council, the General Court's upper house, he was, in the view of Clifford K. Shipton, much more important in promoting the opposition to British policy than were some of the more famous patriots.

Finally, there were the lower-class workingmen's and artisan "mobs" of the North End and South End. The two mobs were in reality social clubs organized to represent the traditional rivalry of the North and South Ends that dated back into the seventeenth century. Composed of rough men who enjoyed a good brawl, the two mobs customarily fought a pitched battle on November 5, Guy Fawkes Day, or Pope's Day as it was known in strongly anti-Catholic Boston—a street war that sometimes, as in 1764, resulted in fatalities. As long as the two mobs fought each other rather than the British and their sympathizers, the dominance that the patriot leaders desired was a practical impossibility. Therefore, one of the truly crucial maneuvers that the patriot chieftains managed successfully was forging an alliance between the North and South End mobs. It was the Loyal Nine in 1765 (probably in close cooperation with Sam Adams, who had Caucus connections in both the North and South Ends) that made peace between the two mobs and welded them together under the leadership of Ebenezer Mackintosh, head of the South End mob. Henry Swift of the North

End mob became the second-in-command of what was virtually a patriotic militia.[52] The result was a new level of violence and intimidation during the anti-Stamp Act riots of 1765, the *Liberty* anticustoms riot in 1768, and the threat of mob violence that caused the evacuation of the two British regiments in the aftermath of the Boston Massacre.

II

In regard to techniques of social violence the Revolutionary period was one of the most creative in American history. It was the Revolutionary generation that developed, intellectually, the majoritarian concept of popular sovereignty, and it was the Revolutionary generation that perfected techniques of violence to enforce popular sovereignty. To this purpose tarring and feathering was levied as a weapon against the unpatriotic, and the broader technique of vigilantism emerged by Regulator action in South Carolina and later "lynch law" in Virginia. To climax the trend a shrewd organizational maneuver produced the means in the Continental Association to intimidate the tories in the crucial transitional period of 1774 to 1776. The idea of the "sovereignty of the people" gave an ideological and philosophical justification and an awesome dignity to the brutal physical abuse or killing of men that tarring and feathering, vigilantism, and lynching came to embody.[53]

Tarring and feathering was a terrifying part of the vendetta that violent patriots carried on against British sympathizers and customs officials in the 1760s and 1770s. Stripping a person naked for the purpose of smearing him with a coat of hot tar and feathers was a punishment that occurred sporadically in America and Europe before our Revolutionary period, but it was in the late 1760s that the practice emerged for the first time

52. Until the appearance of Zobel, *Boston Massacre*, in 1970, all authorities had named Samuel Swift, Boston lawyer and Harvard graduate of 1735, as the "Swift" cited in contemporary sources as the leader of the North End Mob. But Zobel, 321, notes that Samuel Swift lived on Pleasant Street in the South End and thinks it "more likely" that the North End mob leader was one "Henry Swift, Shipwright," who was indicted for the 1764 Pope's Day riot—a surmise that I find persuasive.

53. The origins of the popular sovereignty concept in the Revolutionary period are discussed later in this essay.

as the "popular Punishment for modern delinquents."[54] In Newburyport, Massachusetts, on September 10, 1768, patriots tarred and feathered two customs informers, and a week later in nearby Salem a customshouse functionary was given the same treatment. There were at least five tarrings and featherings in 1769, and in 1770 merchants were tarred and feathered for violating the patriotic policy of the nonimportation of British goods. The tarrings and featherings continued without respite from 1773 through 1775 in such cities as Boston and Charleston and were extended into the countryside of New England and the middle colonies.[55] The tory Peter Oliver climaxed a chronicle of mob violence against loyalists in 1774–1775 with an account of the fate of Dr. Abner Beebe of East Haddam, Connecticut, who had spoken "very freely" in favor of the crown, "for which he was assaulted by a Mob, stripped naked, and hot Pitch was poured upon him, which blistered his Skin. He was then carried to an Hog Sty and rubbed over with Hogs Dung. They threw the Hog's Dung in his Face, and rammed some of it down his Throat; and in that Condition exposed [him] to a Company of Women. His House was attacked, his Windows broke, when one of his Children was sick, and a Child of his went into Distraction upon this Treatment. His Gristmill was broke, and Persons prevented from grinding at it, and from having any Connections with him."[56]

Throughout the nineteenth century and well into the twentieth tarring and feathering was a favorite means of disciplining and punishing when an American mob felt itself in a vindictive but somewhat playful mood. Tarring and feathering was so common in the nineteenth century and the first half of the twentieth that it would be almost impossible to tabulate all such atrocities. Examples abound. One occurred in San Diego in 1912 when Emma Goldman and her manager-lover, Dr. Ben Reitman, visited the city in support of an Industrial Workers of the World (I.W.W.) free-speech campaign. In an event

54. *Boston Evening-Post*, Nov. 6, 1769, 3.
55. Cutler, *Lynch-Law*, 61–72.
56. Peter Oliver, *Origin & Progress of the American Rebellion*, eds. Douglass Adair and John A. Schutz (San Marino, Calif., 1961), 157.

connived at by the police Dr. Reitman was taken out into the country by vigilantes and tarred and feathered.[57] Mitford M. Mathews has cited a tarring and feathering threat as late as 1950,[58] though during the last two decades the practice seems to have faded almost entirely out of existence.

"It has been said," wrote sociologist James E. Cutler in 1905, "that our country's national crime is lynching."[59] From the early twentieth-century vantage point this judgment was correct. Lynch law in the typical nineteenth-century mode, by which thousands of southern and border-state black people were extralegally executed in mass mob spectacles, has disappeared since World War II, but vigilantism in the broad sense of the term is still very much with us today. In fact American vigilantism has experienced a revival in recent years. Significant have been the avowedly self-protective and community patrol organizations that have proliferated by the hundreds among urban and suburban white and black Americans since 1964. Arising chiefly in response to the turmoil in race relations exemplified by the black ghetto riots of the 1960s and to the steeply rising crime rate, these organizations—among them such well-known associations as the "Maccabees" of the Crown Heights neighborhood in Brooklyn and the North Ward Citizens' Committee (headed by Anthony Imperiale) of Newark—have been viewed as vigilante groups by the police, the press, the public, and themselves. Although they have seldom if ever taken the law into their own hands, they have clearly emerged from the vigilante tradition and identify with it.[60]

---

57. Laurence Veysey, ed., *Law and Resistance: American Attitudes toward Authority* (New York, 1970), 208–234.

58. Mitford M. Mathews, *A Dictionary of Americanisms on Historical Principles* (Chicago, 1951), 1706.

59. Cutler, *Lynch-Law*, 1.

60. Richard Maxwell Brown, "The American Vigilante Tradition," in Graham and Gurr, eds., *History of Violence in America*, 201–208; Gary T. Marx and Dane Archer, "Citizen Involvement in the Law Enforcement Process: The Case of Community Patrols," *American Behavioral Scientist*, XV (1971–1972), 52–72. Among the black community, patrol organizations have been the "Deacons" in a Deep South belt from Louisiana to the Carolinas and "Operation Interruption," a Harlem association. Seventeen of the 28 self-defense patrol groups studied by Marx and Archer were black.

The more than two-hundred-year tradition of American vigilantism began during the Revolutionary period in the South Carolina backcountry of 1767. From then until about 1900 vigilantism—in the classic sense of organized extralegal movements that take the law into their own hands—was a constant factor in American life. There was much vigilantism in the eastern half of the nation as well as in the western. As a frequent frontier phenomenon vigilante movements took place in almost all of the states beyond the Appalachians. There were at least 326 known vigilante movements (which took 729 lives from 1767 to 1909), but the actual total may have reached as high as 500.[61]

Launching the vigilante tradition was the South Carolina Regulator movement of 1767 to 1769, the prototype for hundreds of trans-Appalachian vigilante movements of the nineteenth and twentieth centuries. (During the nineteenth century the original terms *regulator* and *vigilante* were synonyms for Americans who took the law into their own hands by participating in an organized movement; by the late nineteenth century *regulator* had faded from general use.) Energized by an outbreak of frontier crime and violence that arose in the aftermath of an especially destructive Indian war and without county courts and sheriffs to combat the banditry, respectable settlers of affluent and average means formed as "Regulators" in late 1767 and began a two-year vigilante campaign. Subscribing to written articles in their pledge to end the problem of crime and disorder, the Regulators attacked and broke up outlaw gangs and communities. The idle and immoral were rounded up, given trials, flogged, and expelled or subjected to forced labor on Regulator plantations. A particularly obnoxious band of outlaws was pursued northward to the North Carolina-Virginia border area, and sixteen of its members were slain.[62]

There was no direct connection between the South Carolina

61. Brown, "American Vigilante Tradition," in Graham and Gurr, eds., *History of Violence in America*, 154.

62. Brown, *South Carolina Regulators*; Brown, "American Vigilante Tradition," in Graham and Gurr, eds., *History of Violence in America*, 154–226.

Regulator movement and the turmoil that brought on the Revolution, but the Regulators as vigilantes were an example of the popular sovereignty impulse of the era that flared up into anti-British rioting in the cities and in the incidents of tarring and feathering. (It is significant, too, that most of the South Carolina Regulators later became whigs during the Revolutionary War and fought on the American side against the British and tories in South Carolina.)[63] There was a direct connection, however, between the Revolution and another phenomenon of the period that was to have an enduring legacy in the history of American social violence. This was the development of lynching in Virginia during the Revolutionary War.

The settlers in Bedford County, Virginia, near the Blue Ridge were plagued in 1780 by numerous tories and by outlaws made bold by the unsettled wartime conditions on the frontier. "Both Tories and desperadoes," James E. Cutler has written, "harassed the [patriots] and plundered their property with impunity. The prices paid by both armies for horses made horse-stealing a lucrative practice, and the inefficiency of the judiciary made punishment practically out of the question. The county courts were merely examining courts in all such cases, and the single court for the final trial of felonies sat at Williamsburg, more than two hundred miles away. To take the prisoners thither, and the witnesses necessary to convict them, was next to impossible. Frequently the officers in charge of the prisoners would be attacked by outlaws and forced to release their men or be captured by British troops and themselves made prisoners."

It was in response to these conditions that the leading men of Bedford County—headed by Col. Charles Lynch, after whom the present city of Lynchburg was named—"after deliberation . . . decided to take matters into their own hands, to punish lawlessness of every kind, and so far as possible to restore peace and security to their community." An extralegal organization for the capture and trial of culprits was formed. Lynch became the presiding justice of a court in which three other leading men—William Preston, Robert Adams, Jr., and James Callaway

63. Brown, *South Carolina Regulators*, 123–126.

—sat as associate justices. This was literally "Lynch-law," as in time it came to be known. Like the Regulators a decade earlier in South Carolina, Lynch and his cohorts conducted regular though illegal trials. The accused "if convicted . . . was sentenced to receive thirty-nine lashes on the bare back, and if he did not then shout 'Liberty Forever' " was "hanged up by the thumbs until he did so." The punishment was immediate and was inflicted under a large and locally famous walnut tree standing in Lynch's yard. Although strictly illegal at the time the Virginia legislature later approved and pardoned the actions of Lynch and his neighbors. Among the other parts of Virginia where lynching took place during the Revolutionary War was Washington County, where in 1779 William Campbell, Walter Crockett, and others caught and punished tories and outlaws.[64]

The practice of vigilantism, lynching, and tarring and feathering might have been abandoned by the American people after the turbulent Revolutionary era had not the Revolution itself with its emergent concept of popular sovereignty furnished a powerful justification for the violent abuse of alleged enemies of the public good. In *The Creation of the American Republic, 1776–1787*, Gordon S. Wood has traced the maturation of the idea of the "sovereignty of the people" in the Revolutionary period and has shown that popular sovereignty was in part the outgrowth of the colonists' "long tradition of extra-legislative action by the people, action that more often than not had taken the form of mob violence and crowd disturbance. . . . Beginning with the Revolutionary movement (but with roots deep in American history) the people came to rely more and more on their ability to organize themselves and to act 'out-of-doors' whether as 'mobs,' as political clubs, or as conventions."[65]

By the 1780s, Wood finds, the emergence of the concept of

64. Cutler, *Lynch-Law*, 24–30. See also William Waller Hening, ed., *The Statutes at Large; Being a Collection of All the Laws of Virginia, from the First Session of the Legislature, in the Year 1619* (Richmond and Philadelphia, 1809–1823), X, 195, XI, 134–135.

65. Gordon S. Wood, *The Creation of the American Republic, 1776–1787* (Chapel Hill, 1969), 319–321.

popular sovereignty was complete—and crucial. The concept was no mere intellectual construct, however. Through activity represented by constitution-making, extralegal conventions, instructions to representatives, and often violent "out-of-doors action," Americans had "infused an extraordinary meaning into the idea of the sovereignty of the people." [66] The thinkers of the time upheld popular sovereignty. For example, in 1787 Samuel Chase of Maryland declared that the people's power "is like the light of the sun, native, original, inherent, and unlimited by human authority. Power in the rulers or governors of the people is like the reflected light of the moon, and is only borrowed, delegated and limited by the grant of the people." [67] About the same time James Sullivan asserted that "there is no supreme power but what the people themselves hold." [68] And John Stevens boldly announced: "All power whatever is vested in, and immediately derived from, the people only; the rulers are deputies merely, and at certain short periods are removable by them: nay, the very government itself is a creature formed by themselves, and may, whenever they think it necessary, be at any time new modelled." [69]

There may be seen a historical connection between the theoretical Revolutionary concept of the sovereignty of the people and the behavioral background of popular sovereignty in the local community of the colonial period. Alexis de Tocqueville's insight that "the doctrine of the sovereignty of the people came out of the townships" at the time of the American Revolution "and took possession of the state" [70] has recently gained support from Michael Zuckerman's *Peaceable Kingdoms: New England Towns in the Eighteenth Century.* Zuckerman contends that on the basis of the New England town meeting's insistence upon harmony "the consciousness of [the town] community, in Massachusetts, continued at least three quarters of the way through the eighteenth century as a prime value of

66. *Ibid.*, 383.
67. *Ibid.*, 371.
68. *Ibid.*, 599.
69. *Ibid.*, 600.
70. Alexis de Tocqueville, *Democracy in America* (New York, 1948), I, 56.

public life" with "consolidation of consensus" as the principle and "control of conflict" as the aim.[71]

The close tie between the nascent idea of popular sovereignty and Revolutionary events may be seen in Boston. G. B. Warden has written that "the growing unity" in Revolutionary Boston "among . . . various groups" was connected to a

> curious, amorphous entity called the "Body of the People." Original-
> ly used by both royal officials and their opponents simply as a
> synonym for "a majority of the people" or "the greater part of the
> people," the vague phrase began to acquire more substance and
> eventually referred to the united will of the people, much as English-
> men referred to the Crown or the King's Person. In more and more
> arguments writers and speakers began to talk of the authority of the
> "Body of the People," its powers, its rights and its duties as a symbolic
> substitute for the "Crown." As the people became epitomized by such
> an abstract symbol, Bostonians of opposing political views tended
> to describe many public gatherings as the "Body of the People" or
> simply the "Body." At times commentators used the phrase to describe
> mobs as well as formal legal assemblies. The people in the town
> meeting began to refer to themselves as the "Body," and ultimately
> in 1773 transformed a town meeting protesting the Tea Act into
> a mass meeting of the "Body" supposedly representing all the people
> in the province.[72]

Revolutionary-period theorists of popular sovereignty probably had not intended to justify vigilantism and lynching, but
to later generations of Americans—including some of the most
eminent Americans such as Andrew Jackson, Theodore Roosevelt, governors, congressmen, senators, lawyers, judges, and
leading capitalists—popular sovereignty was just that: a justification for the people in all their power to take the law into
their own hands and to put the miscreant to death by summary
justice.[73] Typical was the attitude of an Indiana vigilante movement—the Regulators of LaGrange and Noble counties in
northeast Indiana in 1858—who, in justification of a successful

---

71. Michael Zuckerman, *Peaceable Kingdoms: New England Towns in the Eighteenth Century* (New York, 1970), vii, 154, *passim*.

72. Warden, *Boston*, 218–219.

73. Richard Maxwell Brown, "Legal and Behavioral Perspectives on American Vigilantism," *Perspectives*, V (1971), 93–144.

drive on outlaws and blacklegs, stated their belief in "the *doctrine of popular sovereignty*: that the people of this country are the real sovereign, and that whenever the laws, made by those to whom they have delegated their authority, are found inadequate to their protection, it is the right of the people to take the protection of their property into their own hands" and to "deal with these villains according to their just desserts." [74]

In the Revolutionary War and its prelude it was the tories, of course, who bore the brunt of the combination of popular sovereignty and violence. The possibilities for the harassment and oppression of the tories were immensely increased in late 1774 by the Continental Congress's adoption of a Continental Association for a total cessation of trade with the British Isles. To enforce the Continental Association the Congress resolved "that a committee be chosen in every county, city, and town . . . to observe the conduct of all persons touching this association; and when it shall be made to appear, to the satisfaction of a majority of any such committee, that any person within the limits of their appointment has violated this association, that such majority do forthwith cause the truth of the case to be published in the gazette; to the end, that all such foes to the rights of British-America may be publicly known, and universally contemned as the enemies of American liberty. . . ." [75]

It was not really necessary to set up committees in all American communities to meet the stated purpose of the Association (trade stoppage with Great Britain), for the experience of the 1760s had shown that imports from the mother country could be choked off by merely controlling the seaports. But to create a country-wide patriotic movement in support of Sam Adams and the other members of the Continental Congress it was necessary to establish local committees not just in the seaports but on a country-wide basis, and this may have been the main motive behind their establishment. It was particularly impor-

74. Brown, "American Vigilante Tradition," in Graham and Gurr, eds., *History of Violence in America*, 182.
75. S. E. Morison, ed., *Sources and Documents Illustrating the American Revolution, 1764–1788, and the Formation of the Federal Constitution* (Oxford, 1929), 124.

tant to single out for intimidation the tories, and this the committees to enforce the Continental Association were ordered to do. Congress requested only that the tories be subjected to verbal anathema and did not mention violence. But local committees often instigated violence against the tories, as happened in Isle of Wight County, Virginia, in August 1775 when one Anthony Warwick was tarred and feathered immediately after being called to account by the local committee.[76]

III

Long after 1776 the symbols of the Revolution continued to be used with frequency and sincerity by violent movements to enfold themselves in its sanctifying mantle. Thus only twenty years after the first Continental Congress the "Whiskey Rebellion" broke out in western Pennsylvania as a forceful protest against the taxation policy of the federal government. In the summer of 1794 radical participants in the whiskey insurrection "began to revive the Revolutionary custom of erecting liberty poles" in a "call for [a] popular rising against [Federalist] tyranny."[77] In 1844–1845 another farmers' movement invoked the precedent of the American Revolution. This was the violent antirent outbreak in four upstate New York counties to the southwest of Albany. The roots of the antirent protest against the New York tenant system went back to the Revolutionary decade of 1760s, but the movement flamed anew in the 1840s as agricultural decline in the uplands of the Hudson-Mohawk region made the renters desperate. Taking violent and sometimes fatal action against landlords and authorities, the antirenters before committing violence disguised themselves as "Mohawks" in conscious emulation of the patriotic "Indians" of the Boston Tea Party, and they denounced their opponents as "Tories."[78]

76. Ivor Noël Hume, *1775: Another Part of the Field* (New York, 1966), 287–288; see also 32–33 and 285–286. Physical coercion of the tories by the local committees is also noted in William H. Nelson, *The American Tory* (Oxford, 1961), 93–96.

77. Leland D. Baldwin, *Whiskey Rebels* (Pittsburgh, 1939), 103.

78. *Albany Argus*, Aug. 11, 1845, 2, reprinted in Richard Maxwell Brown, ed., *American Violence* (Englewood Cliffs, N.J., 1970), 53–55. See also Henry

In regard to the coming of the Civil War, Charles P. Roland has noted that Southerners "looked upon the American Revolution as the great prototype of their own war for independence."[79] A look at the evidence bears out Roland's statement. Robert Barnwell Rhett, South Carolina's extremist "father of secession," as early as the Nullification movement made "fervent appeals . . . to the example of the Revolution." From then until secession, Rhett, the fire-eating editor of the Charleston *Mercury*, tirelessly promoted Southern independence.[80] The same was true of another "fire-eater," William L. Yancey of Alabama, who in early 1860 "had declared his 'aims and objects' were 'to cast before the people of the South as great a mass of wrongs committed on them, injuries and insults' that had been done, as possible, and thus 'to produce spirit enough . . . to call forth a Lexington, to fight a Bunker's hill, to drive the foe from the city' of Southern rights. He would 'fire the Southern heart' so that 'at the proper moment, by one organized, concerted action' he could 'precipitate the cotton states into a revolution.' "[81] After Lincoln's election and on the eve of secession the Revolutionary heritage was again invoked in South Carolina by the organization of local Minute Men companies whose aim was to march on Washington and forcibly prevent Lincoln's inauguration. Nothing came of this plan, but the Minute Men were significant in whipping up anti-Union sentiment in South Carolina, whose enthusiastic citizens compared their secession convention of 1860 to the Continental Congress of 1776.[82]

The spirit of '76 also flourished in Virginia, where after Lin-

Christman, *Tin Horns and Calico* (New York, 1945), and David M. Ellis, *Landlords and Farmers in the Hudson-Mohawk Region, 1790–1850* (Ithaca, N.Y., 1946).

79. Charles P. Roland, *The Confederacy* (Chicago, 1960), 40–41.

80. Laura A. White, *Robert Barnwell Rhett: Father of Secession* (Gloucester, Mass., 1965 [orig. publ. New York, 1931]), 14–15, 17, 24, 121. I have treated the Revolutionary-era genesis of South Carolina extremism in an unpublished paper, "The Violent Origins of South Carolina Extremism: From the Revolutionary Era to Calhoun to Strom Thurmond."

81. Avery O. Craven, *The Growth of Southern Nationalism: 1848–1861* (Baton Rouge, 1953), 327.

82. Harold S. Schultz, *Nationalism and Sectionalism in South Carolina: 1852–1860* (New York, 1969 [orig. publ. Durham, N.C., 1950]), 226, 229.

coln's election the hallowed tradition of the Revolution was drawn upon to organize local companies of "minutemen" and "committees of safety." [83] Northern "Copperheads" in the midwestern states of Ohio, Indiana, and Illinois during the Civil War also hearkened to the Revolutionary heritage to justify their opposition to the Union war effort. Copperhead sentiment and the vociferous Unionist and Republican opposition that it encountered led to frequent episodes of violence in the lower Midwest—riots and raids, in particular. When Copperheads thought of escalating their insurgency they too called from the past a Revolutionary symbol. This time it was the "Sons of Liberty," which in the Copperhead incarnation was a secret organization with grandiose plans but which according to its historian, Frank L. Klement, had power more in the fears and imaginations of Copperhead-hating Republicans than in actuality. [84]

The Civil War was not the last example of Americans legitimizing violence in terms of the Revolution, for the practice has survived to our own time. A generation ago, in 1932–1933, the Farmers' Holiday Association movement flamed in Iowa and other corn-belt states. This movement, led by Milo Reno, was a protest against adverse economic conditions stemming from the Depression, but with a background of farm grievances that went back to the Grangers, Greenbackers, and Populists of the late nineteenth century. Violent, direct action was a principal feature of the Farm Holiday movement. The farmers defied legal processes, blocked highways, dumped milk from trucks, forcibly halted farm foreclosure sales, and on one occasion assaulted a county judge. The example of the American Revolution was much in the minds of observers, supporters, and members of the Farm Holiday movement. Henry A. Wallace compared the movement to that of the Boston Tea Party, while a sympathizer compared the spirit of the organization to the "spirit of 1776." The farmers themselves drew on the heri-

83. Henry T. Shanks, *The Secession Movement in Virginia: 1847–1861* (Richmond, 1934), 125.
84. Frank L. Klement, *The Copperheads in the Middle West* (Chicago, 1960), 165–166ff.

tage of the Revolution when they enlisted in a violent subgroup of the movement in northwest Iowa whose members called themselves the "Modern Seventy-Sixers."[85]

In our own day talk of revolution is common. We think, correctly, of the current revolutionary fervor as being on the left side of the political spectrum, but the right wing in American history has ever been quick to adopt the symbols of the Revolution, and the present is no exception. It seems that when violence-prone Americans see a crisis approaching their first thought, often, is to organize as "minutemen." Today we have a secret, right-wing, paramilitary organization of eight to ten thousand "Minutemen" founded in 1961 as an anti-Communist movement. Violence is central to the Minutemen's approach to the alleged Communist threat. They train themselves in guerrilla warfare against the expected day when the Communists will attempt a total take-over of the nation. But meanwhile "that the Minutemen are capable of much violence is undisputed. Recent Minutemen-linked events have included an attempted bank robbery, complete with dynamiting of police and power stations, near Seattle; an assault on a peace group in Connecticut; and an attempted assault on three left-wing camps in the New York area." It is also well known that the Minutemen have accumulated huge arsenals of weapons.[86]

In the last few years the violence of the Minutemen has been eclipsed by the violence of extremist elements among the white New Left and the black militant movements. The contemporary white and black revolutionaries have used violent "know-how" gained from the training manuals of the Minutemen in accomplishing some of the 1,391 "guerrilla acts of sabotage in the U.S., 1965–1970" recorded in the January 1971 issue of *Scanlan's Monthly* on "Guerrilla War in the U.S.A." But unlike the Minutemen the current revolutionaries do not identify with the American Revolution. Instead white and black American revolutionaries of today seek their models, not in Samuel

85. John L. Shover, *Cornbelt Rebellion: The Farmers' Holiday Association* (Urbana, Ill., 1965), 46, 59–65, 97, *passim*.
86. Jerome H. Skolnick, *The Politics of Protest* (New York, 1969), 232–238. See also J. Harry Jones, *The Minutemen* (New York, 1968).

Adams, Thomas Jefferson, and George Washington, but in a multiracial galaxy of present-day heroes including Mao Tse-Tung, Che Guevara, Malcolm X, and George Jackson. That current revolutionaries, unlike previous American dissidents, no longer identify with the American Revolution may be one of the most important changes in our contemporary intellectual history. It may suggest that the long-range era of the American Revolution has at last come to an end, for it seems that the Revolution now has little impact as an inspiration for dissent and reform whether peaceable or violent.[87]

87. An exception is the radical historian Staughton Lynd, an advocate of thoroughgoing but nonviolent reform, who in his *Intellectual Origins of American Radicalism* (New York, 1968) seeks to connect the radical reform movement of the present with an American radical tradition represented in the 18th century, so he argues, by the American Revolution.

A Selective Listing of American Colonial Riots, 1641–1759

Year(s)	Colony	Locality	Riot or Riot-producing Event
1641	R.I.	Providence	Liberty of conscience riot
1654	Md.	Severn River	"Battle of the Severn"
1654–1655	R.I.		Political factionalism
1663–1750	R.I.		Boundary riots
1663–1750	Conn.		Boundary riots
1663–1750	Mass.		Boundary riots
1682	Va.		Tobacco plant cutters' riots
1690	N.C.		Capt. Gibbs's gubernatorial claim
1699	N.H.	Portsmouth	Sailors' riot
1699–1700	N.J.		Land riots and mob assaults on courts
1703	S.C.	Charleston	Political factionalism
1703–1710	N.Y.	Jamaica	Nonconformist disturbances
1704	Pa.	Philadelphia	Riot of young gentry
1705	N.Y.	N.Y. City	Privateersman's riot
1710	Mass.	Boston	Food riot
1711	N.Y.	Flatbush	Dutch church riot
1711	N.Y.	N.Y. City	Anti-impressment riot
1713	Mass.	Boston	Food riot
1718	N.Y.-Conn.		Boundary riot
1718	N.C.		Riotous seizure of official records
1719–1764	N.Y.-N.J.		Boundary riots
1719	R.I.	Newport	Anticustoms riot
1721–1737	Pa.-Md.		Boundary riots
1722	Conn.	Hartford	Jailbreak riot
1724	Conn.	Hartford Co.	Riot against ship seizure

1734	N.H.	Exeter	Mast-tree riot
1737	Mass.	Boston	Antiprostitution riot
1737	Mass.	Boston	Antimarkethouse riot
1737	N.C.		Antiquitrent riot
1738	Pa.	Schuylkill R.	Fish-dam riot
1742	Pa.	Philadelphia	Election riot
1745–1754	N.J.		Land riots
1747	Mass.	Boston	Anti-impressment riot
1750	Pa.	York Co.	Election riot
1751–1757	N.Y.	Livingston Manor	Antirent riots by tenants
1751–1757	N.Y.-Mass.		Boundary riots
1754	N.H.	Exeter	Riot against surveyor of woods
1757	N.H.	Brentwoods	Riot against recruiting for royal troops
1757	N.H.	Portsmouth	Mob seizes longboat of H.M.S. *Enterprise*
1759	N.C.		Anti-land-tax riot

NOTE: For the sources of this list see note 23.

A Selective Listing of Riots in the Revolutionary Era,
1760–1775

Year(s)	Colony	Locality	Riot or Riot-producing Event
1760–	N.C.		Regulator riots and disturbances
1760	N.Y.	N.Y. City	Anti-impressment riots (two)
1763–1764	Pa.		Paxton Boys disturbances
1764	N.Y.	N.Y. City	Anti-impressment riot
1764	N.Y.	N.Y. City	"Soldiers Riot and Attempted Rescue"
1764	R.I.	Newport	Anti-impressment riot
1764	Mass.	Dighton	Anticustoms riot
1764	R.I.	Newport	Anticustoms riot
1765	Pa.	Cumberland Co.	Rangers riot against Indian traders
1765	N.C.	Mecklenburg Co.	Riot against land surveyors
1765	R.I.	Newport	Anti-impressment riot
1765–1766	Various	Various	Anti-Stamp Act riots
1766	N.Y.	Hudson River	Antirent riots
1766	Conn.	New London	Riot *v.* Rogerene religious movement
1766	Mass. (Me.)	Falmouth	Anticustoms riot
1766	Conn.	New Haven	Anticustoms riot
1766	Va.	Norfolk	Anticustoms riot
1767	Va.	Norfolk	Anti-impressment riot
1768	Mass.	Boston	Sloop *Liberty* (anticustoms) riot
1768	Va.	Norfolk	Smallpox riot
1767–1769	S.C.		Regulator riots and disturbances
1769	Conn.	New Haven	Anticustoms riot

1769	Conn.	New London	Anticustoms riot
1769	R.I.	Newport	Anticustoms riot
1769	Pa.	Philadelphia	Anticustoms riot
Late 1760s	R.I.	Newport	Riots against unfaithful husbands
Late 1760s	R.I.	Providence	Riots against unfaithful husbands
Late 1760s	N.Y.	N.Y. City	Riots against unfaithful husbands
1769–1770	N.J.	Monmouth Co.	Antilawyer riot
1770	R.I.		Anticustoms turmoil
1770	Pa.	Philadelphia	Anticustoms riot
1770	N.Y.	N.Y. City	Liberty pole riot
1770	Mass.	Boston	Boston Massacre
1770–1774	(Vt.)		New Hampshire grant riots
1771	Mass.	Boston	Riot against whorehouse
1771	R.I.	Providence	Riot against tidesman
1771	R.I.		Anticustoms turmoil
1772	R.I.	Providence waters	Burning of the *Gaspee* (anticustoms riot)
1773	Mass.	Boston	Boston Tea Party
1774	R.I.	Providence	Licensing question riot
1774	R.I.	East Greenwich	Antitory riot
1774	R.I.	Newport	Anticustoms riot
1775	Md.	Sassafrass-Bohemia	Anticustoms riot
1775	Ga.		Anticustoms riot

NOTE: For the sources of this list see notes 23 and 24.

4

The American Revolution

The Military Conflict
Considered as a Revolutionary War

by

JOHN SHY

To ask whether the military conflict of the American Revolution was in any sense a "revolutionary war" is to bring together two distinct and troubled lines of historical inquiry. One is the line followed by military historians, who from the time of Charles Stedman have tried to explain the outcome of the war and especially to answer the question of how one of the greatest military powers in the world could have been defeated by a few million scattered, inadequately armed, and badly trained colonials. The question itself, when posed in this way, has half suggested to some military historians an answer that would necessarily go beyond conventional forms of military explanation and would emphasize revolutionary methods of fighting and revolutionary sources of military strength. But perhaps a majority of the military historians of the American Revolution have rejected any such interpretation; they explain British defeat in terms of British mistakes, without resorting to American marksmanship, Indian fighting tactics, or massive popular resistance as major factors. Between these two schools of thought, a narrowly cast, poorly focused debate has gone on for almost two centuries over whether the war demands a "revolutionary" interpretation.[1]

The other line of inquiry has concerned a greater number of historians, though for a shorter period of time. It became truly prominent less than fifty years ago when J. Franklin Jameson gave his famous lectures on the social effects of the Revolution. Since then, no question has aroused more interest and drawn more scholarly energy than the one posed by Jameson: did the Revolution change American society?[2] Although wars are notoriously effective agents of change, the war of the American Revolution has received little attention from those historians who have tried to answer Jameson's question. Perhaps most of the difficulty lies in Jameson's categories, which were not directly related to the war and its effects. Moreover, the debate among historians over the question of revolutionary change has largely been an argument with Jameson and other historians of the Progressive school, who combined their faith that revolutionary change had indeed occurred with a deep distaste for all things military: neither they nor their critics have been much disposed to consider the possibly revolutionary effects of the war itself.[3]

1. Don Higginbotham, "American Historians and the Military History of the American Revolution," *American Historical Review*, LXX (1964), 18–34, surveys the military historical writing about the Revolution and describes the recent revival of interest in the subject. But it is remarkable how little even this revival has impinged on study of the Revolution as a whole. Higginbotham's recent book, *The War of American Independence* (New York, 1971), more than any previous general account, seeks to relate the military and nonmilitary segments of the war; basic research in this direction, however, has hardly begun.

2. J. Franklin Jameson, *The American Revolution Considered as a Social Movement* (Princeton, 1926).

3. Frederick B. Tolles, "The American Revolution Considered as a Social Movement: A Re-evaluation," *AHR*, LX (1954), 1–12, reprinted in the paperback edition of Jameson (Princeton, 1967), surveys the critical attack on Jameson's argument. Two unjustly neglected books that seek to relate the direct pressure of warfare to major political developments are Bernhard Knollenberg, *Washington and the Revolution* (New York, 1940), and Curtis Nettels, *George Washington and American Independence* (New York, 1951). While both Bernard Bailyn, *The Ideological Origins of the American Revolution* (Cambridge, Mass., 1967), and Gordon S. Wood, *The Creation of the American Republic, 1776–1787* (Chapel Hill, 1969), stress the intellectual and even psychological changes wrought by revolution, the former stresses pre-

It is in this dual sense, then, that we can ask about the military conflict—revolutionary in structure? revolutionary in effects? And, of course, it is likely that the answers to these two questions are related to each other.

Some risk is run by asking questions in this way. Jameson and other Progressive historians projected the social and political concerns of industrial America onto an eighteenth-century screen, thereby confusing their and our understanding of what actually happened in the Revolution.[4] Likewise, much writing on the military history of the Revolution is contaminated with the preoccupations of military theory, especially with the application and illustration of so-called principles of war, which lie near the center of what has passed for military science in the nineteenth and twentieth centuries.[5] Both lines of inquiry have thus been stunted by unhistorical thinking, and the warning to us is plain. When we ask in the 1970s about "revolutionary war" in the eighteenth century, we should admit that our own nightmares, as much as any desire to push back the frontier of historical knowledge, give rise to the question. By being candid about the reasons why "revolutionary war" seems especially interesting at this time, we may be able to avoid some of the pitfalls that our predecessors dug for themselves. We dare not argue that the American Revolutionary War was basically like modern revolutionary wars in Indochina and elsewhere; rather, we ask only whether the doctrines, the studies, and the general experience of "revolutionary warfare" in the twentieth century provide some insight into the American Revolutionary War. The answer, with due caution and qualification, is yes.[6]

---

war whig-tory conflict, while the latter rarely (e.g., 324) sees wartime events as agents of intellectual change. Jackson T. Main, *The Social Structure of Revolutionary America* (Princeton, 1965), finds, on the whole, relatively little perceptible change in socioeconomic structure and so is not disposed to consider the possible effects of the war.

4. Richard Hofstadter, *The Progressive Historians: Turner, Beard, Parrington* (New York, 1968).

5. On military history, see Peter Paret, "The History of War," *Daedalus*, C (1971), 376–396. On the principles of war, see Bernard Brodie, "Strategy as a Science," *World Politics*, I (1949), 467–488.

6. For another, differently directed discussion of the relevance of the 20th century to the 18th, see Thomas C. Barrow, "The American Revolution

I

The social history and the military history of the Revolution have seldom come together in the past because military historians tend to regard the war as an instrument managed on each side with more or less skill, while social historians treat military operations, if at all, as incidental to the study of politics and public finance. But if the war is restored to the central position that it had for the Revolutionary generation, and if it is seen not merely as an instrument but as a process, which entangled large numbers of people for a long period of time in experiences of remarkable intensity, then it may be possible to bring the study of the war and the study of the Revolution more closely together, to the benefit of both.

It is easy to direct attention to the neglected question of the war's impact on society; it is more difficult to discover effective means for answering the question. Tangible effects—death, destruction, the disruption of life and property—seem the obvious and most interesting way to begin. Considering the enormous energy expended on the study of the American Revolution, one is surprised to find information so scarce on the raw quantities of revolutionary violence and upheaval. Except for the laborious military chronicles compiled mainly in the later nineteenth century and some rather tenuous estimates of the magnitude of loyalism, historians have done little to answer the questions of how many? how much? how often? when and where? Though we are told that there were 231,950 separate enlistments in the Continental army, that the logistical requirements of that army generated about $4,000,000 worth of so-called military certificates, and further that the distribution of both enlistments and certificates throughout the society was quite uneven, we have

as a Colonial War for Independence," *William and Mary Quarterly*, 3d Ser., XXV (1968), 452–464. Of the reverse relationship—the relevance of the American Revolution to 20th-century revolution—there is no question here, although Richard B. Morris and Clinton Rossiter, among others, have written books on the subject. J. H. Hexter has some wise thoughts on the tricky question, for historians, of "relevance" in his essay "The Historian and His Day," in his *Reappraisals in History* (New York, 1961), 1–13.

not begun to grasp the historical meaning of those numbers.[7] Several recent studies in social history are at least suggestive in this connection, because from them a hypothesis emerges that one measurable effect of war might have been to widen the gap between richer and poorer Americans.[8] The straightforward if lengthy task of extracting from local histories and records a complete list of all the petty alarms, raids, and skirmishes, the instances when daily routine was disrupted, people harmed, property lost or destroyed, and perhaps atrocities perpetrated, would be a useful exercise.[9] If the list were placed in the context of the then existing patterns of settlement and economic activity, it would restore a part of the Revolution that has become encrusted by neglect, both by historians interested only in military operations on a large scale and by historians not interested in military operations at all. At least such a compilation would correct the illusion that the American Revolution, including its war, somehow took place outside the dynamics of violence that have afflicted revolutionary struggles elsewhere.

7. Allan Nevins, *The American States During and After the American Revolution, 1775–1789* (New York, 1924), 574; E. James Ferguson, *The Power of the Purse: A History of American Public Finance, 1776–1790* (Chapel Hill, 1961), 63, 69. The *specie value* of unredeemed certificates issued by the Quartermaster and Commissary departments was $3,723,000 at the end of the war; the *paper value* of all certificates issued was over $100,000,000.

8. Charles S. Grant, *Democracy in the Connecticut Frontier Town of Kent* (New York, 1961), 96–103; James T. Lemon and Gary B. Nash, "The Distribution of Wealth in Eighteenth-Century America: A Century of Change in Chester County, Pennsylvania, 1693–1802," *The Journal of Social History*, II (1968), 1–24; Allan Kulikoff, "The Progress of Inequality in Revolutionary Boston," *WMQ*, 3d Ser., XXVIII (1971), 375–412. All of these authors found an increase in the relative number of "poor" during the war, but none attempted to connect this change to the war itself.

The question is made more difficult by the lack of systematic thought about the "impact" of war on society. The most recent bibliography, Kurt Lang, *Sociology of the Military* (Chicago, 1969), has 61 entries under "Impact and Consequences of War," but only 2 of them published later than 1960, when revolutionary war began—again—to be a matter of concern. Worth reading is Arthur Marwick, "The Impact of the First World War on British Society," *Journal of Contemporary History*, III (1968), 51–63.

9. The Office of the Chief of Military History, Department of the Army, is now preparing a detailed chronology of the war that should, when completed, be the most comprehensive record of military actions.

Yet this kind of list making and quantification has its limitations; quantities must be translated into qualities. When no testable proposition is put to the evidence, there is the danger of simply piling up data to demonstrate a prior conclusion. How much violence or destruction is consequential? how little, negligible? Moreover, if research of this kind is motivated by the strong impression that a large slice of revolutionary life is being overlooked, it is only fair to take account of another impression, conveyed most readily by travel accounts of the 1780s, that recovery from the direct physical effects of the war was rapid. The second impression does not negate the first, but it does warn us against confusing the compilation of evidence with its analysis. Though the possible revolutionary effects of the war may seem the more accessible and more broadly interesting half of our dual question, we lack any clear conception of "impact" or any satisfactory framework in which to set this raw evidence of wartime destruction and disruption. It may be that the other half of the question, concerning the structure of the war, can lead to a more satisfactory result.

[The structural feature of modern revolutionary wars that has most impressed intelligent observers is not the use of guerrilla tactics but the triangularity of the struggle.[10] Two armed forces contend less with each other than for the support and the control of the civilian population] Invariably, the government and its forces are reluctant to perceive this essential triangularity, while the rebels use whatever strength they can muster to break the links between governor and governed. Revolutionary violence is less an instrument of physical destruction than one kind of persuasion; the aim is to destroy responsiveness to the state, at first within the general population, ultimately among those who man the military and administrative arms of the state. Ideally, government ceases to function because no one any longer obeys; old authority is displaced by revolutionary organization without the massive

10. There is a large but generally polemical and low-grade literature on "revolutionary war." Chalmers Johnson, "Civilian Loyalties and Guerrilla Conflict," *World Politics*, XIV (1962), 646–661, and Peter Paret, *French Revolutionary Warfare from Indochina to Algeria* (Princeton, 1964), are still the best introductions.

confrontations of conventional warfare or the force majeure of the coup d'état. To organize revolution means going beneath the normal level of governmental operation, reaching the smallest social groups and even individuals, indoctrinating everyone so recruited, and of course using those forms of violence, particularly threats, terrorism, and irregular or guerrilla warfare, that are at once most difficult to stop and most likely to change docile, obedient subjects into unhappy, suggestible people. [The keys, if there are any, to modern revolutionary warfare are time and survival: hope remains as long as revolutionary organization survives, and the very passage of time can convince the most skeptical subject and sap the will of the most determined government.]

This model of modern revolutionary warfare is not altogether congruent with the structure of the American Revolutionary War, but the fit at some points is close enough to be worth exploring. [The most important points of dissimilarity are the relative ease with which local instruments of government fell into the hands of American rebels, the relative dependence of the rebels on conventional forms of military action, and their relative innocence of any explicit doctrine of revolutionary warfare, like that developed in our own time by Mao Tse-tung and his admirers.] The latter two dissimilarities, on the forms and doctrine of military action in the American Revolution, deserve further elaboration.

In the first place, the prevalent image of the American Revolutionary War distorts the role of what, then and now, may be designated irregular warfare. Because part-time soldiers involved in small-scale, hit-and-run action were peripheral to the contest between main armies, they have had peripheral attention. Only on the few occasions when there was no rebel main army, as around Boston in the spring of 1775 and in South Carolina during the autumn of 1780, or when militia forces took part (almost always with unhappy results) in a regular military confrontation, have these part-time soldiers come into historical focus. In fact, even the correspondence of Washington, who disliked and mistrusted militiamen because they were not regular soldiers, reveals the neglected importance and frequency of what in the twentieth century is labeled unconventional warfare, and what was called in the eighteenth century *la petite guerre* or "war of posts."[11] This said, there is still no denying that Washington, the Congress, supporters of rebellion, and foreign observers regarded the survival and the success of the Continental army, engaged for the most part in a classical war of maneuver, siege, and battle, as the chief military factor on which the Revolution depended. [The *petite guerre* of the rebel militia had important social consequences, about which more will be said later, but almost certainly these consequences were not of the quality and magnitude that modern doctrines of revolutionary warfare consciously set out to achieve. Instead, the willingness of both British and rebel leaders to accept, if not always enforce, the fairly humane conventions of eighteenth-century warfare served to mitigate some of the radical effects that civil wars often have on society]

The doctrinal divergence between our time and the eighteenth century is the other point of difference to be examined. American strategy from 1775 to 1783 was indeed keyed to conventional operations, not simply to spare women, children, the aged, and property from the horrors of guerrilla warfare, but because a central army visibly helped to meet two acute needs: the need for internal unity and the need for external support. [By being militarily conventional, American revolutionaries created at least the illusion of unified purpose, military strength, and political respectability, both at home and abroad.] Whether they might have done better to be less conventional is an unanswerable, perhaps an idle, question, but it is not an anachronistic one, because it was raised at the time. Charles Lee, the eccentric former British officer who stood second only to Washington in the first years of the war and who was admired

11. Robert C. Pugh, "The Revolutionary Militia in the Southern Campaigns, 1780–1781," *WMQ*, 3d Ser., XIV (1957), 154–175, makes a sensible case for the military importance of the militia without the sentimentalism that impairs other similar efforts. Russell F. Weigley, *Towards an American Army* (New York and London, 1962), 1–9, sketches Washington's view, while Peter Paret, "Colonial Experience and European Military Reform at the End of the Eighteenth Century," *Bulletin of the Institute of Historical Research*, XXXVII (1964), 47–59, clarifies both the tactical and international contexts of the militia question.

by some of the more radical members of Congress, like John Adams and Benjamin Rush, offered an alternative strategic conception.[12] Lee thought that a conventional approach, which he ridiculed as Prussian, played to British strength and from American weakness, and he offered his own Swiss model for revolutionary war. He would have based American strategy on the militia and used regular forces primarily as a means to protect the militia from attack while it was being organized and trained. He would not have faced large British forces in pitched battles, except under the most favorable conditions like those at Bunker Hill or at the attack on Charleston in 1776, but would have given way to strength while nibbling it to death. He said little about the likely social consequences of his Swiss strategy, though presumably—political radical that he was—he was ready to accept them. His thinking was never consciously implemented or even fully developed before his downfall in 1778, but both its existence and its rejection are a measure of the extent to which the American Revolution was *not* a modern revolutionary war.

II

Far more important than the differences between the American Revolutionary War and modern revolutionary warfare are the structural similarities. But rather than becoming mired in the old historical arguments, like those over whether the Continental army or the militia, formal tactics or guerrilla action, French aid or American patriotism, really won the war, we need to detach ourselves from the polemics of American folklore and to view the war as a whole, from outside. There is no better way to do that than by exploiting recent scholarship which makes it possible to see the war in British perspective.[13] British

12. A full development of this argument is in my "Charles Lee: The Soldier as Radical," in George Athan Billias, ed., *George Washington's Generals* (New York, 1964), 22–53.

13. The outstanding recent works on the British side of the war are Piers Mackesy, *The War for America, 1775–1783* (London, 1964); William B. Willcox, *Portrait of a General: Sir Henry Clinton in the War of Independence* (New York, 1964); and Paul H. Smith, *Loyalists and Redcoats: A Study in British Revolutionary Policy* (Chapel Hill, 1964). My under-

understanding of the war was often cloudy and sometimes completely wrong, but the record of British experience provides a uniquely valuable way of looking at the war; like most modern historians, British leaders were less interested in allocating praise or blame among the Americans than in grasping the nature of the phenomenon with which they had to deal. Like other leaders in more recent, comparable situations, they were slow to learn, almost blind to certain key elements of their problem, badly confused beneath a veneer of confidence and expertise, and repeatedly caught in military and political traps of their own creation. But they were not stupid, and their persistent efforts to understand in order to act effectively give us the chance to consider the Revolutionary War apart from the parochial concerns and commitments that have paralyzed so many efforts to analyze it from the inside. Moreover, our own painful experience with revolutionary war may give us an empathetic understanding, a special sensitivity needed for the extraction of meaning from the record of British frustration.

British efforts to interpret and put down rebellion in the American colonies divide into three distinct stages. For almost a decade of agitation before the war, successive British governments had defined their American problem as one of law enforcement and the maintenance of order; in general, legal measures were bound by the belief that, once legitimate grievances were redressed, trouble and resistance was the fault of a few recalcitrant individuals. Policy based on this belief failed, most

standing of the British war effort derives heavily from these three books, although at numerous points their evidence and arguments have been checked by my own research. Mackesy and Willcox also helped to revise the original version of this essay, which they both read, by giving me some incisive criticism, for which I here thank them and absolve them of all responsibility. Several other works are especially valuable: Ira Gruber, *The Howe Brothers and the American Revolution* (New York, 1972); Robert D. Bass, *The Green Dragoon: The Lives of Banastre Tarleton and Mary Robinson* (New York, 1957); George Athan Billias, ed., *George Washington's Opponents: British Generals and Admirals in the American Revolution* (New York, 1969); and Franklin and Mary Wickwire, *Cornwallis: The American Adventure* (Boston, 1970). Troyer Steele Anderson, *The Command of the Howe Brothers During the American Revolution* (New York, 1936), a carefully reasoned study based on limited evidence, is still very much worth consulting.

obviously because these individuals seemed to command wide-spread local sympathy, an attitude that crippled judicial machinery. In early 1774, after the destruction of tea at Boston, the British government adopted a new interpretation of its American problem, which was that insurgency had a center—Boston—and that this center could and ought to be isolated and punished. The new policy assumed that other colonies, and even rural Massachusetts, were disturbed by the extremity of the latest acts of Boston insurgents and could be intimidated by the example made of the Boston community. The policy was thus seen to depend upon the application of overwhelming force, within the framework of civil law, to achieve clear-cut success at a single geographical point.[14]

Of course, the assumption proved completely wrong. Coercive laws and the manifest intention to enforce them with troops gave insurgent leaders greater leverage than ever before outside Boston itself.[15] Despite their misgivings, inhabitants of rural Massachusetts and other colonies concluded that they had no choice but to support Boston, since the new policy of community isolation and punishment seemed to threaten the political and legal integrity of every other community and colony. From this support, Boston acquired sufficient force to make the first military encounters—at Lexington, Concord, and Bunker Hill—inconclusive and thus susceptible to interpretation as moral victories for the insurgents. Nothing did more to expand and consolidate rebel support throughout America.

Some aspects of the British performance in this first stage are worth noting. The outbreak of open fighting came in an attempt to break up what may be described as an insurgent base area whose existence cast doubt on the basic assumption.

14. The final crisis, and the thinking that shaped it on the British side, can be traced in Bernard Donoughue, *British Politics and the American Revolution: The Path to War 1773–1775* (London, 1964); Benjamin W. Labaree, *The Boston Tea Party* (New York, 1964); and John Shy, *Toward Lexington: The Role of the British Army in the Coming of the American Revolution* (Princeton, 1965), chap. 9.

15. How Boston kept itself from being effectively isolated can be followed in Richard D. Brown, *Revolutionary Politics in Massachusetts: The Boston Committee of Correspondence and the Towns, 1772–1774* (Cambridge, Mass., 1970).

British intelligence of the target was good, but it failed in two other critical respects. It could not prevent the transmission of every British order and movement throughout the civilian population, and it grossly underestimated the rebel will and capability for large-scale combat: "These people show a spirit and conduct against us that they never showed against the French, and everybody has judged them from their former appearance and behavior, which has led many into great mistakes," General Gage reported after the battles of Lexington and Concord.[16] Related to this failure was the psychology of the British command. The long period of relative inaction before the outbreak and Gage's increasingly pessimistic estimates of the situation during that period finally put him in the position of having to take some action in order to redeem himself in the eyes of his own government. The first setback at Lexington in April prepared the way for the second at Bunker Hill in June, since an even more sensational success was required to redeem the initial failure. General Burgoyne explained why a tactically reckless assault was made at Bunker Hill when he wrote that "the respect and control and subordination of government depends in a great measure upon the idea that trained troops are invincible against any numbers or any position of untrained rabble; and this idea was a little in suspense since the 19th of April."[17]

With the outbreak of actual fighting, the concept of the problem as essentially a police action, however massive and extraordinary that action might be, quickly faded away and was replaced by the belief that the government faced a fairly con-

16. Gage to Secretary at War Barrington, "Private," June 26, 1775, Clarence E. Carter, ed., *The Correspondence of General Thomas Gage . . . 1763–1775* (New Haven, 1931–1933), II, 686–687.

17. Burgoyne to Germain, Aug. 20, 1775, Germain Papers, William L. Clements Library, Ann Arbor, Mich. The psychological effects of Bunker Hill, of course, were the opposite of those expected by Burgoyne. One British officer, who had a line to general headquarters, wrote: "Our confidence in our own troops is much lessened since the 17th of June. . . . We have a great want of discipline both amongst officers and men." Lord Rawdon to his uncle, the earl of Huntingdon, Charlestown, Mass., Aug. 3, 1775, *Report on the Manuscripts of the Late Reginald Rawdon Hastings . . . ,* III (Historical Manuscripts Commission, *Twentieth Report* [London, 1934]), 159, hereafter cited as *MSS of Hastings,* III.

ventional war that could be conducted along classical lines. The American rebels were hastily organizing an army on the European model, and the game now seemed to be one of maneuvering in order to bring the rebel army to decisive battle or, better still, to destroy it without costly fighting. Accordingly, the British shifted their base from Boston, a dead end in terms of classical strategy, to New York, which was a superior port with access to the best lines of communication into the American interior. An incidental consideration, but no more than that, was the greater friendliness of the civilian population in the Middle Atlantic theater of operations as compared with New England.[18]

[The underlying policy assumption of this second stage, not very closely examined at the time, was that success in conventional operations against the main rebel army would more or less automatically bring a restoration of political control in the wake of military victory.] The assumption proved to be not wholly wrong. A series of tactical successes through the summer and fall of 1776 not only secured the New York port area but produced a striking collapse of resistance in New Jersey as well. Without any special effort by the British command, local rebel leaders fled or went into hiding as the main rebel army with-

18. Mackesy, *War for America*, 35, 42; Willcox, *Clinton*, 55, 58; Smith, *Loyalists*, 41. The question of strategic intentions and expectations, especially in the case of General Howe, is murky. Although he said that he expected to destroy Washington's army in battle, there is some reason to believe that he hoped to win a decisive victory in the chess-like manner idealized by Maurice de Saxe (see Jon M. White, *Marshal of France* [London, 1962], 272–273), by maneuvering Washington out of richer, more populous areas and into a tactically hopeless position, where the only rational choice would be for the rebel army to break up and flee, all without major bloodshed. This kind of strategic thinking, so characteristic of the ancien régime, would later move Clausewitz to scorn (*On War*, trans. O. J. Matthijs Jolles [Washington, D.C., 1950], 210); but even Clausewitz elsewhere admitted that battles unfought, like the unpaid bills of commercial credit, functioned as the nexus of strategy (*ibid.*, 27, 123). The point here is that Howe, by threatening to fight only under favorable circumstances, no doubt hoped to minimize fighting. The tension, obvious to Clausewitz and to ourselves, between the conquest of territory and the destruction of enemy armed force, was less felt in the 18th century, when the very objects of war tended to be territorial and the costs of major battle, even to the victor, seemed extraordinarily high.

drew. The local rebel militia, which had firmly controlled the communities of New Jersey, tended to disintegrate and to be replaced by an improvised loyal militia. It is clear that almost every civilian in New Jersey believed that the rebellion would collapse completely and that it was not too soon to reach an accommodation with the royal authorities. The government granted free pardon to all civilians who would take an oath of allegiance, and almost three thousand Americans accepted the offer in a few weeks, including one signer of the Declaration of Independence.[19]

The failure of the British campaign in New Jersey, after such a promising start, had two major causes, one external, the other internal. The internal cause is summarized in the remarks of two British observers: one noted that the lenient policy toward the civilian population "violently offends all those who have suffered for their attachment to government"; the other noted "the licentiousness of the troops, who committed every species of rapine and plunder."[20] There is ample evidence from both sides to confirm these observations. British regulars and especially their non-English-speaking German auxiliaries—products of the hard school of European warfare—tended to regard all civilians as possible rebels and hence fair game. Even if civilians avoided the regular foragers, they were not permitted to relapse into passive loyalty if they had ever shown the slightest sympathy for the rebel cause. Loyal bands of native militia regarded retribution as their principal function and were determined that no rebel should escape, pardon or no pardon. [In many cases, former neutrals or lukewarm rebels found no advantage in submission to government and came to see flight, destruction, or resistance as the only available alternatives.[21]]

19. Leonard Lundin, *Cockpit of the Revolution: The War for Independence in New Jersey* (Princeton, 1940), 157*ff.*

20. E. H. Tatum, ed., *The American Journal of Ambrose Serle, Secretary to Lord Howe, 1776–1778* (San Marino, Calif., 1940), 155; "Journals of Lieut.-Col. Stephen Kemble," *The Kemble Papers*, I (New-York Historical Society, *Collections*, XVI [New York, 1884]), 160.

21. W. A. Whitehead *et al.*, eds., *Archives of the State of New Jersey, 1631–1800*, 2d Ser., I (Trenton, 1901), 276*ff*, contains numerous accounts of minor skirmishes and affrays, reported in newspapers on both sides. Col. Charles Stuart to his father, the earl of Bute, Feb. 4, 1777, E. Stuart-Wortley,

The other, external cause of failure stemmed from the British attempt to control and live off the central part of the state: brigade garrisons were deployed among towns, mainly for administrative convenience. Not surprisingly, the rebel main army, weak as it was, managed to achieve local superiority and exploit its excellent tactical intelligence to pick off two of these garrisons, at Trenton in late December and at Princeton in early January. The tactical effects of these small battles were modest, but the strategic and psychological effects were enormous. British forces withdrew from all exposed locations and henceforth concentrated in the area from Perth Amboy to New Brunswick. The morale of rebels, already sensitized by harsh treatment, soared; while the morale of loyal civilians, now out of range of British regular support, dropped sharply. Almost all New Jersey quickly came under insurgent control. The international repercussions of Trenton and Princeton were likewise serious.[22]

One noteworthy point: in the only intensive study made of a single community during this period (Bergen County, New Jersey), it is apparent that the local and bloody battles between rebel and loyal militia were related to prewar animosities between ethnic groups, political rivals, churches, and even neighbors.[23]

---

ed., *A Prime Minister and His Son* (London, 1925), 99, is an especially clear statement of the problem. Some British officers, like the young Lord Rawdon, had expected positive results from the brutal conduct of the army in New Jersey. While still at New York he had written: "I think we should (whenever we get further into the country) give free liberty to the soldiers to ravage it at will, that these infatuated creatures may feel what a calamity war is." To the earl of Hastings, Sept. 25, 1776, *MSS of Hastings*, III, 185.

22. The loss of British control in New Jersey is illustrated in a letter written by James Murray, a British officer, to his sister, from Perth Amboy, Feb. 25, 1777: "As the rascals are skulking about the whole country, it is impossible to move with any degree of safety without a pretty large escort, and even then you are exposed to a dirty kind of *tiraillerie*. . . . Would you believe that it was looked upon as a rash attempt to go [to New Brunswick] by land accompanied by two Light Dragoons, tho' there are not above 5 or 6 miles of the road, and these next to the shore, but what are occupied by our troops?" Eric Robson, ed., *Letters from America, 1773–1780* (Manchester, 1951), 38–42.

23. Adrian Leiby, *The Hackensack Valley in the American Revolutionary War* (New Brunswick, N.J., 1962), 20.

[The campaign of 1777 was essentially a continuation of the strategy of 1776; its object was to destroy, disperse, or demoralize the rebel main army and to quarantine New England insurgency by gaining control of the Hudson valley. But the assessment of civilian attitudes became more important than it had been in 1776 and affected planning in two ways:] because the unexpected continuation of the war for another year strained British military manpower, one British force would move to Philadelphia, not only luring the main rebel army to defend its capital but also permitting the recruitment of badly needed provincial troops from the supposedly friendly population. Another British force would move down the Champlain-Mohawk-Hudson corridor on the assumption that the scattered population of the area was loyal or at least not actively hostile and that Indian auxiliaries could intimidate those who might lean toward rebellion.[24] The campaign was a disaster, in large part because the intelligence estimates, gleaned mainly from exile sources, were much too optimistic. The Canadian force simply drowned at Saratoga in a hostile sea, which its Indian allies had done something to roil and its commander had not foreseen and done little to calm. The army at Philadelphia, whose commander had assumed that the northern army could take care of itself, found that the march of his men through the countryside from Chesapeake Bay had created new rebels and that Pennsylvania "friendliness" did not go beyond selling what was needed to feed the troops penned up in the city.[25] Other

24. Mackesy, *War for America*, 103–124; Smith, *Loyalists*, 44–59. Although the basic strategic concept remained that of "proving the superiority of the British troops over the army of the rebels" in order to produce a collapse of American morale and a more or less automatic political settlement (Germain to Gen. Howe, Oct. 18, 1776, Germain Papers, Clements Lib.), there is evidence of growing British interest in the attitudes of the local population. See, for example, Burgoyne to Clinton, Quebec, Nov. 7, 1776, Clinton Papers, Clements Lib.; Gen. Howe to Germain, Dec. 20, 1776 (extract), and Howe to Carleton, Apr. 5, 1777, Germain Papers.

25. On the popular response to the British march from Elkton, Md., to Philadelphia, see Bernard A. Uhlendorf, ed., *Revolution in America: Confidential Letters and Journals, 1776–1784, of Adjutant General Major Baurmeister of the Hessian Forces* (New Brunswick, N.J., 1957), 95–113, and Alexander Graydon, *Memoirs of His Own Time* (Philadelphia, 1846), 285, 306. In Uhlendorf, ed., *Revolution in America*, 134–139, 148, 157, 162, 169,

factors contributed to the disaster of 1777, especially a three-way failure to agree on the basic idea of the whole operation, which was attributable only in part to the slowness of transatlantic communications.[But primary was the miscalculation of objectives and of time-space factors through an erroneous conception of the civilian environment within which military operations were to be conducted.[26]]

Throughout this second stage of the war, the British military and naval commanders, the brothers Howe, were empowered to negotiate with rebel leaders. These negotiations came to nothing because the rebel military situation was never truly desperate except briefly at the end of 1776 and because rebel unity so patently depended on adherence to political demands that the British government was not yet willing to concede. It has sometimes been argued that the British attempt to unify politics and warfare inhibited military operations, because the Howe brothers allegedly withheld the full force of the military stick in order to dangle the political carrot more enticingly. Little contemporary evidence supports the criticism, though the Howes were bitterly attacked once their failure was apparent. The effects that a ruthless naval blockade and the pursuit of armed rebels to utter destruction might have had on any real pacification of the troubled areas were unpredictably double-edged. The Howes knew this, and so did everyone else; awareness did not depend on having formal powers to negotiate.

Baurmeister gives a graphic account of guerrilla warfare around Philadelphia during the following winter and spring.

26. Mackesy, *War for America*, 121–144. Historians continue to explain the failure of the campaign almost solely in terms of the famous "forgotten despatch," though, as Mackesy, 117–118, demonstrates, long-available evidence does not confirm the emphasis given to this incident, in which General Howe allegedly was not told that General Burgoyne might be needing some help around Albany. The reasons for the failure of the campaign are far more complicated and in a sense more damning of the British high command, but the story and its point are apparently too good to give up. Additional evidence is in the letter of Adj. Gen. Edward Harvey to Lt. Gov. James Murray of Minorca, May 16, 1777; Harvey in London clearly understood what Howe and Burgoyne planned to do: "I think that we may place H[owe] in possession of Philadelphia and a great part of Pennsylvania in the month of June. If the Canada Army can get, in tolerable time to Albany, much may be done, but much certainly depends on that measure." W.O. 3/23/214–215, Public Record Office.

Only after their strategy had failed, and especially after the fiasco of 1777, did their critics become retrospectively wise about the campaign of 1776. In fact, the Howes conducted operations in that first year with great skill and smoothness; understanding between army and navy was never better. Washington's army had been shattered at minimal cost; to have expected relentless exploitation of success was to ignore the basic character of eighteenth-century armies, technology, and military doctrine. Battles were murderous, desertion rates soared whenever an army became dispersed and control relaxed, tactical fortunes often turned abruptly at just the moment when one side tried to push an advantage beyond the limits of a powerful but rigid system of fighting, and trained replacements were pure gold. All these characteristics of eighteenth-century warfare were more acute when operations occurred in a large and distant country, against a semiskilled but numerous and enthusiastic enemy; but they were by no means peculiar to American conditions. If anything, the lessons learned from the American campaigns of the Seven Years' War, not to mention Lexington, Concord, and Bunker Hill, pointed to the need for more, not less, than the usual amount of tactical caution. The most serious criticism of the Howes' campaign in 1776 is simply that it failed to end the rebellion.[27]

27. The special constraints on strategy imposed by 18th-century tactics and organization are discussed and revealed in Stanley M. Pargellis, "Braddock's Defeat," *AHR*, XLI (1936), 253–269, and *Lord Loudoun in North America* (New Haven, 1933), and in C. P. Stacey, *Quebec, 1759* (New York, 1959). The Wickwires, *Cornwallis*, 90, refuse to accept at face value the testimony of Cornwallis when he said, concerning Howe's failure to destroy Washington's army at Long Island in August 1776, "that I never did hear it suggested by anyone that those lines could have been carried by assault." But other eyewitness accounts, written during the events of the campaign of 1776, bear out Cornwallis's words. The young Lord Rawdon wrote to his uncle, from New York, Sept. 25, 1776, "that everything is at stake and that one daring attempt, if unsuccessful would ruin our affairs in this part of the world, and the difficulty of getting troops, and such troops, is so great that we ought not to hazard our men without the evident prospect of accomplishing our purpose." *MSS of Hastings*, III, 186. The more experienced Frederick Mackenzie, during the pursuit of Washington later in the fall, noted in his diary on Nov. 3, 1776, only the question of whether the British army would extend its winter quarters into New Jersey, not whether Wash-

The outline of the third and last stage of British strategy took a year to emerge from the confusion that followed the defeat at Saratoga. The French fished more openly and aggressively for advantage in North America, and the British response was to escalate by declaring war against France. The West Indies, where both powers had large economic and military stakes, pulled the strategic center of gravity southward and seaward. During 1778, the British army on the continent remained on the defensive, cut its commitments by evacuating Philadelphia, and used bases at New York and Rhode Island to carry out a campaign of coastal harassment, while Indian allies put pressure on the rebel frontiers. Meanwhile, a general reevaluation of British strategy was taking place.[28]

[For the first time, the civilian population came to be the major factor in planning. As never before, it was seen that loyal and neutral civilians had to be organized and protected before any lasting results could be achieved and that the great pool of civilian manpower largely accounted for the surprising resilience of the rebel main armies.] Because civilian response had so far been disappointing in New England and the Middle Atlantic states, because West Indian and mainland operations now had to be coordinated, and because earlier, small-scale operations had produced an unexpectedly favorable response from civilians in the southern colonies, it was decided to begin the new campaign in the South. Some British officials had always seen the South as the soft underbelly of the rebellion, with its scattered population, its fear of slave uprisings, strong Indian tribes at its back, and a split between tidewater and upcountry societies in the Carolinas that approached a state of civil war. A heavy stream of information from loyal Americans supported this kind of thinking. At last it was understood that the recruitment of loyal provincial troops merely for use in conventional

---

ington would be pursued to destruction. *The Diary of Frederick Mackenzie* . . . (Cambridge, Mass., 1930), 95. Military historians have tended to judge Howe and other 18th-century military leaders by Napoleonic standards, which are simply not appropriate to the historical situation. See note 18, above.

28. Mackesy, *War for America*, 156–158, 252–256; Willcox, *Clinton*, 26off.

operations often had deprived an area of the very people who might control it; [high priority would now be given to the formation of local self-defense forces. The basic concept was to regain complete military control of some one major colony, restore full civil government, and then expand both control and government in a step-by-step operation conducted behind a slowly advancing screen of British regulars. From a police operation, and then a classical military confrontation, British strategy had finally become a comprehensive plan of pacification directed against a revolutionary war.29]

The new strategy was linked to the political situation in Britain itself: increasingly, the government had justified a costly and controversial war to members of the House of Commons on the ground that Britain had an unbreakable commitment to defend loyal Americans against rebel vengeance. The government thus staked its political life on the success of pacification in the South. The decision, however, was not seen as a gamble so much as the pursuit of a logical course, because [the government, especially the king and his principal strategic planner, Lord George Germain, had always believed that most Americans, given a chance to choose freely, would support the crown.] When Lord North, nominally prime minister, but in a weak position within his own government, expressed an opinion that the war was no longer worth its cost, the king rebuked him by saying that "this is only weighing such events in the scale of a tradesman behind his counter" and that American independence would surely lead to the loss, piece by piece, of the rest of the British Empire, including Ireland. It might be said, without exaggeration, that North's cost-benefit analysis of the situation lost out to the king's domino theory.30

29. Smith, *Loyalists*, 79–99; Mackesy, *War for America*, 252ff.

30. The king to Lord North, June 11, 1779, John W. Fortescue, ed., *The Correspondence of King George the Third* . . . (London, 1927–1928), III, 351. Almost five years earlier, Lord Barrington, secretary at war until 1778 and a fairly consistent hard-liner on American policy, had used North's logic and reached the same conclusion: "Our disputes with North America have not at present the foundation of Interest, for the contest will cost us more than we can ever gain by our success." Even if the Americans were defeated, Barrington thought that they would have to be held down by armies, "which would be ruinous and endless." To Dartmouth, Dec. 24,

The new campaign began well. Amphibious attack captured Savannah at the end of 1778 and led to a collapse of rebel resistance in the more densely populated part of Georgia. Twenty loyal militia companies were organized, and fourteen hundred Georgians swore allegiance to the king. Yet certain problems appeared that would never be solved. In attempting to clear rebel remnants away from pacified areas, British regulars pushed detachments to Augusta and toward Charleston, beyond the limit where they could be permanently maintained at that time. Subsequent withdrawal of these detachments led to the deterioration of loyal militia units left behind in the outlying areas and to an adverse effect on the future behavior of their loyal and neutral residents. Furthermore, regular commanders revealed themselves as unduly optimistic in deciding that any particular area had been pacified and could safely be left to defend itself. Finally, the troops, and even some of their commanders, simply could not be made to treat civilians—except those actually in arms for the crown—as anything but suspected rebels despite explicit directives from London and headquarters to the contrary.[31]

Large reinforcements in 1780 brought about the capture of Charleston and its large rebel garrison in May; a small rebel army that entered the Carolinas in August was quickly destroyed at Camden. Now British mounted forces successfully employed irregular tactics and achieved tactical mobility equal or superior to that of the rebels themselves. Upcountry, the loyal militia was organized district by district; men over forty were assigned to local defense, while those younger served as territorial auxiliaries. Every effort was made to meet the rebel threat

1774, Barrington Letterbook 1766–1775, East Suffolk Record Office, Ipswich, England, HA 174 acc. 1026, 283–289. Thomas Hutchinson, however, former governor of Massachusetts and a man of penetrating intelligence, used cost-benefit analysis in a letter to Lord Hardwicke, Aug. 31, 1778, to reach the opposite position; without some great military victory, Hutchinson argued, Britain would lose not only the 13 colonies but the West Indies and the Newfoundland fisheries as well, and he stated that whatever the cost of defeating the colonies it would be far less than the harm done by such a loss. Additional Manuscripts 35427, fol. 141, British Museum.

31. Mackesy, *War for America*, 267–268; Smith, *Loyalists*, 100–105, 126–142.

by effective countermeasures at the local level. Moreover, the orders from General Clinton to the inspector of militia show the spirit in which these measures were undertaken: "You will pay particular attention to restrain the [loyal] militia from offering violence to innocent and inoffensive people, and by all means in your power protect the aged, the infirm, the women and children from insult and outrage." [32]

In the end, the policy failed; the question is why? Small groups of rebel irregulars could not be eliminated altogether. They hid in some of the least accessible swamps and mountains or operated from unpacified prorebel locations on the periphery —in upper Georgia or southern North Carolina. These irregular bands made complete physical security unattainable for many pacified areas. Rebel guerrillas and militia could achieve local superiority against any particular body of loyal self-defense militia and sometimes even against mobile detachments. In an action reminiscent of both Trenton and Saratoga, a group of rebels quickly built up strength in October to wipe out an overextended loyal force of a thousand men at King's Mountain, North Carolina. Thus, neither side had the capability of fully protecting its supporters among the civilian population, and a ferocious guerrilla war spread throughout South Carolina and into Georgia and North Carolina. Areas thought to have been pacified quickly slipped out of control, sometimes because loyal forces fought their own little wars of counterterror against rebels, rebel sympathizers, suspects, and anyone else they disliked.

Almost every British action appears to have exacerbated this situation. The chronic rough treatment of civilians by regulars simply could not be curbed to any significant extent. Moreover, the British force under Tarleton that had successfully employed irregular tactics soon acquired in the course of its operations a reputation for inhumanity that drove apathetic civilians toward the rebels for protection. A proclamation offering full rights of citizenship and pardon to all who would take the oath

32. Quoted from the Clinton Papers, Clements Lib., in Wickwire, *Cornwallis*, 427, n.55. On the success of British irregular tactics, see *ibid*., 132–133, 164–165, and Bass, *Tarleton*.

of allegiance, but declaring all others as rebels, drove many paroled rebel prisoners out of the neutral position that they had assumed and back into active rebellion. At the same time, the conciliatory aspect of this policy infuriated loyal auxiliaries, militia, and irregulars, who increasingly ignored official policy and orders and took matters into their own hands. A loyalist observer, who had defected some time before from the rebel side, described South Carolina as "a piece of patch work, the inhabitants of every settlement, when united in sentiment, being in arms for the side they liked best, and making continual inroads into one another's settlements."[33] During this civil war, there was little difference between loyalists and rebels in terms of organization, tactics, or the use of terror. Pacification had failed well before a new rebel army was organized under Gen. Nathanael Greene in central North Carolina.

The failure of pacification, and the appearance of this large rebel force to the northward, led General Cornwallis to return, almost with a sigh of relief, to more conventional operations. Priorities were shifted, mobile forces were concentrated, and the principal objective became the destruction of the rebel army through maneuver, battle, and pursuit.[34] This reversion to the strategy of 1776–1777 ended in the disaster at Yorktown in October 1781, when the British navy momentarily lost control of sea lines of communication with its southern army. From that time on, all serious attempts to pacify the American interior were given up, and only New York and Charleston were kept as impregnable enclaves until the declaration of peace in early 1783.[35]

33. "Colonel Robert Gray's Observations on the War in Carolina," *South Carolina Historical and Genealogical Magazine*, XI (1910), 153. This is a remarkable document, conveying a vivid sense of the chaotic situation in those areas of South Carolina not occupied in strength by British forces. On the failure of British pacification even before the appearance of Greene's army, see Lord Rawdon to Maj. Gen. Leslie, Oct. 24, 1780, *Report on the Manuscripts of Mrs. Stopford-Sackville* . . . , II (Hist. MSS Comm., *Fifteenth Report* [London, 1910]), 185, hereafter cited as *MSS of Stopford-Sackville*, II.

34. Wickwire, *Cornwallis*, 169–195. But see also Willcox, *Clinton*, 352–353, and Mackesy, *War for America*, 343–345.

35. Mackesy, *War for America*, 404–436, 473–477, 487–494. On p. 512, the author suggests that the British might reasonably have continued the war

Certain aspects of the failure of this third stage of British strategy require emphasis. One is that neither British nor rebel leaders regarded the bloody civil war in the South as "favorable" to their side; both tried to curb it in order to gain political control and to prevent large-scale alienation of potentially friendly civilians. But it *was* beneficial to the rebels inasmuch as they could choose to operate in prorebel areas while the British were constrained to operate everywhere. Furthermore, the relative proximity of a large British regular army had a surprisingly unfavorable effect on civilian attitudes. Civilians tended to overreact to the army. Depending on the particular circumstances, civilians were intimidated by it and so behaved "loyally," for which they later suffered; or they were disillusioned by its predatory conduct and lack of sympathy for the precarious position of the civilian; or they felt secure in its presence and committed violent acts under its aegis, which ultimately created prorebel sympathy; or they saw it as an alternative, a place of flight and refuge; or they were demoralized when it moved away and refused to protect them, their homes, and families.

This last point is most important to our subject: [every major British troop movement in the American Revolution created shock waves of civilian behavior in the surrounding area. Only the scale of British operations in the South, where the British were more aware of the problem and tried to control it, makes those shock waves especially visible in the latter stages of the conflict. But repeatedly, throughout the war, loyal and neutral civilians had responded excessively, prematurely, and unwisely, at least in terms of their own personal security, to the appearance of British troops, only to see those troops withdraw or move elsewhere.] British leaders throughout the war had assumed that civilian attitudes and behavior were more or less constant factors that could be measured by civilian actions;

---

after Yorktown. He makes a strong case, but it rests on his belief that American rebels by 1781 were too war-weary to survive the withdrawal of French and Spanish support. I do not agree; American complaints are not to be taken at face value.

American behavior on any one occasion was taken not only to indicate attitudes but also to predict behavior on the next occasion. In fact, each of these occasions brought about a permanent change in the attitude and behavior of those civilians who were involved in, or even aware of, what happened; over time, these occasions had a major, cumulative effect. By 1780–1781, earlier in some places, most Americans, however weary, unhappy, or apathetic toward the rebellion they might be, were fairly sure of one thing: the British government no longer could or would maintain its presence, and sooner or later the rebels would return. Under these circumstances, civilian attitudes could no longer be manipulated by British policies or actions.[36]

36. Among the senior commanders, General Clinton, for all his faults, had the clearest and earliest grasp of what was happening. In planning for the campaign in the South, he wrote to Secretary of State Germain, Apr. 4, 1779, cautioning against a premature capture of Charleston: "It might induce a number of persons to declare for us whom we might afterwards be obliged to abandon, and thus might destroy a party on whom we may depend if circumstances will permit a more solid attempt in proper season." *MSS of Stopford-Sackville*, II, 125. See also the observation of Frederick Mackenzie, Aug. 5, 1781, *Diary of Mackenzie*, 581–582.

A decade after the war, Charles Stedman, in discussing the reversal of popular attitudes in New Jersey in 1776–1777, gave a succinct version of how the British lost their ability to control public opinion. Before the battle of Trenton, Stedman wrote, many New Jerseyans were "well affected" and ready to fight for the king.

But when the people found that the promised protection was not afforded them; that their property was seized, and most wantonly destroyed; that, in many instances, their families were insulted, stripped of their beds—nay, even of their very wearing apparel; they then determined to try the other side. . . . And it is but justice to say that the Americans never took anything from their friends, but in cases of necessity; in which cases they uniformly gave receipts . . . always living, as long as they could, upon their enemies; and never suffering their troops to plunder their friends with impunity. But at the same time it is to be noticed, that the American troops were suffered to plunder the loyalists, and to exercise with impunity every act of barbarity on that unfortunate class of people; frequently inflicting on them even scourges and stripes.

Stedman, *The History of the Origin, Progress, and Termination of the American War* (London, 1794), I, 242–243.

Some argued, both at the time and subsequently, that a more wholehearted resort to fire and sword would have terrorized the Americans into submission. For example: Thomas Hutchinson to Lord Hardwicke, May

III

British strategy may seem but distantly related to the war's impact on American society; in fact, analysis of the first illuminates the second, leading us directly back to the question of effects posed by Jameson. Reflected in the foregoing account of British operations and their difficulties is a changing pattern of American behavior. More direct kinds of evidence, generated by the American war effort itself, distort the picture by concentrating either on a committed but small minority or, in the tones of Jeremiah, on the failure of others to do all that they could or should have to support the Revolution. What the British record on the other hand reveals is something rather different: the response of the whole population to the multifarious stimuli of war. British estimates of American attitudes were frequently in error, but seldom were they completely mistaken. They were prone to exaggerate the intensity of loyalism, they usually blurred the relationship between attitude and likely behavior, and they often mistook loyal behavior as a sign of unshakable loyalty. But these estimates, when placed in the context of the British experience and when tested against evidence from the other side, give us a way of understanding the effect of the war on American society.

In the first place, two standard versions of the war are called into question, if not discredited altogether, by a British perspective. One is the interpretation that turns the fact of British military failure into a hymn to the American spirit, recounting how revolutionary courage, belief, and solidarity frustrated every British design. The other interpretation would reverse

---

31, 1779, Add. MSS 35427, fol. 186, Brit. Museum. But young Col. Charles Stuart, who had served in America for several years and could hardly be suspected of prorebel sympathies, rejected a strategy of terror on other than humanitarian grounds. He not only questioned the physical capacity of the British army and navy to carry on "a war of ravage and destruction" but argued that there was no reason to believe that "acts of severity will cause these people to submit." Everywhere the British army had gone, Stuart wrote to his father on Sept. 16, 1778, "every species of barbarity has been executed," doing nothing more than to plant "an irrecoverable hatred." Stuart-Wortley, ed., *Prime Minister and His Son*, 132.

the emphasis; according to it, nothing but luck, timely French aid, and a tiny group of dedicated men stood between American liberties and British repression. The British version of the war indicates that the Revolution was neither as irresistible nor as fragile, respectively, as these other versions suggest.

What emerges from the British record, especially when an effort is made to distinguish between the earlier wishful fantasies and the cold insights wrung from later disillusionment, is a picture of the great middle group of Americans.[37] Almost certainly a majority of the population, these were the people who were dubious, afraid, uncertain, indecisive, many of whom felt that there was nothing at stake that could justify involving themselves and their families in extreme hazard and suffering. These are the people lost from sight in the revolutionary record or dismissed as "the timid." With not even poverty to redeem them, they are also passed over by historians who believe that the inert mass of people in any epoch deserve nothing better than obscurity. These people, however, did count, because they made up a very large proportion of a revolutionary republic whose very existence depended on counting.

From a British perspective, it appears that a great many of these people were changed by the war. Beginning as uneasy but suggestible, manipulable, potentially loyal subjects of the crown, they ended as knowing, skeptical, wary citizens of the United States. In this sense, the war was a political education conducted by military means, and no one learned more than the apathetic majority as they scurried to restore some measure of order and security in their disrupted lives. The British army was, of course, one of the chief political teachers; in its erratic progress from North to South over the course of seven years, the army directly touched hundreds of thousands of individuals, eliciting behavior that would identify each in political terms while teaching him something about politics. Nothing shows better the success of its instructional effort than its ever-greater difficulty in predicting and controlling the behavior of the pre-

---

37. Barrow, "American Revolution as a Colonial War for Independence," *WMQ*, 3d Ser., XXV (1968), 459, also thinks that neutral or moderate elements were "often a majority."

sumably apathetic majority. And as we examine the British record for more specific clues to the impact of the war, a second institution, which also played the role of political teacher, comes into clearer focus.

The British and their allies were fascinated by the rebel militia.[38] Poorly trained and badly led, often without bayonets, seldom comprised of the deadly marksmen dear to American legend, the revolutionary militia was much more than a military joke, and perhaps the British came to understand that better than did many Americans themselves. The militia enforced law and maintained order wherever the British army did not, and its presence made the movement of smaller British formations dangerous. [Washington never ceased complaining about his militia—about their undependability, their indiscipline, their cowardice under fire—but from the British viewpoint, rebel militia was one of the most troublesome and predictable elements in a confusing war. The militia nullified every British attempt to impose royal authority short of using massive armed force. The militia regularly made British light infantry, German jäger, and tory raiders pay a price, whatever the cost to the militia itself, for their constant probing, foraging, and marauding. The militia never failed in a real emergency to provide reinforcements and even reluctant draftees for the state and Continental regular forces. From the British viewpoint, the militia was the virtually inexhaustible reservoir of rebel military manpower, and it was also the sand in the gears of the pacification machine.[39]]

38. Uhlendorf, ed., *Revolution in America*, contains the most revealing account of British and Allied day-to-day awareness of rebel militia.

39. Baron Ludwig von Closen, a member of the French expeditionary force, noted in his journal on Apr. 12, 1781: "The Americans lose 600 men in a day, and 8 days later 1200 others rejoin the army; whereas, to replace 10 men in the English army is quite an undertaking." Evelyn M. Acomb, ed. and trans., *The Revolutionary Journal of Baron Ludwig von Closen, 1780–1783* (Chapel Hill, 1958), 75. In Uhlendorf, ed., *Revolution in America*, esp. 353–354, Baurmeister describes the rebel militia at its best, near the end of the war. See also the "Journal of John Charles Philip von Krafft, of the Regiment von Bose, 1776–1784," N.-Y. Hist. Soc., *Colls.*, XV (New York, 1883), 43–142.

When we look more closely at the rebel militia, an interesting if obvious fact confronts us: the prudent, politically apathetic majority of white American males were not eager to serve in the militia, but many of them did nonetheless. Their wives were even less enthusiastic; in an agrarian society with a chronic labor shortage, manpower was too important to the welfare, even the survival, of the family. But the sheer busyness of British strategy in the early years of the war—from Boston to New York to Philadelphia, into Long Island and Rhode Island, across New Jersey and Delaware, along the Carolina and Connecticut coasts, up Lakes Champlain and George and down the Mohawk River—made it difficult to know how to be prudent. In the later years of the war, growing British sophistication about the nature of the war made prudence increasingly dangerous, especially from Virginia southward and in a great arc around New York City. Under the circumstances, enrollment in the militia could be a test of loyalty to one side or the other, and it could be a kind of insurance—the readiest form of personal security in a precarious world. But the militia was also a coercive instrument: it was the ultimate sanction of political authority in its own district, and in the mysterious way of all large organizations it kept its own grumbling membership in line. Of course, whole districts might go tory, just as whole militia units crumbled under pressure, but rarely were nearby rebel forces unable to intervene, salvage, and restore these situations. A reservoir, sand in the gears, the militia also looked like a great spongy mass that could be pushed aside or maimed temporarily but that had no vital center and could not be destroyed.

Take a concrete example: in December 1776 the new state of Connecticut passed a law, not very different from old laws in Connecticut and elsewhere, establishing a military organization. It reiterated the obligation of all males between sixteen and sixty to serve in the militia, excepting only congressmen, certain members of state government, ministers of the gospel, Yale tutors and students, and Negroes, Indians, and mulattoes. Officers were to be elected, and no one over fifty could be forced to march out of the state. As in the past, it was legally possible to provide a substitute or pay a £5 fine, but only if drafted for active service.[40]

Five months after the passage of the new militia law, a committee of the Connecticut assembly reported on the case of Nathaniel Jones and seventeen other men from Farmington.[41] Jones and his associates, imprisoned "on suspicion of their being inimical to America," had petitioned for pardon and release and swore that they were now "ready and willing to join with their county and to do their utmost for its defence." They found themselves in jail because, a month before, they had failed to join their militia unit in opposing Governor Tryon's destructive raid on Danbury; their negative act had identified them as suspected persons, if not outright tories. In order to clear themselves, they were forced to undergo individual grilling by the legislative committee, which finally reported favorably on the men from Farmington in the following terms: ". . . They were indeed grossly ignorant of the true grounds of the present war with Great Britain. . . . They appeared to be penitent of their former conduct, professed themselves convinced since the Danbury alarm that there was no such thing as remaining neuters. . . . The destruction made there by the tories was matter of conviction to them."

It is a simple story, repeated hundreds of times in the course of the Revolutionary War, and it makes a simple but very important point. While military historians have generally clucked over the failure of the Connecticut militia to trap and destroy Tryon's raiders, the real significance of this episode is that Nathaniel Jones and many other apathetic, apolitical men, who simply did not want to become perilously involved in a civil war, learned that trying to "remain neuter" was also perilous. In late April 1777, they had tried to evade a political choice,

40. Charles J. Hoadly, ed., *The Public Records of the State of Connecticut*, I (Hartford, 1894), 91*ff*.

41. *Ibid.*, 259–260. An interesting study of the Maryland militia, its sociology and political role, during the early years of the war, is an unpublished paper by David C. Skaggs, "Flaming Patriots and Inflaming Demagogues." It confirmed my own belief that mobilization often meant politicization. I understand that Richard Buel of Wesleyan University is undertaking a general comparative study of this process in the American Revolution.

but in the end they had to beg, in the old language of religious conversion that spoke of "matter of conviction," for a second chance to choose. The mechanism of their political conversion was the militia. Unlike other tests of allegiance, which either applied to only a few of the most prominent or notorious, or else, like the oath, lacked both the urgency and the administrative machinery needed to make it effective, the military obligation sooner or later thrust itself directly into the lives of even the most apathetic. Mere enrollment and occasional drilling were not all that the militia demanded, because eventually almost every colonial county had its equivalent of the Danbury raid, when men actually had either to take arms in an emergency or to do something that would visibly label them as suspicious or disloyal persons. Popular military service was as old as the colonies, but never before had its performance or avoidance defined political categories.

Evidence from both sides records how time and again, in place after place, the movement of British forces combined with the American obligation of universal military service to politicize communities and individuals. John Davies of Charlestown, South Carolina, was able to evade the rebel oath until 1779, when he was obliged to take up arms; having refused, he spent four months on a prison ship. The same thing happened to John Pearness, Thomas Mackaness, David Lorimer, and Col. John Philips and his two sons, who learned that refusal to serve in the militia meant trial by court-martial. Alex Chesney, on the other hand, gave in and served actively in the American forces on three separate occasions. In England after the war, Colonel Philips testified in Chesney's behalf: "He does not think the worse of him because he served in the Rebel Army," said Colonel Philips, "many good men were obliged to do it." [42] While these good men and others were suffering for their reluctance to serve in the South Carolina militia, George Grant was being hauled before the Commissioners for Detecting and Defeating Conspiracies in Albany County, New

42. H. E. Egerton, ed., *The Royal Commission on the Losses and Services of American Loyalists, 1783 to 1785* (Oxford, 1915), 49; also 10, 32, 35, 41, 43–44, 48.

York, "as a Person of suspicious Character"; he was given the choice of jail or "enrolling himself in some Militia Company." [43] To the Albany commissioners, the militia was as much a political as a military organization; when they learned that some of the people who lived on the frontier and enrolled in Maj. Ezekiel Taylor's militia regiment were rumored to be "disaffected," they asked the major for a regimental roll with the "Political Character of Each Man" noted so that the "disaffected" might be "removed" from this sensitive part of the state.[44] A similar crunch had come for many Pennsylvanians in late 1776; it did not come for most Virginians until the spring of 1779.[45] But virtually everywhere, in time, it came.

The pattern of wartime politicization may be seen in dozens of minor military actions; one last example will suffice. When the British established a small post on the Penobscot River in June 1779, Brig. Gen. Francis McLean, an exceptionally able officer, found the local settlers terrified by their belief "that His Majesty's troops were accustom'd to plunder and treat the Country where their operations led them with the greatest inhumanity." McLean set out to correct this mistaken idea. Through promises and humane treatment, he persuaded some five hundred people to come in and take the oath to the king; "yet numbers of the young men of the country have gone westward," he reported, "and attempts have been made to raise the people tho' hitherto without success." He was sure that most of the settlers between Boston and the Penobscot were loyal, but he also saw that "the impossibility in our present circumstances of affording them protection from the threats of the opposite party obliges them to act with caution. . . ." For three weeks in July and August, McLean's force was

43. V. H. Paltsits, ed., *Minutes of the Commissioners for Detecting and Defeating Conspiracies in the State of New York: Albany County Sessions, 1778–1781* (Albany, 1909), I, 369.

44. *Ibid.*, II, 735.

45. Minutes of the Council of Safety, *Pennsylvania Archives*, 1st Ser., XI, 38, 54–55, 94; Edmund Pendleton to William Woodford, May 24, 1779, David J. Mays, ed., *Letters and Papers of Edmund Pendleton* (Charlottesville, Va., 1967), I, 285–286.

under attack and siege by an amphibious expedition sent from Boston. The siege failed and the American fleet was driven off, but McLean had to report that "most of the inhabitants . . . notwithstanding their oath of allegiance, and fidelity to His Majesty were compelled to join the enemy. . . ." He still had hopes and worked to recapture the popular support enjoyed by the British in June. Tories from Boston swore that a strong force of loyal militia could be organized around the Penobscot garrison. But by October, McLean had all but given up; in spite of his gentle policy and their oaths of allegiance, he did not believe that the king could count on more than ten of the inhabitants along the whole river. Things looked a little brighter in November, but only because refugees from the rebels had begun to stream into the area around the British post. Eighteen months later, McLean's successor begged to evacuate the Penobscot post because he could not stop the local settlers from enticing his redcoats to desert.[46] As in New Jersey earlier and the Carolinas later, the dynamics of British intrusion and American reaction produced first a change, then a hardening of the local political situation. A tough or desperate few fled to the British for protection, while the rest gave at least the appearance of zeal for the American cause. But whether sham or not, their new revolutionary commitment could rarely be reversed again, either by the tact of a McLean or the terrorism of a Tarleton.

IV

It has always seemed slightly implausible that the American Republic was born out of a congeries of squabbling, unstable colonies and that labor was induced by nothing more than a few routine grievances expressed in abstract if elegant prose.

46. The Penobscot episode can be followed in the reports to Clinton in Hist. MSS Comm., *Report on American Manuscripts in the Royal Institution of Great Britain* (London, 1904–1909), I, 458–460, II, 14–18, 45, 52, 66, 83, 144, 258. Some interesting observations are in Uhlendorf, ed., *Revolution in America*, 313, to the effect that McLean "is probably the first Briton who understands the art of winning the confidence of the inhabitants. He has organized militia twenty miles inland." See also 342.

The Revolutionary War, considered as a political education for the masses, helps to fill the explanatory gap, provided we are willing to extrapolate a little from the evidence.

The broad popular basis of military organization forced thousands of more or less unwilling people to associate themselves openly and actively with the cause. In an age when single-shot muzzle-loaders were the standard instrument of coercion, sheer numbers were most important, and naked majoritarianism grew from the barrels of muskets. The absolute need to organize and hold a majority of gunmen had still wider implications: it required some kind of consensus, at least among the armed majority, in order to ward off incipient mutiny and dissolution. In the last years of the war, consensus probably operated to ease some of the pressure within the militia itself; derelictions of duty, once minimal loyalty could be taken for granted, were no longer treated as political crimes, but rather were punished as minor offenses. Likewise, the readiness shown soon after the war of the whole society to stop persecuting those loyalists who had not actually emigrated, despite the desire of many to purge the Republic of toryism, may be a measure of the curiously moderating effect of mass military participation.

Another effect of the war was the rapid erosion of deferential political behavior, which had characterized above all the apolitical majority; once they had seen and even taken part in hounding, humiliating, perhaps killing men known to them as social superiors, they could not easily reacquire the unthinking respect for wealth and status that underpinned the old order. And in a time of notorious duplicity and corruption, evident by 1779 in contemporary accounts from every hand, it was equally difficult to defer to new leaders, though many of them had been part of the old elite.

American laments for the decline of public virtue in the later years of the war may be read simply as so many jeremiads, but British evidence points to the sordid reality beneath the rhetoric. The British interpreted what they saw as war-weariness; what they really saw was the extent to which rebellion had successfully recruited the apathetic.[47] The continuing obsession with virtue, so central to political discourse during the postwar years, derived as much from the depressing spectacle of the compromises forced by the irresistible demands of revolutionary warfare as it did from the logic of classical republican theory.[48] In the end, of course, military and diplomatic success colored memory. Reluctance and resentment were readily forgotten, and the bare record of participation was all that mattered. After the fortunes and pressures of war had destroyed his other alternatives, each member of a large majority could claim his tiny but concrete share in the creation of the United States.

Beyond this hothouse nationalism, whose strengths and weaknesses would baffle observers for decades, there was at least one more visible effect that the war, working through the agency of the militia, had on American politics: the sharpening of the struggle between central and local authority. The many bitter words of Washington about the militia, the public outburst between Aedanus Burke and Alexander Hamilton over the respective roles of militia and regular forces in the southern campaign, prefigure the constituencies who fought over the Constitution and later organized as political parties.[49] If the Revolutionary militia is considered in its political role, then the relative apathy of the more numerous Antifederalists in 1787–1788 is less puzzling.

That a long, straggling, often disruptive and sometimes atrocious war had lasting effects on a society of three million people is not surprising. The difficulty has always been in discerning and describing those effects and in explaining them, without resort to some mystical notion of American character. The cor-

47. Certain strongly held opinions appear with greater frequency in the British record near the end of the war: that the Americans were war-weary; that the Americans were virtually unanimous in opposition to royal government; that British leniency was losing the war; that British brutality was losing the war; and that British inconsistency toward the Americans was losing the war.

48. On virtue, see Wood, *Creation of the American Republic*, 65–70.

49. For the exchange between Hamilton and Burke, see Harold C. Syrett and Jacob E. Cooke, eds., *The Papers of Alexander Hamilton* (New York, 1961–), VI, 333–337, 357–358.

rectness in detail of my own oblique attack on this problem through the medium of British strategy and American response is less important than the concept of the Revolutionary War, not as an instrument of policy or a sequence of military operations, but as a social process of political education that can be explored and should be analyzed.

5

The Structure of Politics

IN THE

Continental Congress

by

H. JAMES HENDERSON

I

The Continental Congress has been interpreted in the general literature of the American Revolution as a kind of antitype of the Federal Congress, just as the Articles of Confederation have often served as an antitype of the Constitution. George Bancroft's contention that the Continental Congress left "a people without a government" persists. Even Edmund Cody Burnett, whose work remains the standard treatment of the Continental Congress, was so struck by its failures to draw funds from the states that he sometimes hardly took its deliberations seriously. While it is not the intention of this essay to resuscitate the first national government of the United States—nor should it be necessary to do so after the admirable work of Merrill Jensen—it is important to reiterate that the Continental Congress did serve as a stage for the national politics of the Revolutionary era, that its influence upon institutional development was significant, and that it was sufficiently consequential even to produce a tradition of partisan politics that affected the formation of the first party system.[1]

During the war years the national establishment, because of the existence of the Continental army, was actually larger and more authoritative than during the early national era. It is likely that the average citizen near the battle regions was more aware of the coercive power of the national government in 1778 than in 1793 or 1803. Conscriptions of wagons and wagoners, grains, and other foodstuffs were palpable examples of the press of national power. If Congress could not tax, it could issue money and in certain instances force its acceptance. Lacking the power to regulate trade, it could and did stop commerce through embargo. Lacking an independently constituted executive, the Congress nonetheless created departments that were sufficiently vigorous and extended to excite fears of executivism. Because the Congress also had judicial powers in admiralty cases and therefore combined all of the legislative, executive, and judicial authorities of the national government, there was a natural reluctance to grant it authority at the expense of the states.

While it is true that much of the power of the national government derived from the Continental army and that its influence declined after the end of hostilities, it should be stressed that civil control of the military was maintained. This was itself remarkable, for legislative bodies in other colonial revolutions have tended to abdicate authority to military dictators or juntas. In the Spanish viceroyalties of New Grenada and La Plata, for example, congresses met and drew up constitutions, but proved incapable of directing the revolutionary movement. Washington's rectitude was admirable, but had he attempted to politicize his command in the manner of a Simón Bolívar, he doubtless would have been displaced. Even after the war when congressional influence was at its nadir, the Continental Congress organized a western empire in such manner as to have

1. George Bancroft, *History of the United States* (Boston, 1834–1874), X, 168–180; Edmund Cody Burnett, *The Continental Congress* (New York, 1941); Merrill Jensen, *The New Nation: A History of the United States during the Confederation, 1781–1789* (New York, 1950).

incalculable and enduring importance. Above all, it was in the Continental Congress that a tradition of national representative government was established, a government in which interests could be advanced and conflicts frequently resolved.

Partly because of the presumed impotence of the Continental Congress and partly because of its constitution as an assembly of delegates from sovereign states, each with an equal voice in policy formulation, historians have tended to interpret the partisan politics of Congress either as a formless confusion of faction or as a struggle between states' rightists and nationalists. Recent historians of the first party system, for example, have generally subscribed to William Nisbet Chambers's characterization of pre-Constitutional national politics as coalitions of individuals or interests that were transitory, unextended, and without ideological definition. Early historians in the Bancroft tradition, who saw only the debility of Congress, and Merrill Jensen, who has refuted John Fiske's contention that the nation under the Articles had fallen into depression and anarchy, have at least one thing in common: they interpret the partisan politics of the Congress as a contest between centralists and parochialists over the kinds of powers to be granted to the national government.[2] Both interpretations are partially true, but insufficient.

Because many colonials believed that parliamentary innovations of the decade before Lexington and Concord were the product of a conspiracy hatched by corrupt ministers and their legislative cohorts, Americans were particularly sensitive to the dangers of legislative combinations. The words *party* and *faction* were part of the vocabulary of members of Congress, but they were used most frequently as terms of opprobrium to describe an organized opposition. It is easy to read the strictures

2. William N. Chambers, *Political Parties in a New Nation* (New York, 1963), esp. chap. 1; John Fiske, *The Critical Period of American History* (Boston, 1888); Jensen, *New Nation*. Fiske, Bancroft, and others in the nationalist tradition portrayed the centralists as enlightened statesmen and the states' rightists as benighted parochialists, while Jensen views the parochialists as defenders of democratic accomplishments in the states and the centralists as conservatives who would curb social and economic change through political consolidation.

against factionalism in the press and pamphlet literature of the Revolutionary era and arrive at the conclusion that Congress was indeed a dangerous and chaotic assembly of factions.

But from another angle of vision—that of the voting record of the Congress—different interpretations are possible. From the time roll calls were recorded in the journals, that is, August 1777 (and even before then if one includes fragmentary reports by delegates such as John Adams), it is evident that members of Congress grouped in blocs that were enduring and cohesive. These legislative voting blocs, to be scrutinized momentarily, were not explicitly organized, but functioned as if they were. Confined largely to the Congress, they had important links with the embryonic party system of Pennsylvania. Far from being momentary aggregations of politicians with personal interests, they persisted in the shape of coalitions of states and even individuals throughout the entire history of the Continental Congress. Despite the fact that members of Congress were legally delegates from sovereign states and in status were not unlike diplomatic envoys, they frequently behaved as legislators representing popular constituencies.

There was a disjunction between the formal constitution of Congress as created under the Articles of Confederation and the practical operation of the Congress and its agencies that made it much more than a diplomatic assembly. The Articles provided, for example, that each state should be represented by from two to seven delegates who should collectively cast one vote. But the one-state, one-vote rule simply could not erase the distinction between Virginia and its diminutive neighbor, Delaware. In practice the larger states, particularly Virginia, Massachusetts, and Pennsylvania, sent more delegates than did the smaller states, even those located close to the Congress such as New Jersey and Delaware. For this reason, and because of their influence, they dominated congressional committees and the diplomatic and fiscal apparatus. The smaller states did not lack political talent—Rhode Island, New Jersey, and Delaware were being well served by men such as William Ellery, John Witherspoon, and John Dickinson. But it was not by chance that the men who were designated to negotiate the treaty of peace came from Pennsylvania, New York, Massachusetts, Virginia, and South Carolina, or that the ministers to France and England after the war should have come from Virginia and Massachusetts. It was only partially accidental that the superintendent of finance, the most powerful individual in domestic affairs, was a Pennsylvanian and that both secretaries for foreign affairs were New Yorkers.

Nor did the unit rule of voting preclude cleavages within states. The Lees of Virginia and certain cohorts such as Theodorick Bland frequently split with the other members of the Virginia delegation, as did the Adamses with John Hancock in the Massachusetts delegation. These divisions were in part simply factional disagreements related to the struggle for power among notables in their respective states, but they had ideological implications as well and, most important, created a bond between political conflict on the state and national levels. That the Lees and Adamses combined in the Continental Congress had important consequences for the politics of the Revolution.

The most active interplay between national and state politics occurred, not in the extremities of the Confederation, however, but in the middle states. This was a natural consequence of what might be roughly termed a factor of social communication —the closer a state was to the national capital, the more immediate was the influence of national policy making, all other factors being equal. There were other reasons for this interplay, particularly between Congress and Pennsylvania. Party politics in Pennsylvania were more fully developed than in other states as a consequence of the sharp division between the radical "Constitutionalists" led by the Bryans and the conservative "Republicans," the most notable of whom were Robert Morris and James Wilson. These conflicts have been described by Robert Brunhouse and need no reiteration here, but it is less fully appreciated that the partisan politics of the Continental Congress and the party struggles in Pennsylvania were closely related.[3] The influence of Robert Morris in both political situa-

3. Robert L. Brunhouse, *The Counter-Revolution in Pennsylvania, 1776–1790* (Harrisburg, 1942). For the relationship between congressional and Pennsylvania politics, see H. James Henderson, "Constitutionalists and

tions would alone have guaranteed such a connection, but beyond that, the posture of the Pennsylvania delegation in the context of congressional legislative blocs was almost entirely predictable, depending upon which party happened to control the state legislature at the time of election. Delegates elected by a Constitutionalist-dominated assembly aligned with an "eastern" party led by the New Englanders and their supporters from the South such as the Lees and Henry Laurens of South Carolina. Delegates elected by a Republican legislature either aligned with a "southern" party with middle states support from conservative New Yorkers such as Gouverneur Morris and John Jay or, as was more frequently the case, took the lead in forming a third, "middle states" party with southern support and strongly nationalistic leanings.

At the same time, the ability of congressmen to act as popular representatives was severely limited by the Articles. It was only through inadvertence or mixed signals that both Pennsylvania parties happened to be represented in Congress at a given moment. Samuel J. Atlee, for example, appears to have been elected by the Constitutionalists, but he aligned with their congressional opponents in 1779 and was later displaced. Not until the principle of popular representation was embodied in the election of Congress under the Constitution was a simultaneous two-party representation assured. Nonetheless, the Continental Congress was more sensitized to segments of the national constituency than has usually been recognized. Even notables such as Richard Henry Lee were not free to ignore the interests of their constituents without risking reelection to Congress. Lee's support of the eastern party in Congress prompted his opponents in Virginia to launch an attack against him in the assembly that almost succeeded in removing him from the delegation.

II

The comments made above are based in part on a comprehensive examination of the voting records of the Continental

Republicans in the Continental Congress," *Pennsylvania History*, XXXVI (1969), 119–144.

Congress. This computerized method pairs the votes of all members of the legislature between 1777 and 1786, establishes indexes of agreement for each pair, and makes possible the separation of "cluster blocs" of legislators who have a high level of agreement with each other. Partisanship can be discerned in the results by the existence of voting blocs that have high internal cohesion and low indexes of agreement with other blocs. The technique used is similar to that recently employed by Mary P. Ryan in her analysis of the party structure of the first four Federal Congresses.[4]

Historians have often used voting records in the writing of legislative history, but generally in a selective fashion. Before the advent of the computer it was a severe strain on the patience and even the sanity of the researcher to undertake the massive correlations necessary in a wholesale examination of a substantial legislative population casting a sizable number of votes. It was thus natural to select for close scrutiny what the researcher deemed significant votes. The peril of such an approach, however, is that controlling assumptions as to what is and what is not significant directly structure the outcome of the analysis. If, for example, it is assumed at the outset that the basic division in the Continental Congress was between nationalists and states' rightists, by no means an implausible assumption, it is possible to develop a persuasive argument supporting this thesis from selected roll calls in conjunction with other traditional materials such as correspondence and newspapers.

The technique used in the analysis that follows makes no such assumption—or indeed any qualitative assumption other than the contention that legislators voted intelligently, that is, they understood the meaning of the issue and voted their sentiment. Certain roll calls have been excluded, but only for quantitative reasons that might have skewed the results. Since unanimous or near-unanimous roll calls tell nothing about partisanship, roll calls on which there was less than 10 percent dis-

4. Mary P. Ryan, "Party Formation in the United States Congress, 1789–1796: A Quantitative Analysis," *William and Mary Quarterly*, 3d Ser., XXVIII (1971), 523–542.

agreement were eliminated on the assumption that such an elimination would not obscure a small faction that voted consistently in opposition to the congressional consensus. A check of the relatively few near-unanimous votes reveals no such consistency. In any case, the mere demand for a roll call was almost always the consequence of significant disagreement. Repetitive roll calls on the same question that occurred as the result of attempts to bring the issue to a vote but that resulted in no shift in the voting alignment were also excluded, since their inclusion would give undue stress to a given issue. All told, not more than one-quarter of the total roll calls were eliminated. Had all been included, in all probability the bloc structures would not have been appreciably different.

Two classes of bloc membership have been arbitrarily designated: "core" members, who agreed with all other members of the core on at least 66.7 percent of all the votes they cast in common, and "marginal" members, who had that same minimal level of agreement with at least half of the core of the bloc. Generally marginal members agreed with well over half of the core on the minimal level and had an average level of agreement in excess of 66.7 percent with the entire bloc, including both its core and margin. Because some blocs were rather closely associated, it is possible that a single delegate might belong to more than one bloc. Usually this characterized the middle states and southern blocs and entailed core membership in one bloc and marginal membership in another. Finally, delegates who were in attendance for only short intervals were not included in the analysis. There are four delegates from Virginia listed in the blocs for 1779, for example, but another five attended for too brief a time to be included.

The bloc structures for 1779, 1783, and 1786 have been delineated in table 1 because these were years of somewhat sharper partisanship than was customary and because they embody the peaks of what will be described as party ascendancies that had periodic fluctuations.

Before scrutinizing the structure and the meaning of the voting blocs, it would be well to define what they were—factions, haphazard combinations, diplomatic groupings, parties, or whatever. As previously suggested, the voting blocs were not haphazard, but rather were consistent groups with a strongly regional complexion. Nor were they diplomatic groupings, for diplomats cover disagreements and certainly never cancel each other out in the casting of a single vote. As is evident from table 1, this was not true of the Continental Congress.

TABLE 1

Voting Blocs in the Continental Congress, 1779, 1783, 1786

1779

Eastern Bloc	Middle Bloc	Southern Bloc	Independents
Peabody* (N.H.)	Duane (N.Y.)	Floyd* (N.Y.)	Collins (R.I.)
Whipple (N.H.)	Floyd (N.Y.)	Jay* (N.Y.)	Ellery (R.I.)
Adams, S. (Mass.)	Jay (N.Y.)	Plater* (Md.)	Root (Conn.)
Gerry (Mass.)	Morris, G. (N.Y.)	Paca* (Md.)	Lewis (N.Y.)
Holten (Mass.)	Fell* (N.J.)	Griffin (Va.)	Scudder (N.J.)
Lovell (Mass.)	Atlee (Pa.)	Fleming (Va.)	Forbes (Md.)
Marchant (R.I.)	Dickinson* (Del.)	Smith, M. (Va.)	Henry (Md.)
Spencer (Conn.)	Carmichael* (Md.)	Burke (N.C.)	Jenifer (Md.)
Huntington, S.* (Conn.)	Plater* (Md.)	Harnett (N.C.)	Laurens (S.C.)
Sherman (Conn.)		Hill (N.C.)	Mathews (S.C.)
Houston (N.J.)		Penn (N.C.)	
Witherspoon* (N.J.)		Sharpe* (N.C.)	
Armstrong* (Pa.)		Drayton (S.C.)	
Muhlenberg* (Pa.)		Langworthy (Ga.)	
Searle (Pa.)			
Shippen (Pa.)			
McLene (Pa.)			
Lee, R. H. (Va.)			

1783

Eastern Bloc	Middle Bloc	Southern Bloc	Independents
Higginson (Mass.)	Duane (N.Y.)	Mercer (Va.)	Foster (N.H.)
Holten (Mass.)	Floyd (N.Y.)	Williamson (N.C.)	White (N.H.)
Osgood (Mass.)	Hamilton (N.Y.)	Hawkins (N.C.)	Gorham (Mass.)

Eastern Bloc	Middle Bloc	Southern Bloc	Independents
Howell (R.I.)	L'Hommedieu (N.Y.)	Izard* (S.C.)	Collins (R.I.)
Ellery* (R.I.)	Boudinot (N.J.)	Read (S.C.)	Huntington, S.
Wolcott (Conn.)	Fitzsimmons (Pa.)		(Conn.)
	Montgomery (Pa.)		Clark (N.J.)
	Peters (Pa.)		McHenry (Md.)
	Wilson (Pa.)		Bland, T. (Va.)
	Carroll, D. (Md.)		Lee, A. (Va.)
	Jones, J. (Va.)		Rutledge (S.C.)
	Madison (Va.)		Gervais (S.C.)

1786

Eastern Bloc	Middle Bloc	Southern Bloc	Independents
Livermore (N.H.)		Harrison* (Md.)	Symmes (N.J.)
Long (N.H.)		Henry (Md.)	Pettit (Pa.)
Dane (Mass.)		Ramsey (Md.)	
King (Mass.)		Carrington (Va.)	
Gorham* (Mass.)		Grayson (Va.)	
Sedgwick* (Mass.)		Lee, H. (Va.)	
Manning (R.I.)		Monroe (Va.)	
Miller (R.I.)		Bloodworth (N.C.)	
Johnson* (Conn.)		White (N.C.)	
Sturges* (Conn.)		Bull (S.C.)	
Haring (N.Y.)		Huger (S.C.)	
Smith (N.Y.)		Parker (S.C.)	
Cadwalader (N.J.)		Pinckney (S.C.)	
Hornblower (N.J.)		Few (Ga.)	
Bayard* (Pa.)		Houstoun (Ga.)	
St. Clair (Pa.)			

NOTE: Asterisks indicate "marginal" members, as previously defined.

In 1779 John Fell of New Jersey broke with his colleagues William Houston and John Witherspoon, and Samuel J. Atlee separated from his fellow delegates from Pennsylvania. The example of Richard Henry Lee is admittedly extreme, but it is worthy of mention that his ratio of agreement with Meriwether Smith of Virginia was 40 percent on seventy-five votes the two cast in common, while Lee's level of agreement with William Whipple of New Hampshire was 83 percent on seventy-one votes.

The word *faction* seems at once appropriate and insufficient as a description of the blocs. Despite the existence of a closer relationship between the people and the Congress than is generally recognized, congressional blocs were far from being organized in a formal sense and clearly lacked the kinds of contacts with the grass roots that we associate with the modern party. The term *faction* conventionally refers to personal alliances within the government, and such a description does help characterize certain members of the blocs. Richard Henry Lee's membership in the eastern bloc was attributable in part to the support the New Englanders gave his brother Arthur during his controversy with Silas Deane and Benjamin Franklin in France. The connection between the Adamses and the Lees was described by John Jay as a "Family compact."[5] Lee had familial connections of the most direct sort with the eastern bloc, for William Shippen was the father-in-law of Alice Lee, Richard Henry Lee's sister. Robert Morris, whose influence was always felt in Congress whether he happened to be a member or not, was the brother-in-law of William Paca. James Duane and John Jay were connected by marriage with the Livingstons, who like Morris were generally connected with congressional business whether or not they were members. (Four were delegates and two held important administrative offices.) Factions traditionally are also stitched together by personal economic interests, and many middle and southern bloc delegates were connected through business ties in commerce and land speculation—most strikingly with Robert Morris. As a result of Morris's enterprise in the flour and tobacco trade, land speculation, and the organization of the Bank of North America, he was connected to one degree or another with Gouverneur Morris, Thomas Fitzsimmons, James Wilson, William Paca, and Thomas Adams —all members of the Congress in 1779 and 1783. But this is only a reflection of a larger network involving members of Congress and their connections during the Revolutionary era. In the Virginia delegation alone Morris had business relationships

5. John Jay to George Washington, Apr. 26, 1779, Edmund C. Burnett, ed., *Letters of Members of the Continental Congress* (Washington, D.C., 1924–1936), IV, 176–177.

with Carter Braxton, Benjamin Harrison, Jr., John Harvie, and John Banister between 1774 and 1778.[6]

For a number of reasons, however, the congressional blocs were more than traditional factions. The Lee-Adams connection dated back to 1770, and it was more a political than an interest-oriented relationship. It involved Samuel Adams much more than John Adams, both in its inception and in its sustained involvement in congressional activity. Samuel Adams, who sought neither profit nor national office from the Revolution, found that his political opponents in Massachusetts (a scene in which he did have constant political ambitions) were attempting to "prejudice the People against the Lees, and propagate that I am a Friend to them."[7] Richard Henry Lee, as previously indicated, almost lost his seat in Congress because of charges that he had "favored New England to the injury of Virginia."[8] In short, factional activity on the national stage prejudiced the political positions of both Adams and Lee in their respective states. While there are clear indications of a mixture of public and private business in the dealings of many delegates, particularly those in the middle bloc of 1783, that bloc was not formed simply as a result of personal "connections" in the eighteenth-century mode. Individuals such as Hamilton, Wilson, and Madison were brought together more by nationalist political objectives than by the perquisites of office. In any event, all three shortly left Congress.

The term *legislative party* probably serves best to describe the blocs in table 1. The parties at once included factions and transcended them. Restricted largely to the Congress, they were not unknown on the outside. An anonymous letter writer in the

6. Morris's business connections are described in many sources, but the evidence of these particular relationships can be traced in his papers at the Library of Congress and in the Holker Papers in the Library of Congress and the William L. Clements Library, Ann Arbor, Mich. See, e.g., Morris to Holker, Oct. 6, 8, 1778, Morris Papers, Lib. of Congress. Morris also lent money to Thomas Burke, the North Carolina delegate; Burke to Morris, Nov. 4, 1780, *ibid.*

7. Samuel Adams to James Warren, Mar. 23, 1779, Harry A. Cushing, ed., *The Writings of Samuel Adams* (New York, 1904–1908), IV, 140.

8. Richard Henry Lee to Gov. Patrick Henry, May 26, 1777, Burnett, ed., *Letters*, II, 374.

Pennsylvania Gazette under the pseudonym "O Tempora! O Mores!" complained in June 1779 of a "junto" that had been "early formed in Congress" when the northern and southern states suspected some middle states "on many real grounds as well as some pretended ones" of being unsympathetic with the Revolution. The writer (probably Edward Langworthy of Georgia) went on to describe the junto as being composed of "certain of the delegates from New England, New Jersey, and this state Pennsylvania, and of two or three members to the southward." Allowing for a strong tendency for Henry Laurens of South Carolina (an independent in 1779) to align with the bloc, or "party," the description is accurate. The French officer Louis Fleury described a two-party division in Congress in 1778 in which New England, New Jersey, Pennsylvania, and South Carolina were aligned against Virginia, Maryland, New York, North Carolina, and Delaware. The French minister Conrad Alexandre Gérard filled his dispatches to the comte de Vergennes with detailed and generally correct descriptions of congressional parties.[9]

These legislative parties achieved an impressive cohesion over time despite fluctuations in personnel and changes in issues. Indeed, the average level of agreement on roll calls within the blocks was higher than in the parties of today.[10] Of course, such comparative data are not strictly compatible, since the situation in the Continental Congress was in a sense precisely the opposite of that in today's Congress. In the Revolutionary era legislators accepted regional interests as the norm and resisted formal and extended party organization; today officeholding parties are the norm and regional differences are the anomalies with which they must cope. But the analogy with the early legislative parties that formed the nucleus of the first party

9. "O Tempora! O Mores!" *Pennsylvania Gazette* (Philadelphia), June 23, 1779; B. F. Stevens, ed., *Facsimiles of Manuscripts in European Archives Relating to America, 1773–1783* (London, 1889–1895), XVII, no. 1616; Gérard to Vergennes, June 12, 1779, John J. Meng, ed., *Despatches and Instructions of Conrad Alexandre Gérard* (Baltimore, 1939), 717–724.

10. Party unity scores during the 1970 session of Congress were just 57% among Democrats. *Congressional Quarterly*, XXIX (1971), 237.

system under the Constitution is very comparable and much more relevant. It remains, however, to investigate the meaning of the blocs, or legislative parties—terms that will be used interchangeably below.

III

Sectionalism is the most obvious factor in the bloc alignments shown in table 1. Whether in the form of a tripartite division following the traditional eastern, middle, and southern colonial components or in the more menacing dichotomy of the middle eighties, the North-South tension of national politics was unmistakable. A delegate in the Continental Congress from one of the four New England states would be over thirty times more likely to join the eastern party than the southern party (or parties, as the case might be). The same tendency to identify with one's section held true for delegates from the five southern states. Table 2 illustrates this generalization. That the sectional tendency of political alignments was neither haphazard nor the product of personal connections is apparent from the data, which reflect the voting behavior of 186 different delegates[11] over a ten-year span from August 1777, when roll calls were first recorded in the congressional journals, until the end of 1786, when the Congress had reached the end of its effectiveness (excepting only its passage of the Northwest Ordinance). The posture of the Massachusetts delegation in 1778, when it was represented by Samuel Adams, Elbridge Gerry, James Lovell, Francis Dana, and Samuel Holten, differed very little from that of 1786, when the delegates were Nathaniel Gorham, Rufus King, Nathan Dane, and Theodore Sedgwick. Likewise, Cornelius Harnett, John Penn, and Thomas Burke in the North Carolina delegation of 1778 were almost as parochial in their attachments as Timothy Bloodworth and James White in 1786. Actually sectional divisions increased rather than diminished over time, as is evident in table 3. Another indication of the

11. It should be noted that this total does not equate with the entire membership of the Congress during that time span. Delegates with low attendance records were eliminated, but rarely was a member who was present for even 25% of the total roll calls not included.

TABLE 2

Percentage of Pairings of Individual Delegates, 1777–1786
(66.7 Percent Agreement)

	Eastern Blocs	Middle Blocs	Southern Blocs	Unaffiliated
Eastern blocs	68%	10%	2%	20%
Middle blocs	28%	48%	16%	16%
Southern blocs	3%	8%	65%	23%

NOTE: The pairings are based on 66.7% or more agreement between all pairs of delegates from annual analysis of nonrepetitive roll calls on which there was at least 10% disagreement in the entire Congress. Percentages have been worked out for a weighting of "core" and "marginal" members of the various blocs. Core members were given a value of 1, marginal members, .5, and unaffiliated delegates, a value of 0. Generally unaffiliated delegates skittered about the fringe of their own regional bloc. (Thus inclusion of unanimous and near-unanimous roll calls would in all likelihood have accentuated the sectional character of the blocs by including such members as marginal members. Clearly the inclusion of repetitive votes would have had that effect, as in 1779 when the debates over the fisheries as a peace "ultimatum" produced many rigidly sectional roll calls that were not included because they represented persistence on the part of dedicated supporters of the fisheries rather than an actual change of the issue.) It should be added that totals need not equal 100%.

pervasive influence of sectionalism can be seen in the ambiguous stance of the delegations from the middle states. Often showing the potential of establishing an independent third force, they were constantly pulled toward a dichotomization of the Congress around the New England and southern extremities.

This should not be surprising. While it would be erroneous to classify the American Revolution simply as a colonial war for independence, it did share certain problems common to such wars, particularly the problem of constructing a new nation from differentiated materials of the colonial past.[12] In the twentieth century there are many examples of bitter regionalism in Asia and Africa, which are by no means unique in the difficulties

12. For an argument that puts the American Revolution in the paradigm of the colonial revolution, see Thomas C. Barrow, "The American Revolution as a Colonial War for Independence," *WMQ*, 3d Ser., XXV (1968), 453–463.

TABLE 3

Sectional Pairings, 1777–1786
(Expressed in Percentages of Possible Pairs)

	1777–1779	1780–1783	1784–1786
South	55%	60%	83%
Middle states	19%	58%	64%*
New England	66%	62%	83%

NOTE: *This middle states percentage for 1784–1786 is inflated by the classification of the northern bloc that formed in 1786 in response to the Jay-Gardoqui negotiations as a New England-middle states alliance. Delegates belonging to that coalition were scored as New England if from that section and as middle states if from there.

colonial nations experience in achieving coherence. When the Spanish Empire dissolved as a consequence of Napoleon's dethronement of the Spanish Bourbon monarchy, the efforts of Bolívar to form a grand continental Spanish-American republic foundered on the resistant materials of parochial loyalties. It was Bolívar's lament at the end of his illustrious but ultimately unsuccessful career that he had "ploughed the sea." Even the viceroyalty of New Grenada, one of four subdivisions of the Spanish Empire, resisted the inspired rhetoric and commanding generalship of the great Venezuelan liberator. Bolívar died an exile, as did the Argentinean liberator, San Martín, who was equally dedicated to the ideal of molding a nation out of the viceroyalty of La Plata and equally unsuccessful in achieving it.

The struggle for political coherence in La Plata is instructive both as regards the problems encountered by the Confederation and the remarkable character of the achievement of the political leadership of the American Revolution in establishing an enlarged republic. The political leaders of Buenos Aires, the *porteños*, not only fought a war for independence but also put together an ambitious program of social and economic reform and connected it with a consolidated and democratic national political system. The program foundered before it was launched because of internal resistance that congealed about deep attachments to locality, the church, and provincial leadership among the people. The battle between tradition and innovation was won by what the recent Argentinean political historian Romero has called "inorganic democracy," or the populist elements of diffusion in the Banda Oriental and the Platan interior.[13] In a ferment of anarchy the La Platan viceroyalty finally split into the three nations of Argentina, Uruguay, and Paraguay.

One might have anticipated the same outcome in the American Revolution. Indeed, tory prophecies of disaster during the Resistance period, British intelligence, and strategy during the War for Independence all assumed the incapacity of the various parts of the thirteen colonies to form a homogeneous republic. Paul Wentworth, the New Hampshire informer from the illustrious and powerful clan of that colony, reported to the crown that "there is hardly any observation moral or political, which will equally apply either to the Individuals or the Collective Bodys of the Colonies, at large. . . ." Straining his argument, which he titled "Minutes respecting political Parties in America and Sketches of the leading Persons in each Province," he asserted there were greater differences between the colonial regions than between the countries of Europe. He called New England the "Eastern Republick of Independants in Church and State," a region similar to the Swiss Confederation. The "Middle Republick of Toleration in Church and State" embraced the nondissenting portion of New York down to the Potomac and was analagous to the Dutch Republic. The remaining four states constituted the "Southern Republick, or Mixed Government Copyed nearly from Great Britain."[14]

13. José Luis Romero, *A History of Argentine Political Thought*, trans. Thomas McGann (Stanford, Calif., 1963), chaps. 3, 4. Romero's use of the terms organic and inorganic democracy are the reverse of what others might prefer. By "organic" Romero means a rational, constitutional order, while "inorganic" refers to the more elemental, irrational force of unstructured, communal, populist democracy. This usage is similar to that of the great Argentinean patriot Bartolomé Mitre, who struggled himself against the "reactionary" interior populism of the gaucho, aligned behind local *caudillos*, or strongmen. Mitre's lament, enunciated later than that of Bolívar, was essentially the failure of La Plata to achieve a constitutional form that could provide coherence for what Mitre believed was the basic democratic tendency of the Argentinean people. That Mitre was instructed by the example of the United States hardly needs reiteration.

14. Paul Wentworth, "Minutes respecting political Parties in America

Wentworth doubtless intended that British policy take advantage of such sectional differences, and while it is questionable that he received a careful hearing by British policy makers, English military strategy seems to have been predicated upon just such regional disparities.

Congressional politics, though structured in a highly sectional fashion, were not static. Beneath the constant sectional character of congressional factionalism there was a dynamic progression of sectional ascendancies. Three essential phases of Confederation politics may be delineated. The first lasted from 1774 to 1779 and may be termed the period of eastern ascendancy,[15] when the New England party dominated congressional deliberations. A second interval, lasting roughly from 1780 to 1783, was marked by a shift in the locus of power to the middle party. The remainder of the era of nominal congressional authority, 1784 to 1787, was basically a period when southern delegates, hitherto often divided, achieved a level of cohesion sufficient to lead in the shaping of policy.

Regional ascendancies are apparent, at least in a superficial sense, from the bloc configurations in table 1. In 1779, the high point of eastern power, the eastern party was the largest of the three blocs, not only in terms of individuals but in its capacity to deliver state votes. There were six votes in the party, while the middle bloc could deliver only New York, and the southern party only the three votes of Virginia, North Carolina, and Georgia with any certainty. In 1783 both the eastern and southern parties were fragmented, while the middle party had superior cohesion. In 1786, while the eastern party had a larger number of votes than were commanded by the South, the south-

---

and Sketches of the leading Persons in each Province," Stevens, ed., *Facsimiles*, XVII, no. 487.

15. The term "eastern" rather than "New England" is used because it was conventional at the time and because, as Wentworth noted in his characterization of the three colonial regions, the New England influence extended beyond the borders of Massachusetts and Connecticut into portions of New York. Thus Gouverneur Morris, who had only disdain for the populist tendencies of the early Revolutionary politics of New England, described William Clingan, the Pennsylvania Constitutionalist, as a man made of "the true Eastern Stamp and Clay." Gouverneur Morris to Robert Morris, May 11, 1778, Burnett, ed., *Letters*, III, 230.

ern party had unparalleled cohesion, with no independents and only one marginal member. Even with the vagaries of attendance and the defections that occurred even in a sharply divided Congress such as that of 1786, the South acquired an influence it had not had since the first Congress.

It should be stressed that full party representation was crucial in a Congress often marked by nonattendance. Lengthy tenures were also very important. That the eastern party had both representation and tenure during the 1770s gave it a real tactical advantage. The Adamses, Elbridge Gerry, James Lovell, William Ellery, Oliver Ellsworth, Roger Sherman, Samuel Huntington, and Eliphalet Dyer all had sustained tenures when there was great flux in the delegations from the middle and southern states. This contributed greatly to their effectiveness on the floor and in committees. Elbridge Gerry's name is attached to 115 motions resulting in roll calls during the period after August 1777, when roll calls were recorded—an extraordinary statistic when contrasted with the next highest number of 43 motions offered by both Thomas Burke and Charles Pinckney.[16] The reason is not simply Gerry's penchant for legislative involvement, remarkable in itself, but also that he served six terms after 1776. The eastern influence prompted Francis Lewis of New York to remind his home state that it had been deprived of its vote for the previous six weeks because he was the only New Yorker on the floor of Congress. He concluded, "Permit me to observe that the four N. E. States are allways represented. . . ." The consequence was felt in all the business of Congress. John Jay reported to Washington in 1779: "The Marine Committee consists of a Delegate from each State. It fluctuates, new Members constantly coming in and old ones going out. Three or four indeed have remained in it from the Beginning, and have a proportionate Influence, or more properly *Interest* in it. Very few of the Members understand even the State of our naval Affairs or have Time or Inclination to attend to them."[17] Just

16. The tabulation is from the index of Clifford Lord, ed., *The Atlas of Congressional Roll Calls* (New York, 1943).

17. Francis Lewis to the president of the New York Convention, Jan. 31, 1777, John Jay to George Washington, Apr. 26, 1779, Burnett, ed., *Letters*, II, 230, IV, 176–177. Jay went on to charge that the committee system

as eastern influence was enhanced by its ubiquitous presence on congressional committees during the 1770s, so the ascendance of the middle states was achieved in great measure by domination of the executive departments created and staffed during 1780 and 1781. Robert Morris's joint administration of finance and marine affairs, Robert R. Livingston's secretaryship of foreign affairs, and the offer of the secretaryship of war to Alexander McDougall caused Samuel Adams to warn from Boston of "a compleat NY Administration. It may be well to enquire, what Influence has brought this about. . . ."[18]

While the southern faction never achieved the executive power wielded by the centralists from the middle states during the early 1780s, the role of Jefferson in the original committee on the organization of the West in 1784 is suggestive of a significant southern presence. Jefferson symbolizes as well another factor that contributed to the ascendance of a given regional party at a particular moment: quality of leadership.

It is a commonplace to state that the Revolutionary generation produced an extraordinary list of political talents. It is less recognized that there were exceptionally able members constantly in attendance in Congress (for there was no wholesale exodus to the army and the states) and, more important for

---

remained unchanged because it was "convenient to the Family compact," presumably the Lee-Adams connection. Jay was partially correct, but the Marine Committee was dominated by New England delegates, as was the Committee on Foreign Affairs, where the influence of James Lovell was paramount. It should be added that the eastern faction did not have absolute hegemony, despite its domination as well of the Board of War, created in 1777. The eastern bloc was less well represented in the standing Committee on Commerce, where the influence of Robert Morris was strongly felt. Nonetheless, New England and the South had disproportionately large representation on standing and special committees, as has been pointed out by George Wood, *Congressional Control of Foreign Relations during the American Revolution, 1774–1789* (Allentown, Pa., 1919). Although Wood focused on foreign relations, he also surveyed the general composition of the hundreds of standing and special committees concerned with all varieties of business. The eastern thrust can be seen in the presence of one of the Adamses or Richard Henry Lee (one of the few southern members of the eastern bloc) on each of the 20 committees Wood selected at random for the year 1776. *Ibid.*, 32–36.

18. Samuel Adams to Thomas McKean, Aug. 29, 1781, Cushing, ed., *Writings of Samuel Adams*, IV, 261.

the purposes of this argument, that there were moments when one region was represented by superior political talents. Perhaps no Congresses were more illustrious than those that met before Independence. However, the continued presence of the Adamses and Lees during the later 1770s was one guarantee of eastern predominance. Likewise the presence of Hamilton, James Wilson, and Madison (a core member of the middle faction in 1781 as well as 1783), along with the absence of many eastern leaders, enormously enhanced the potential of the middle states group during the early 1780s. During the third period of congressional history, however, the middle states were represented by men whose names are familiar only to scholars— DeWitt, Paine, Haring, Laurance, and Melancton Smith from New York; Beatty, Cadwalader, Stewart, Hornblower, and Symmes from New Jersey; Gardner, William Henry, David Jackson, Pettit, John Bayard, and Arthur St. Clair from Pennsylvania. Delaware went largely unrepresented. It was at this time that southern delegations included James McHenry, Jefferson, Monroe, William Grayson, Henry Lee, Hugh Williamson, and Charles Pinckney. James Madison, moreover, although eliminated during the mid-eighties by the three-year tenure rule of the Articles, was in constant contact with Congress and returned as a delegate in 1787. In an age that placed a high premium on political intelligence, such men inevitably made a mark on congressional deliberations.

The New England delegations also included men of ability during the middle and later eighties. Rufus King, Nathan Dane, and Theodore Sedgwick from Massachusetts, David Howell and James Manning from Rhode Island, Roger Sherman and William Samuel Johnson from Connecticut were larger talents than those in the middle states delegations. That the middle states bloc fused with the eastern states in the voting of 1786 was in all probability partially due to this fact, as well as to the increased influence of the Constitutionalists in the Pennsylvania assembly.

The regional tendency of congressional partisanship inherited from the colonial past posed one particularly perplexing problem. No sectional bloc could take command against united opposition, since none had a majority of the votes. After the Articles of Confederation, which required an absolute majority of seven votes for routine questions and nine for all consequential matters regarding war, diplomacy, and finance, went into effect, the problem became even greater. Even before the Articles became operative in March 1781, it was difficult for a single party to establish a working majority. Intersectional support was therefore crucial. That decisions were made testifies to the capacity of members of Congress to compromise (a matter that should not be forgotten in an analysis that is directed largely toward the anatomy of congressional divisions). The ability of a party to achieve compromise or to overcome opposition by drawing support from outside a regional nucleus was also affected by factors outside Congress that were related to the changing circumstances of the Revolution.

IV

The early phase of the Revolution was marked by a high level of ideological fervor as the decision to separate from the mother country was legitimized through appeals to charter liberties, traditional rights, republican principles, natural law, divine imperatives, and the threat that a corrupt ministry was scheming to enslave the colonies—an elaborate ideological orchestration that, as Bernard Bailyn has suggested, powerfully influenced the decision to revolt. As Gordon Wood and Alan Heimert have also shown, there was an anticipation, voiced most forcibly by the Calvinist clergy, that a republican revolution would achieve a moral regeneration of the American people. No particular region had a monopoly on the vocabulary of republicanism, particularly in terms of the legal authenticity of the resistance to parliamentary taxes—a point well established by Edmund S. Morgan in his study of the Stamp Act.[19] But the greatest flood of the rhetoric of regeneration came from the active presses and

19. Bernard Bailyn, *The Ideological Origins of the American Revolution* (Cambridge, Mass., 1967); Gordon S. Wood, *The Creation of the American Republic, 1776–1787* (Chapel Hill, 1969); Alan Heimert, *Religion and the American Mind from the Great Awakening to the Revolution* (Cambridge, Mass., 1966); Edmund S. and Helen M. Morgan, *The Stamp Act Crisis: Prologue to Revolution* (Chapel Hill, 1953).

pulpits of New England. Even the more straightforward statements of grievances from all the colonies regarding traditional
liberties and the dangers of distant consolidated power contain
subtle differences in accent that suggest the ideology of discontent reached its highest level in New England.

Samuel Adams's anticipation of a reformation of public morality—even the creation of a "Christian Sparta"—as a consequence of a republican revolution was consonant with the
Suffolk Resolves, but much less so with the forebodings of
Dickinson in the Olive Branch Petition and, less conspicuously,
in the Declaration of the Causes and Necessity of Taking up
Arms. It would not be too much to say that Adams's perception
of the Revolution lacked congruence with the secular liberalism
of such an enthusiastic republican revolutionary as Jefferson.
In the more limited sphere of the Continental Congress, the
ideological separation of the New Englanders from delegates
representing the middle and southern colonies after 1776 was
even more marked.

As the final break with England approached, there was a
natural tendency for the New Englanders to interpret the
"spirit of '76" as a peculiarly New England phenomenon, and
for New England delegates in the Congress to think of themselves as the "Party of the Revolution," representing the most
uniformly patriot area of the nation and therefore uniquely
competent to translate the republican spirit of the Revolution
into concrete policy.[20]

20. Thus the loss of Ticonderoga was blamed by John Adams on the
ineptitude of the middle states officers George Schuyler and Arthur St. Clair.
The North Carolina delegate Thomas Burke was incensed at this, complaining that the New England delegates were "very unwilling to admit
that any of our misfortune has happened through a weakness which they
share in common with the rest." Burke to Gov. Richard Caswell, July 30,
1777, Walter Clark, ed., *The State Records of North Carolina, 1777–1790*
(Winston and Goldsboro, N.C., 1895–1905), XI, 550. After the defeat of
Burgoyne, New Englanders "dispaired" of expelling the British "but by
New England Exertion." Henry Marchant to Samuel Adams, Dec. 22, 1777,
Joseph Ward to Samuel Adams, Jan. 14, 1778, Samuel Adams Papers, New
York Public Library. The strenuous involvement of the New England
militia at Saratoga under the "republican" General Gates was contrasted
with the failures of Washington's generalship and the soft resistance put
up by the Pennsylvanians against Howe.

A second factor contributing to New England ascendancy during the early phase of the Revolution was the promising military resistance against the vaunted British army that had taken place in Massachusetts, largely with New England arms. If, as John Shy suggests elsewhere in this volume, large-scale popular involvement in military action—or even the organization for action—served to politicize and nationalize the population, clearly the New England region had an early start.

The eastern posture as the party of the Revolution had political and social implications beyond parochial claims to superior patriotic commitment. Because of tory propaganda about the dangers of aggressive New England republicanism, because of gaps in social communication that led to simplistic generalizations about regional character, and because of genuine regional differences, New Englanders acquired the reputation of radical levelers, and southerners gained the reputation of conservative aristocrats. The behavior of delegates from the two sections gave a measure of plausibility to this distinction.

The dour, puritanical qualities of many of the easterners doubtless gave credence to their posture as the party of the Revolution. By design and accident the eastern delegations were gradually rid of moderates such as Thomas Cushing, profiteers such as John Langdon, who chose to tend to his naval contracts in Portsmouth rather than suffer financial loss as a delegate, and high livers, such as John Hancock, who was denied a vote of appreciation at the end of his term as president of Congress by the New Englanders themselves.[21] Most New Englanders who remained by the time of Saratoga and the French alliance—the Adamses, Shermans, and Whipples—had impeccable credentials as virtuous republicans.

The socioeconomic characteristics of congressmen during the late 1770s tended to substantiate contemporary impressions that easterners were democrats and southerners were elitists. The average New England delegate was a professional man—a lawyer,

21. Worthington C. Ford *et al.*, eds., *Journals of the Continental Congress, 1774–1779* (Washington, D.C., 1904–1937), IX, 854. Interestingly, this very vote delineates the eastern faction and its fringe in 1777.

physician, or schoolteacher—without extensive property, while the average southerner was also a lawyer, but with substantial property in land and slaves. Behaviorally the two factions were poles apart. The eastern faction supported sumptuary legislation to purify cosmopolitan Philadelphia, while the southerners tried to civilize the "Bestian" land of York, a congressional sanctuary during Howe's occupation of Philadelphia, with bucolic teas on an island dubbed "Daphne."[22] Considering the Continental Congress as a transient community, as James Young has described the Federal Congress between 1800 and 1828, such distinctions were not without consequence during the early ideological phase of the Revolution.[23]

Although in all probability the snap judgment of a parochial Yankee, John Adams's contention that the delay in moving toward the creation of state constitutions, and ultimately independence, arose "from a single source—the Reluctance of the Southern Colonies to Republican Government"—appears significant. The creation of constitutions in the colonies and a confederation between them could be accomplished only on the basis of "popular Principles and Maxims" that were "abhorrent" to the proprietary interest of the middle colonies and the "Barons of the South. . . ."[24] Much later, in 1779, the delegate from New Hampshire, Nathaniel Peabody, complained of "the Tyrannic strides of Certain Aristocratical Gentry . . . Using their Hostile influence to Subjugate the E.[ast] and force them to a Compliance with Measures injurious degrading, and Contrary, to every republican principal."[25] Although the precise grievance Peabody had in mind is not clear, it is probable that he was objecting to cooperation of the southern faction (and its middle states allies) with the French request that the American

22. John Banister to Mrs. Bland, June 19, 1778, Historical Society of Pennsylvania, Philadelphia.

23. James Sterling Young, *The Congressional Community* (New York, 1967), esp. 89–94.

24. John Adams to Horatio Gates, Mar. 23, 1776, Peter Force, comp., *American Archives* . . . , 4th Ser. (Washington, D.C., 1837–1846), V, 471.

25. Nathaniel Peabody to Josiah Bartlett, Aug. 17, 1779, Burnett, ed., *Letters*, IV, 382.

claim to the fisheries not be included in the United States's peace demands. In any event it is clear that social and ideological antagonisms were kindling congressional factionalism.

Disputes between the eastern and southern factions were not confined to exaggerated and stylized regional characterizations or petulant outbursts of parochial frustration. Southerners were inclined to favor a professional Continental Line and to sympathize with the demand of officers for half-pay pensions. Thomas Lynch of South Carolina urged Washington to force New England officers not to "cheat or to mess with the Men" and to "do their Duty and look as well as act like Gentlemen." James Lovell, the Boston schoolteacher, on the other hand deplored that "our Continental Gentlemen" should ask for half-pay pensions in the European manner. He warned that in America, as in Europe, such favoritism would create "a lot of haughty idle imperious Scandalizers of industrious Citizens and Farmers. . . ."[26] As republican purists, the easterners generally were less tolerant than southerners of the mixture of public and private enterprise that Robert Morris and the commercial community surrounding him came to symbolize. James Searle from Pennsylvania argued that no one could be a good whig "unless he grows poor during the war."[27] It was these qualities that made it rather natural for Richard Henry Lee to join the New Englanders against the Deane-Morris connection that had aligned against his brother Arthur in Europe.

Interestingly the divisions between and within delegations in the middle states indicate that delegates did not vote according to their geographic proximity to New England so much as their social and ideological compatibility with one of the two sectional factions. During 1778 and 1779, a time of extreme partisanship, members from the New York elite such as Gouverneur Morris, William Duer, John Jay, Philip Schuyler, and James Duane aligned either with the southern party or with the middle states bloc of 1779, which was closer to the southern than

26. Thomas Lynch to George Washington, Nov. 13, 1775, *ibid.*, I, 253–254; James Lovell to Samuel Adams, Jan. 13, 1778, Samuel Adams Papers, N. Y. Pub. Lib.

27. Quoted by Benjamin Rush in Rush to Searle, Jan. 21, 1778, *Pennsylvania Magazine of History and Biography*, III (1879), 223.

the eastern party. Because they dominated the delegation, they usually cast New York's vote on partisan issues against the eastern bloc. Pennsylvania, on the other hand, almost always supported New England at this time—even on roll calls in 1779 dealing with the fisheries in which Pennsylvania had little if any economic interest. That this was because the delegation was dominated by the radical Constitutionalist party is evident from the fact that, when the Republican opposition won control of the Pennsylvania legislature, congressional delegates such as Robert Morris, James Wilson, and Thomas Fitzsimmons abruptly shifted toward a southern orientation.

In 1779 there was a convergence of eastern revolutionary purism and the radical-conservative party conflict in Pennsylvania that seemed to have the potential of providing the nucleus of a national party system organized on the basis of an opposition of what might be termed populist and elitist interests. Evident in the eastern-Constitutionalist alliance in the Congress, it was activated as well by extralegal, price-control committees in Pennsylvania that opposed profiteers and among other actions impounded a shipment of flour under the account of Robert Morris. Nothing significant came from this flurry, however, and clearly the fears of conservatives that the eastern alliance represented a leveler threat were grossly exaggerated.

Actually the radical reputation of the easterners was not entirely warranted; at least it must be carefully qualified. There were profoundly conservative dimensions to the "Christian Sparta" that remained Sam Adams's ultimate revolutionary purpose. Adams's populism, in contrast to the ideology of Gouverneur Morris or John Jay or Edward Rutledge, was predicated upon the expectation that the people would naturally cling to older, even seventeenth-century, corporate Christian values that stressed denial more than opportunity and social order more than mobility. If his inclination was more toward democracy than deference (in contrast to John Adams and the Federalists of a later decade), it was hardly attuned to the expansive and materialistic liberalism that would characterize post-Revolutionary American society—a society that Sam Adams was never really able to accept.

The republican purism that had been the mainstay of the eastern faction proved to be as fragile an instrument for sustaining power as it was dynamic in generating the Revolution. Compromised by parochialism, diluted by the passage of time, and flawed by the natural obligation of eastern delegates to promote concrete eastern interests such as the fisheries and high interest rates on loan office certificates, its power declined by the winter of 1779/1780.

There were compelling practical reasons for the termination of this first phase of the Revolution, however. British military pressure was mounting in the South. Depreciation of Continental bills of credit had become so critical that financing a new campaign seemed problematical. National honor, if not survival, dictated that a more efficient central government shape the revolutionary commitment, particularly in view of the French involvement that obligated the Congress to prosecute the war with vigor at the same time that it raised the specter of outside contamination of the republican revolution.

That the creation of quasi-independent executive departments to replace the committee system during 1780 and 1781 constituted a conservative turn away from the legislative and parochial thrust of revolutionary republicanism hardly needs elaboration. Bureaucratization was an indication of the failure of revolutionary commitment; it also created dangerous concentrations of power. The office of superintendent of finance in the hands of Robert Morris was particularly threatening because of the economic and political influence that naturally attached to the office and the aggregations of "interested" men in the army, government, and the states who looked to the financier. While it would be wrong to view Robert Morris as capable of launching a grand program of political consolidation in the mode later accomplished by Hamilton, the fact remains that a large portion of the measures effected by Hamilton in the early 1790s was anticipated and partially put into practice by the financier and his able assistant, Gouverneur Morris.

This concentration of power, this creation of a new "aristocracy," a term employed not only by Morris's inveterate enemies such as Arthur Lee or Timothy Matlack but by such a deeply conservative man as Stephen Higginson of Massachusetts,[28] was not only a perversion of the original Revolutionary principles but also a triumph of the middle states nationalists in the Congress and in the executive apparatus. This too was a product of the changing circumstances of the Revolution. The central location and multiple interests of the Morris mercantile apparatus, as well as the practical expertise of Morris and his associates, constituted an appropriate center of gravity for the moment when, as Robert Morris saw it, "the convulsive labors of enthusiasm" would be replaced by "the sound and regular operations of order and government."[29]

Although deeply divisive in its effects by 1783, Morris's initial assumption of power tended to unite a body seriously torn by the bitter partisanship of the Lee-Deane imbroglio. In the expectation that Morris could revitalize Continental securities, some eastern delegates who had security-holding constituencies voted for him. Likewise southern delegates were sympathetic with a program that would improve finances, placate the Continental Line through half pay (part of the nationalist program), and thereby strengthen the military effort. Only by recognizing that it was the day of the technician, not the ideologue, can one appreciate the appropriateness as well as the irony in Thomas Burke's motion that Morris be given the powers of appointment and removal he demanded as a condition of his acceptance of the superintendency of finance, for Burke had been the author of Article II of the Confederation, which guaranteed the states their independence and sovereignty. It was the North Carolina delegation, traditionally the parochial nucleus of the southern faction, that first proposed a Continental impost —later an essential part of Morris's financial program.

So strong was this marriage of convenience between the mid-

28. Higginson, an aggressive, even warlike, New England Federalist in 1798, complained to Samuel Adams in 1783 of the "extensive influence" of Morris, whose "Friends in Congress are many and powerful," and to Theodorick Bland about the "Designs of the Aristocratic Junto in Congress. . . ." Higginson to Samuel Adams, May 20, 1783, and to Theodorick Bland, Oct. 6, 1783, Burnett, ed., *Letters*, VII, 167, 323.

29. Robert Morris to Benjamin Franklin, Nov. 27, 1781, Francis Wharton, ed., *Revolutionary Correspondence of the United States* (Washington, D.C., 1889), V, 12.

dle states and the South in 1781 that the entire span of delegations from New York to Georgia may be said to have formed a single coalition. Even the New Hampshire delegates, Samuel Livermore and John Sullivan, joined in.

Yet the middle states nationalists had less staying power as an organized party than did the easterners. The Morris plan of fiscal rehabilitation foundered on the Articles of Confederation, which allowed the single legislature of Rhode Island to block the impost amendment. The nationalists were forced to rely on French support to a degree that opened them to charges of subservience to France—or worse, of conspiring with France to create an aristocratic political establishment.[30] From inclination and necessity Morris so merged public and private finance in his issuance of the so-called Morris notes and his use of the Bank of North America that enemies found new ammunition for charges of profiteering and influence, and even conservatives outside the seat of power were alienated. Above all, the cessation of hostilities eliminated that sense of crisis that had drawn the South to the support of the middle states' Morrisonian brand of nationalism. By 1783, the year when the middle states achieved their greatest cohesion as a legislative bloc under the leadership of Hamilton, Fitzsimmons, Wilson, Boudinot, Duane, and others, including most significantly the two Virginians, James Madison and Joseph Jones, the middle party had lost the support of the South. Even the nationalists Oliver Wolcott of Connecticut and Nathaniel Gorham of Massachusetts did not align with the middle bloc, although they were also unaffiliated with the weakened New England party. The failure of the impost (now made more certain by new reservations in Virginia and New York), the counterproductive threat by Morris to resign, and the futile and bungling attempt to use officer unrest at Newburgh to effect political consolidation capped the nationalist failure.

Without adherence to the ideology of republican regeneration, the eastern party seemed incapable of dominating con-

30. See Stephen Higginson to Theophilus Parsons, Sr., Apr. [7?], 1783, Burnett, ed., *Letters*, VII, 122–123.

gressional politics, and without pragmatic success, the nationalist, middle states party dispersed to the states in search of other
alternatives to what must be considered as much a fiscal as a
nationalist goal. That the southern bloc achieved an unparalleled cohesion and became the dominant force in Congress at
this time was not simply the result of another turn of the wheel.
There was more than one avenue to national coherence, as the
history of the next quarter century would demonstrate, and the
South, in conjunction with the middle states—particularly Pennsylvania—was uniquely poised to map out that avenue.

In an overwhelmingly agrarian nation the vast unoccupied
lands of the West won in the Treaty of Paris at the very moment
of the collapse of fiscal consolidation constituted a "pay-off"
more than adequate to absorb the public debt. The West also
offered opportunities for countless thousands to repair their fortunes, and, for many advocates of western expansion in Congress, a new means of reinvigorating the Republic. The West
thus constituted an acceptable combination of ideology and
interest, the twin strands of previous factional development.

The perception of this crucial role of the West was not confined to any particular section, to be sure. Middle states land
companies had long agitated the question of ownership of western lands; delegates from landless states with a high stake in
state regulation of import duties such as David Howell of
Rhode Island were thoroughly alert to the revenue-producing
potential of the West. That other New Englanders were not
indifferent to western development is attested not only by Connecticut's insistence upon the Western Reserve but also the influential roles of Rufus King and Nathan Dane of Massachusetts
in the organization of the western territory.[31]

Nonetheless, the Ordinance of 1784 was preeminently the
work of Jefferson, and before that the insistence that the right
of navigation on the Mississippi be placed on a par with fishery
rights, the work of James Madison. There were excellent rea-

31. Francis S. Philbrick, *The Rise of the West, 1754–1830* (New York,
1965), 130–132, contends Dana's responsibility for the Ordinance of 1787
has been greatly underestimated.

sons for their involvement. The South, and especially Virginia, was in a prime situation to take advantage of western development, not only from the moral if not legal force of its claim to the Old Northwest but also its central location on the Potomac, which many expected to be the major avenue into the interior.

Further, the South, and particularly Virginia with its declining tobacco economy, needed the potential of lateral movement. It is even possible that some Virginians such as Madison, Washington, and Henry Lee hoped to change the socioeconomic makeup of Virginia by developing a maritime capacity, stimulating commerce with the interior, cultivating a middle class, and discouraging the growth of plantations and slavery. The political organization of the western territory, the location of the national capital on the Potomac River, and the addition of new states from the western counties in Kentucky and Tennessee (and ultimately the whole trans-Appalachian area) would enhance such a policy.

The implicit social values in the southern program for western expansion—values occasionally made explicit in discussions of the land ordinances and the navigation of the Mississippi—actually constituted an ideology that may be distinguished from that articulated in the New England press and pulpit and in the correspondence of members of Congress during the early years of the Revolution and the years immediately preceding. Having enough in common with the earlier eastern attitudes toward the dangers of power and the need for constitutional restraints to belong to a common vocabulary of republicanism, the liberal, expansive republicanism of the southern advocates of westward development was different in a number of ways from earlier regenerative republicanism. Secular rather than religious in its frame of reference, it created a religion of republicanism rather than a republican credo out of religion. Anticipatory rather than regressive, it looked forward to continental grandeur rather than back to ancestral virtue. Individualistic rather than corporate, it stressed personal liberties rather than communal obligations. Accepting, rather than being disturbed by, conflict, it seems to have incorporated the assumption that disharmonies could be resolved less through surveillance and constraint than through spatial separation. It was the latter notion that Madison had in mind when he advocated a substantial increase of national authority, confident that an enlarged republic was not only possible but indispensably necessary to prevent the collapse of the republican revolution in a jumble of sectional rivalries, doctrinal antagonisms, and internal class conflict.

The southern program was not restricted to western expansion, nor was the philosophy of its proponents simply agrarian. It was James Monroe who chaired a committee in 1785 that recommended that the Articles be revised to allow Congress to regulate foreign and coastal trade, prohibit foreign carriers and imports in American harbors, and levy duties on foreign imports. Jefferson was in accord with the measure and agreed with Monroe that the modification should be effected before admission of new states from the West, which would be unsympathetic with maritime objectives.[32] Ironically, the proposal encountered opposition from the Massachusetts delegates Gerry, Holten, and King, who also opposed a request from the Massachusetts legislature that a general convention be held to consider revision of the Articles.[33] Another southerner, Charles Pinckney, moved that Congress call a convention to revise the Articles in May 1786. Failing to gain approval, Pinckney was successful in promoting the formation of a committee that recommended seven amendments granting Congress the kind of authority over commerce that Monroe had advocated a year earlier and, in addition, the power to collect revenues in states that failed to meet their requisitions.

Pinckney's plan was cumbersome in many respects, but it was a feasible attempt to strengthen the national government within

32. Papers of the Continental Congress, Committee Book No. 186, Lib. of Congress; James Monroe to Thomas Jefferson, June 16, 1785, Burnett, ed., *Letters*, VIII, 143; Jefferson to Monroe, Aug. 28, 1785, Julian Boyd, ed., *The Papers of Thomas Jefferson* (Princeton, 1950–), VIII, 445.

33. The Massachusetts delegates to Gov. Bowdoin, Sept. 3, 1785, Burnett, ed., *Letters*, VIII, 208. King, Gerry, and Holten warned that a general convention would stimulate "the Friends of an Aristocracy, to send Members who would promote a Change of Government."

the framework of the Articles. That it was never seriously considered was due to the drastic division of Congress over the Jay-Gardoqui negotiation in process at the same time.

The Jay-Gardoqui negotiation appeared to barter navigation rights on the Mississippi in exchange for commercial concessions from Spain that would benefit the Northeast without any compensation for the South. The result was a sharp division of Congress in 1786. Even Virginians whose Potomac waterway scheme stood to gain in importance from a closure of the Mississippi were distraught by the reaction in the West, by Jay's handling of the negotiation, and above all by the menacing division of the Confederation along the North-South axis. Monroe warned Patrick Henry that "the Eastern people talk of a dismemberment so as to include Pena (in favor of which I believe the present delegation Petit and Bayard who are under the influence of eastern politicks would be) and sometimes all the states south to the Potomack."[34] Henry Lee and Theodore Sedgwick echoed Monroe's concern from different points of view.[35] Sedgwick wrote to Caleb Strong that "even the appearance of a union cannot in the way we now are long be preserved. It becomes us seriously to contemplate a substitute; for if we do not controul events we shall be miserably controuled by them."[36] Evidence indicates, however, that it was the southern leadership that mainly shaped events at this alarming juncture. Madison especially was moved to a level of action that was not even remotely matched by the disjointed middle states nationalists. Consequently the Philadelphia Convention was primarily a Virginia production. And with good reason, for Virginia had more to lose from a division of the Confederation along a North-South line than any other state.[37]

34. James Monroe to Patrick Henry, Aug. 12, 1786, *ibid.*, 425.
35. *Ibid.*, 462, 439, 415–416.
36. Sedgwick to Strong, Aug. 6, 1786, *ibid.*, 415–416.
37. Historians have not fully appreciated the extent to which the Convention was a Virginia production. Most would agree with Charles Warren, *The Making of the Constitution* (Boston, 1928), 11–12, that sentiment for a stronger national government can be found in the correspondence of "Washington, Hamilton, Jay, Madison, Jefferson and many others, both in the South and the North." While this is not untrue, the inference that it was these men who engineered the Convention is false—with the exception

The Constitutional Convention must thus be placed in a complex web of developments involving not simply conservative alarm over the quality and disposition of state governments, the preservation of social order, and the management of the public debt but also the extension of a western-oriented southern congressional policy. The crucial involvement of Virginia in the calling of the Convention and the sharp debates over the admission of new western states evidence this aspect of the tangle of issues.[38]

---

of Madison, who of all men was most responsible for it. Warren demonstrates that Hamilton was concerned about the weakness of the Confederation and advocated changing it as early as 1780, but can cite no letter even mentioning the Convention at the moment of truth in 1786. Hamilton, despite his presence at Annapolis, was more involved in his law practice than in political reform. The same can be said with greater emphasis about the other New York nationalists—Robert R. Livingston and James Duane, both of whom declined to attend the Annapolis Conference, even though elected as delegates. Most of the letters cited by Warren in his history of the background of the Constitutional Convention are from Virginians during the years 1784–1787. The same is true of Bancroft's earlier treatment, *History of the Formation of the Constitution of the United States of America* (New York, 1882). Citing a larger number of letters relevant to the constitutional movement than Warren, Bancroft includes a heavy collection of Virginia correspondence. That collection makes possible a rough sort of index of involvement by tabulating all letters to and from the middle states nationalists and comparing them with all letters to and from Virginians. Including Hamilton, Duane, Jay, Robert R. Livingston, Robert Morris, George Plater, Thomas Fitzsimmons, Gouverneur Morris, and Robert Schuyler (9 individuals), there were 34 letters cited in the indexes of Bancroft's two volumes. By contrast, 11 Virginians, including Grayson, Jefferson, Joseph Jones, Richard Henry Lee, Madison, Monroe, Edmund Randolph, Washington, Edward Carrington, Cyrus Griffin, and Henry Lee, wrote or received 225 letters. Of course this is only a very rough indication of involvement, for the statistic reflects in part Bancroft's ability to acquire the correspondence, as well as the chances of survival. Washington's 67 letters doubtless reflect in part the fact that his correspondence was carefully preserved by all. Yet it still seems striking that not a single letter written by Hamilton, Gouverneur Morris, or Robert Morris is included in Bancroft's collection. The 3 letters received by Hamilton may be compared with 74 sent to Madison. The conclusion that the middle states nationalists were tending to business and the Virginians to national politics is not automatic, but strongly suggested from surviving evidence.

38. Staughton Lynd, *Class Conflict, Slavery, and the United States Constitution: Ten Essays* (Indianapolis, 1967), may make too much of the unanimity of the South in support of its slavery interest, but his stress on the vital stake of the South in western expansion, as well as the anticipation

V

A major problem, perhaps the major problem, in the construction of a viable nation-state out of the experience of the War for Independence was the sectional tendency of congressional factionalism. It is apparent in retrospect that a basic source of the problem was that regional cleavages and controversies not only were a result of economic sectionalism (as when rights to the fisheries were pitted against rights to Mississippi navigation in 1779) but were freighted with ideological content involving the meaning of the Revolution and the definition of republican purity. That elitist and populist viewpoints should have emerged from the early Revolution was natural, but that they should have been associated with regional value systems was a less natural product of gaps in communication and the circumstances of the revolutionary process. However inaccurate a reflection of reality, such perceptions jeopardized the success of the Revolution and the emergence of a cohesive nation-state.

Simply enlarging the sphere of national competence would not necessarily resolve the difficulty. It was the redefinition of the national constituency, an integral part of the Virginia plan in the Constitutional Convention, which, by generating a coalescence of interests, offered the greatest potential for national coherence. In a sense the achievement of this coherence was precisely the reverse of the relationship between factionalism and stability formulated by Madison in his celebrated *Federalist* Number 10. It was not so important that an augmentation of national authority should produce checks against propertyless majority factions in individual states as that faction should be redefined along sectional axes. Thus it appears that in this instance Madison's keen political instincts faltered. Probably anticipating more generous national commitments in a central government with more consequential authority and doubting that in an enlarged republic comprehending many interests a dichotomization of the sort that obtained in 1786 would be repeated, he was confident the new federal form would produce

---

that the West would be prosouthern in sympathy, seems to me well grounded.

stability as well as protect property. The history of the formation of the first party system during the subsequent decade
shows both the proximate error and the mediate wisdom of his
expectations.

Neither a filtration of talent nor an enlarged, nationalized
constituency altered the strong tendency toward regional partisanship. During the formation of the first party system, the
extremities of the Union continued by and large to oppose each
other, and the middle states divided between them. Ideology
was again identified with regional loyalties. Parties began to
take shape first as legislative blocs and then extend beyond the
national government, as had been faintly prefigured in 1779.
The dangers of executivism continued to excite alarm, and foreign policy, to produce the sharpest partisan antagonisms. Appropriately John Jay was in the very center of the storm in 1795
and 1796, as he had been in 1786 and 1779.

There were nonetheless two crucial differences between the
patterns of partisan politics in the Continental Congress and
the House of Representatives, the first as subtle as the second
was dramatic and overt. When the middle states divided in the
Revolutionary years, the general pattern had been for delegations to shift from one year to another, depending on the composition of the state legislatures that elected them. (This was
above all true in Pennsylvania.) With a national constituency,
however, the correlation between national and state party systems began to take place on a continuous basis, first in Pennsylvania, soon afterward in New York, and ultimately in New
England. The more startling difference was, of course, the inversion in the ideological postures of the eastern (Federalist)
and southern (Republican) political groupings: levelers had
become monocrats, and aristocrats, Jacobins.

There are many plausible answers for the anomaly: Shays's
Rebellion may have converted eastern parochialists into conservative centralists; southern agrarians may have been forced
to seek support from the yeoman democracy in order to oppose
Hamilton's fiscal program; each region may have simply found
new leaders to supplant the early Revolutionary generation. All
three explanations (and many others might be added) are par-

tially true and at the same time insufficient. The notion of a change in leadership begs the question, and there were many early Revolutionaries who made an apparent change themselves: Richard Henry Lee became a Federalist despite his having delivered one of the best expressions of the Antifederalist position in his *Letters of a Federal Farmer* and despite his early revolutionary radicalism; Roger Sherman and Artemas Ward were puritan revolutionaries who became pious Federalists; Charles Pinckney was a South Carolina elitist who became a Jeffersonian Republican; John Langdon, chastized by William Whipple for his lack of republican virtue and his ostentatious style of living, was wooed and won by the "Jacobin" Democrats.[39] If Shays's insurrection had a determinative role in converting eastern democrats to conservative centralists, it is incongruous that New England was so slightly involved in the organization of the Constitutional Convention; if Hamilton's program created a yeoman democratic opposition, it is also incongruous that the opposition was led by gentry, supported in many instances by tradesmen, and rejected by broad segments of the northern yeomanry.

There is, in short, an almost unreal quality about the inversion of populist and elitist regional postures from the 1770s to the 1790s. Perhaps the most concrete illustration of this is in the reaction of a New Englander from a staunchly Federalist family to the Virginia House of Burgesses. Peregrine Foster, the younger brother of both Theodore Foster, senator from Rhode Island, and Dwight Foster, representative from Massachusetts, journeyed to western Virginia and was eventually elected to the Virginia assembly in 1795. Commenting on "the Enemies to the Federal Government and most especially so to the Officers and Administration of it" who dominated the Burgesses two to one, he was struck by their calling themselves "true Democrats" while in reality they were "the most haughty People of America." Noting that "our political as well as moral

---

39. William Whipple to John Langdon, Apr. 29, 1776, Force Transcripts, Lib. of Congress, I, 115; Jeremiah Smith to William Gordon, Dec. 17, 1794, in J. H. Morrison, *Life of the Honorable Jeremiah Smith, LL.D.* (Boston, 1845), 66–67; Henry Mayo, *John Langdon* (Concord, N.H., 1937), 248–249.

and religious Sentiments are apt to be biased and influenced thro Life by the earliest part of Our Education," he concluded: "I find my Situation less agreeable than it would be had my whole Education been with these Lords of the Soil who are taught from their Infancy to consider the industrious Poor man of their own colour as little above the Africans. . . ."[40] Peregrine Foster's impression of Virginia politics raises the question of whether even the Federalism of New England may not have been preformed in the Revolutionary era.

The Adamses, Whipple, Sherman, and other old eastern revolutionaries had joined their radical republicanism with many of the values that, dressed in Federalist garb and associated with the executivism of Hamilton, left the impression of rank conservatism. The stress on public virtue, individual asceticism, corporate obligation, and deference to properly constituted authority was characteristic of presumed eastern levelers as well as the Federalists. Recalling the politics of the Continental Congress, it was perfectly appropriate for the New England party, again in the ascendancy as Federalists, to join its corporate philosophy with the old role of party of the Revolution—now translated into the party of constitutional legitimacy—and to perceive the traditional southern opposition as subversive of the commonweal. (That extreme Federalists were willing to go to almost any lengths to suppress such "subversion" is, it should be noted, characteristic of nation-states emerging from colonial revolutions. Viable two-party systems rarely emerge in new nations where the highest priority is placed on national cohesion.[41]) That the opposition should have been associated with a revolutionary philosophy that seemed to challenge all of the verities further exacerbated the problem, as did the traditional anti-Gallicanism of the New England bloc.

The hyperbolic character of the politics of the Federalist decade suggests among other things that gaps in communication continued to exist and that it would be in the middle

40. Peregrine Foster to Dwight Foster, Nov. 30, 1795, Dwight Foster Papers, Massachusetts Historical Society, Boston.

41. See Fred R. von der Mehden, *Politics of the Developing Nations* (Englewood Cliffs, N.J., 1964), chap. 4.

states that the two-party system would first cohere. It might be added that the new nation was unusually fortunate in that it was after all unnecessary to apply the full press of a definitive solution to the problems of national political coherence. In the last analysis Madison's formula for the extended republic proved to be a workable solution.

6

The Role of Religion

IN THE

Revolution

*Liberty of Conscience and Cultural Cohesion
in the New Nation*

by

WILLIAM G. McLOUGHLIN *

"This is a Christian nation."
—Associate Justice David Brewer, 1892

The role of religion *in* the American Revolution cannot be
understood apart from its role *before* and *after* the Revolution.
If we define religion as the philosophical outlook, the set of
fundamental assumptions, ideals, beliefs, and values about
man's relationship to his neighbors, his environment, and his
future, that provides the cultural cohesion for a community,
then the Revolution was both a culmination and a beginning
of the process that produced American cultural cohesion. In
this sense the Revolution was a religious as well as a political
movement.

* I am indebted to Gordon Wood and Oscar Handlin for their comments
on an early version of this essay and to the detailed comments of Sidney
E. Mead and Richard Bushman at the conference at Williamsburg, Mar.
8–12, 1971.

The salient religious development of the Revolution has variously been referred to as disestablishment, the rise of religious liberty, the adoption of voluntaryism, or the separation of church and state (not all the same thing, but all closely related). From a moderately long-range view, this was an irreversible development in America from the time of the Great Awakening and reached one of its logical conclusions a century later with the final abolition of the system of compulsory religious taxes in Massachusetts. An even longer-range view would push the development back to Roger Williams, the Scrooby Separatists, or the Anabaptists of the Reformation and forward to today's problems over federal aid to parochial schools. In the more common and short-range view disestablishment began with George Mason's article on religious liberty in the Virginia Declaration of Rights in 1776 and was "substantially" complete, as J. Franklin Jameson said, by 1800, with the passage of the First Amendment and the abolition of religious tests for office-holding in most state constitutions.[1]

I have chosen in this essay to take the moderately long-range view, concentrating upon the efforts to work out the principles and practical definitions of voluntaryism in the original states from 1776 to the middle of the nineteenth century. But this obliges me to begin with at least a cursory glance at the development of religious and political liberty in the period from 1740 to 1776.

As I see it, the Great Awakening, sometimes seen as a religious reaction to Arminianism and sometimes as the upthrust of the Enlightenment in the colonies, was really the beginning of America's identity as a nation—the starting point of the Revolution.[2] The forces set in motion during the Awakening broke

1. By "substantially" complete Jameson presumably meant that the principles of religious liberty and equality were accepted by 1800. But of course they were by no means yet worked out in practice. See J. Franklin Jameson, *The American Revolution Considered as a Social Movement* (Boston, 1956 [orig. publ. Princeton, 1926]), 90–91.

2. Alan Heimert, *Religion and the American Mind from the Great Awakening to the Revolution* (Cambridge, Mass., 1966), sees the Awakening in terms of the beginning of the battle of the evangelical Calvinists and the liberal rationalists for the mind of America in which the former played the more influential role. Richard L. Bushman, *From Puritan to Yankee:*

the undisputed power of religious establishments from Georgia to the District of Maine, but more than that, the Awakening constituted a watershed in the self-image and conceptualization of what it meant to be an American. The old assumptions about social order and authority that underlay colonial political economy and produced cultural cohesion dissolved. The corporate and hierarchical ideal of society began to yield to an individualistic and egalitarian one. While the medieval concept of a Christian commonwealth lingered, its social foundations crumbled.

A description of the complex forces that led to the breakdown of the old order and hastened the modernization of American institutions (of which the Revolution was the modus operandi) cannot be attempted here.[3] Nor have I space to trace the subtle theological shifts that sustained this social reformation. But, in essence, between 1735 and 1790 the American colonists redefined their social principles into a cohesive structure sufficiently radical to necessitate a political break with the Old World and sufficiently conservative to sustain a new nation.

The historian of religion would stress three interrelated intellectual strands that gave the pattern to the new national consciousness: the new emphasis in evangelical Calvinism (the prevalent religious commitment of the people), stressing the individual's direct, personal, experiential relationship to God; the general acceptance of the deistic theory of inalienable natural rights and contractual self-government; and the resurgence of the radical whig ideology with its fear of hierarchical tyranny (the united despotism of church and state) epitomized in John Adams's *Dissertation on the Canon and Feudal Law*.[4]

Before the Awakening most individuals gladly yielded their judgment and conscience to the superior claims and knowledge

---

Character and Social Order in Connecticut, 1690–1765 (Cambridge, Mass., 1967), sees the Awakening in terms of the rise of democratic self-government.

3. Gordon S. Wood, *The Creation of the American Republic, 1776–1787* (Chapel Hill, 1969), has stressed this modernization process as well as the religious fervor of the Revolutionary era.

4. Bernard Bailyn has stressed this hitherto neglected element in pre-Revolutionary American thought in his *Ideological Origins of the American Revolution* (Cambridge, Mass., 1967).

of their "betters," the ruling elite in church and state, who derived their authority from God and as his vicegerents administered the ordinances of government for the good of the people. After the Awakening this order of things became reversed: the state and church were considered by increasing numbers of Americans to be the creatures of the people and subject to their authority. Prior to the Awakening the king, his bishops, judges, and governors interpreted the will of God, and deference was their due. Afterwards the people considered themselves better able than any elite to interpret God's will and expected their elected officials to act as *their* vicegerents under God. The channel of authority no longer flowed from God to the rulers to the people but from God to the people to their elected representatives. State and church were henceforth to serve the needs of the people as defined by the people—or rather, by the people's interpretation of God's will. Intermediaries were dispensed with; every individual was assumed to be in direct relationship to God and responsible only to him, and therefore their collective will was God's will. Or so, in its extreme and logical form, this theory evolved by the time of Thomas Paine's *Common Sense* and came into practice by the age of Jackson.

Psychologically the Awakening may be seen as the traumatic conversion of a whole society from a burden of frustration, guilt, and anxiety to a buoyant assertion of self-assurance, self-confidence, and self-righteousness: frustration because the old institutions and behavioral patterns no longer satisfied needs or made sense; guilt because in order to break loose the people had to assault their father figures. Given the essentially pietistic context of the thirteen colonies, this breakthrough took the form of a religious revival before it assumed its more pragmatic task of social and political reform. The impact of this sociopsychological awakening fell first upon the existent religious establishments; the rise of rampant sectarian pluralism among a people no longer satisfied with the parish church and its official religion destroyed the homogeneity upon which territorial parish systems depended. The essence of the New Light Calvinism or evangelical pietism that formed the central and driving force of popular action in the Awakening was to place the individual experience and judgment of the regenerated man, the New Adam, above the doctrines and practices, traditions and rituals of established civil and ecclesiastical authority. George Whitefield did not give a fig for the rulings of his own denominational authorities against him; the nominal Anglicans in Virginia used the Two Penny Act to vent their dissatisfaction against their church, and the New Lights in the Presbyterian, Dutch Reformed, Lutheran, and Congregational churches pitted their individual consciences against the rulings of presbyteries, synods, classes, and consociations in their denominations and against the ecclesiastical laws of their colonial governments. Newly awakened converts positively courted censure and excommunication, fines and imprisonment, "for consciences' sake." As one New Light wrote to his brethren from Plymouth jail in 1749, "I shall bring glory to God in my bonds . . . the Lord hath made those bonds my liberty." [5] Hosts of people simply refused to believe any longer that the duly constituted authorities in church and state knew best what was right for them, good for the commonwealth, or approved of God. Standing upon nothing but their own common or moral sense of what was right (as God gave them to see the right), Americans engaged as individuals and groups in more and more extensive passive and active civil disobedience, asserting as plainly as they could that the powers that be were not in their judgments ordained by God and therefore ought not to be obeyed. [6]

The religious and political establishments did not fall under these first radical onslaughts of pietistic individualism. But their authority eroded steadily before the rising tide of alienation. The Congregational establishments in New England,

5. William Hooper to the [Separate] Church of Christ in Middleborough, [Mass.], Apr. 4, 1749, Isaac Backus Papers, Andover Newton Theological School, Newton, Mass. So extreme did this kind of behavior seem to the leaders of the old order that they could only describe the protesters as out of their minds.

6. For a dramatic account of how this popular zeal made itself felt in the political sphere, see Edmund S. and Helen M. Morgan's chapter on the mobbing of Jared Ingersoll in *The Stamp Act Crisis: Prologue to Revolution* (Chapel Hill, 1953), 220–238.

always under a measure of popular control, responded to the challenge by altering their posture—yielding power to the New Lights within the structure and granting greater religious liberty to those without.[7] But the Anglican establishments turned more strongly than ever to authoritarian control, and that meant reliance upon the power of kings and bishops across the sea and insistence upon the need for bishops in America.[8] Once the Revolution started, Anglican authority and power immediately ceased.

The Revolution—an essentially irrational impulse despite the eloquent rationalizations provided for it—combined this popular spirit of pietistic self-righteousness with a new commitment to inalienable natural rights (fostered by the Enlightenment). Both fed upon the heady fruits of a long-brewing commonwealth radicalism to produce an ecstatic enthusiasm for national self-assertion. Ostensible rationalists fervently upheld the innate, God-given rights of Englishmen and mankind against a despotic George III; evangelical pietists zealously insisted that Christ died, not for the divine right of kings or hierarchies, but for the Christian liberty of his saints. Both relied ultimately upon their own heartfelt judgments, for which God, but no one else, could hold them responsible. And when, in the final "appeal to heaven" after 1775, God judged for the patriots and pietists, it seemed proof positive that whatever divine right once existed within the British Empire had been corrupted beyond redemption. The power of crown and mitre had passed to the people, and the future site of the millennium had once again moved westward toward its final, and probably imminent, fulfillment. The Peace of Paris brought from the pietists cries of "Come quickly, Lord Jesus" and from the ra-

7. Clarence C. Goen, *Revivalism and Separatism in New England, 1740–1800: Strict Congregationalists and Separate Baptists in the Great Awakening* (New Haven, 1962), has indicated how the homogeneity of the New England parish life was broken up by schisms from both sides; i.e., radical New Lights separating to become Baptists or Separates, while conservative Old Lights separated to become Anglicans or, intellectually at least, Unitarians.

8. See A. L. Cross, *The Anglican Episcopate and the American Colonies* (New York, 1902), and Carl Bridenbaugh, *Mitre and Sceptre: Transatlantic Faiths, Ideas, Personalities, and Politics, 1689–1775* (New York, 1962).

tionalists the belief that the United States of America were "God's last best hope" for mankind.

The Revolution as an act of individual and communal self-assertion, being both a culmination of a long-smoldering revolt against dysfunctional colonial institutions and theories and also an opportunity for new beginnings, led inevitably to confusion and experimentation once the colonists were on their own. As an act, a process, a time of internal stress and enforced cooperation, the Revolution itself profoundly affected the religious life of the colonies. For example, when the Sons of Liberty began to—had to—use radical, abstract, absolutist arguments to rationalize their rights against king and Parliament, all segments of discontent in the crumbling established order rushed to apply these arguments to their own needs and ambitions. The dissenters were among the most zealous of these malcontents. And since most of the political leaders of the Revolution were themselves associated with the established churches in their respective colonies, it became increasingly difficult for them to press their own claims against the mother country without accepting at least some of the similar claims of the dissenters at home. At the same time the needs of temporal self-preservation became so immediate that religious worship and churchly activities were seriously disrupted, if not totally neglected, throughout the colonies for almost two decades. It is hardly surprising that Timothy Dwight, upon assuming the presidency of Yale in 1795, found a young generation (which had come of age in the Revolution) more interested in the radical political philosophies of the French Revolution than in the evidence for the divine authority of Scriptures.

I will cite briefly here ten of the most obvious ways in which the political rhetoric, mood, and actions of the Revolutionary era interacted with the critical issues of religious liberty and equality. All ten in some measure hastened the development of what we now call the separation of church and state. The first five relate to the early phases of the revolt; the second, to the efforts to construct the new states and nation.

First, and most obvious, the attacks by leading patriots upon the dangers of the Anglican establishment inevitably provided ammunition for dissenters in each colony against their own religious authorities. Isaac Backus and other dissenters in New England had a field day with Charles Chauncy and John Adams for denouncing all establishments and claiming that New England never had such a thing.[9] By their own definition Chauncy and Adams were right, for by an establishment they meant a confessional state, and the Puritans had from the outset drawn a clear line forbidding the state to interfere with the autonomy of the Congregational churches or to demand conformity to any legally defined creed or ritual. Yet dissenters were able to convince their neighbors by 1775 that the system of compulsory religious taxes imposed upon all inhabitants in the Puritan colonies did in fact seriously infringe upon their conscientious scruples. Dissenters in the Anglican colonies had an even easier case to make.

Second, the incidence of civil disobedience incited and engaged in by patriot leaders for political and economic causes gave example and encouragement to dissenters to participate in their own conscientious rebellion against the religious laws of the colonies. New Light Baptist and Presbyterian itinerants in Virginia defied laws requiring licenses to preach or build meetinghouses and won increasing sympathy after 1776 from nominal but alienated Anglicans (many of whom joined their ranks). New Light Baptists and Separates in New England refused to pay religious taxes or even to turn in the certificates that would have entitled them to exemption from them. Defiance of authority was infectious and could not be kept within the narrow bounds that the leaders of the Revolution desired.

Third, the rhetoric of natural rights and radical whig ideology was as easily adapted by dissenters or alienated Anglicans as by respectable patriots within the establishments. New England Baptists insisted that "no taxation without representation" applied to their case against compulsory taxes to support

9. John Adams told the Baptist protesters at the First Continental Congress in 1774: "There is indeed an ecclesiastical establishment in our province, but a very slender one, hardly to be called an establishment." Alvah Hovey, *Isaac Backus* (Boston, 1859), 210. For Backus's criticism of Charles Chauncy, see William G. McLoughlin, ed., *Isaac Backus on Church, State, and Calvinism: Pamphlets, 1754-1789* (Cambridge, Mass., 1968), 346-360.

Congregational churches. And John Adams's fulminations against canon and feudal law aroused fear of even the "slender" establishment that he admitted existed in New England. Virginia's patriots included most of the laymen in the Church of England.

Fourth, as the rebellion pushed toward open warfare, it became evident that the colonists must hang together or they would all hang separately. Dissenters restrained their actions against rebel legislatures, and the legislatures in turn offered more leniency toward them. Even at the local level, town and parish animosities were muted in the effort to maintain unity against a common external enemy. Concessions clearly had to be made, and were promised on both sides in the interest of colonial harmony. Even the legitimate enforcement of prevailing ecclesiastical laws was held in abeyance. Most New England towns, for example, ceased after 1773 to collect religious taxes from dissenters who conscientiously refused to pay them, even when they did not turn in certificates; Virginia ceased to imprison itinerant dissenting preachers and from the outset of the war forbade parishes to collect money to pay parish ministers.

Fifth, since all patriots believed their cause was just and would obtain the support of heaven, all believed that their neighbors, no matter how they might differ in some respects, were on the side of the angels. When the dissenters proved as ready to take arms and risk their lives against the king as the conformists, it was difficult to maintain animosity toward them. Consequently the rationalistic utopians and the pietistic millennialists, the former defenders of good order and the latter "enthusiasts" and "fanatics," could join hands in the belief that a benevolent God had taken them both under his protection and promised them both a second Eden in the New World. Patriotism helped pietism cross denominational lines and fused a new religious and cultural core for America.

Once the Rubicon was crossed and the break with Britain made, a new set of circumstances brought political and religious forces into conjunction. Rhetoric had to be put into practice in the construction of bills of rights and state constitutions.

Undertaken in the midst of the struggle for independence, these formulations of the social contract required mutual give-and-take if harmony were to be maintained and the needs of all religious persuasions fairly met. The opportunity—the need—to do away with the old established churches necessitated co-operation in the creation of new religious structures in each state.

Having put the ideals of religious liberty into bills of rights, constitutions, and statutes, Americans had then to work them out in practice. Here the pragmatic temper of a frontier people, combined with the multiplicity of sects and a decentralized system of government, enabled a host of different ways of working out the frictions of religious pluralism. The absence of a strong national government, and even of effectively centralized state governments in the Revolutionary years, meant that the treatment of religious dissent often varied within the same state. Geographical regions, towns, and counties were able to respond to diversity in terms of their own local inclinations and groupings. An extraordinary variety of experiments in religious freedom took place, which over time could be taken as precedents for more flexible statewide approaches to the problem. Some fears proved groundless; some experiments proved impracticable.

As the new states began to develop new political institutions, new socioeconomic alignments of the population arose. With expansion of the suffrage dissenters took more important roles in the varying clusters of power—especially in the western areas where so many of them had gone to escape the frustrations and inequities of the old system. The dissenters in western Virginia were the most obvious example, joining forces with Jefferson and Madison against the conservative tidewater electors to advance their radical reforms of colonial institutions. The Separate-Baptists in western Massachusetts were prominent among the supporters of Daniel Shays. Elected to the legislatures in ever-increasing numbers, concomitant with their rapidly increasing membership, citizens of differing denominations formed coalitions that often gave them a balance of power between two factions (especially where the old elite was divided). Dissenters, instead of being despised or ignored, found themselves courted by their former harassers.

The strain and stress of establishing new institutions and governments broke down in many respects the denominational unity of dissenters. In the various debates and controversies that were not in the specific area of religion—paper money, higher taxes, indebtedness, Federalism versus Antifederalism—dissenters not only began to act in concert with their neighbors of different denominations but also began to divide among themselves. Baptist leaders in eastern New England tended to deplore Shays's Rebellion, paper money, and Antifederalism. Baptists in western and rural areas differed with them. Formerly excluded from political participation and under oppression from the establishment, the sectaries had thought of themselves first and foremost as beleaguered bodies of united believers. Now they began to react in terms of their social and economic needs, finding often that they had more in common with nearby neighbors of different denominations than with their distant or socially differentiated brethren.

So ultimately the Revolution brought the dissenting sects out of their apolitical pietistic shells and within the pale of political power. Ceasing to be outgroups, they entered the mainstream of the nation as participating partners. The favored status of one Protestant denomination gave way to the equal status of all Protestants. In addition, as colonial boundaries broke down and the nation united, denominations formed interstate or national bodies and sometimes joined formally with other denominations in evangelistic or benevolent activities. Parochialism gave way to wider national horizons. Becoming respected and respectable, dissenters found men of rank and position willing now to join their churches. In the southern states Baptists, Methodists, and Presbyterians rapidly became the dominant denominations not only in numbers but in power and wealth.

These are only the most obvious and general ways in which the Revolution, by breaking the cake of custom and opening new opportunities, interacted with the ideals, the hopes, and the allegiances of all religious groups, uniting individual, sectarian, and local interests to those of the nation at large. A vital cultural reformation was taking place. While, as I have said, this process had begun a generation before the Revolution, that event provided so many changes in so short a period that Jameson may have rightly described it as a social revolution, at least in the area of religion. Under the urgent need to create one out of many, even Roman Catholics and Jews, the most extreme outsiders, found themselves included in the new nation. Many even talked as though Buddhists and Mohammedans would have been equally welcome.

Yet the harmony was deceptive. Beneath the abstract rhetoric and universal ideals of the Revolution—sufficiently powerful to break the vital bonds to the mother country—there yet remained assumptions, beliefs, and values that were far from universal or absolute. Americans did not cease at once to think like Englishmen, and their cultural heritage and homogeneity produced a very relativistic and ethnocentric definition of religious liberty. The Protestant establishment of the nineteenth century, so obvious to Tocqueville and Lord Bryce, may seem a betrayal of the Revolution if one thinks of Thomas Jefferson as its spokesman or if one reads the religious clauses of the bills of rights and the First Amendment with the deistic gloss that the Supreme Court has applied to them in the twentieth century. But, as I hope to indicate below, Americans were clearly committed to the establishment of a Protestant Christian nation.[10] Religious liberty was to be granted to all, but the spiritual cement that was to hold the nation together had to be Protestant.

To understand the means by which these two commitments —to liberty of conscience among individuals and Protestant hegemony among religious faiths—were implemented is to probe the essence of the role of religion in (and after) the Revolution.

10. I agree with Mark DeWolfe Howe's statement that "the predominant" view of church-state relations in 1790 "was not the Jeffersonian but rather the evangelical. . . . " *The Garden and the Wilderness* (Chicago, 1967), 19. Howe's book addresses itself to many of the same questions I raise here, and I wish to express my indebtedness to it as well as to his article, "Problems of Religious Liberty," in Carl J. Friedrich, ed., *Nomos IV: Liberty* (New York, 1962), 262–275.

Phrased as a question, my subject is, How did the universal spirit of the rights of man become in the end a new national establishment that excluded non-Protestants from full religious equality? Since, as Sidney E. Mead has rightly said, establishments rest upon placing the coercive power of the state behind the institutions responsible for the definition, articulation, and inculcation of those commonly shared religious beliefs upon which the safety and well-being of the society are thought to depend, the answer lies in the highly original manner in which Americans institutionalized their religious life in terms of congregations or religious societies voluntarily associated, democratically controlled, and legally incorporated.[11]

Free now to construct their own civil and ecclesiastical institutions, Americans faced the issue first in terms of how much of the old system was to be retained and how much had to be reconstituted from rational or scriptural scratch. The most radical pietists, the New Light Baptists, were for scrapping all ecclesiastical systems and laws and leaving each individual church reliant solely upon the voluntary control and support of its gathered saints. In this proposal they were joined by some equally radical rationalists whose secular pietism equaled the zeal of the Baptists to *écrasez l'infame*—to destroy all traces of an establishment and its priestcraft. The former trusted God to preserve his church; the latter, wanting to keep the state free from religious pressures, was willing to let each denomination sink or swim on its own merits. Each pietistic group expected in the end that his own sect, being the Gospel truth, would soon sweep the nation, while radical deists thought that natural religion, inculcated via public education, would triumph over all sectarian corruption.[12] The deist opposed state

11. Sidney E. Mead, *The Lively Experiment: The Shaping of Christianity in America* (New York, 1963), 63. Mead, however, presents a rather different answer to this question.

12. For conflicting and strangely inconsistent interpretations of the role that public schools might play in the indoctrination of religious truth as seen by two notable spokesmen for the Revolutionary generation, see the essays by Benjamin Rush and Noah Webster in Frederick Rudolph, ed., *Essays on Education in the Early Republic* (Cambridge, Mass., 1965). Rush, though a Jeffersonian in general orientation, demanded denominational indoctrination by the schools, while Webster, a New England Federalist,

encouragement to religion because it would leave the state open to those with a vested interest in promoting superstition and because there was sufficient ethical truth in all forms of Christianity to consider them all, in their voluntary form, of some benefit to the state. The sectarian opposed state encouragement to religion for fear that it would provide assistance to false religions and thereby impede true religion.

At the other extreme were those moderate Anglicans in the South and conservative Congregationalists in New England who feared the zeal of enthusiastic zealots and perfectionists, doubted the perfectibility, rationality, and benevolence of human nature, worried over the future stability, morality, and prosperity of the nation, and were hesitant to jettison too much of the old forms and traditions lest the new ship of state capsize in the winds of doctrine. These conservative religionists felt that it was possible, as well as necessary, for the states to find some way to encourage and support Christian worship without impeding Christian liberty.

In between these extremes stood the great bulk of Americans, who considered themselves Protestant Christians by profession, if not by conversion, and who believed that the state should encourage religion. They felt strongly that Americans owed a special debt to God for his favor; they thought it man's duty to worship God; they were convinced—all Americans were convinced—that the safety and prosperity of the nation depended upon inculcating into its citizens the fear of God and the love of one's neighbor.[13] Cautious about moving too fast, doubting their own ability to pay heavy taxes, and suspecting that they would not be as generous as they should be in their freewill offerings to support religious worship, the middle-of-the-road Americans tended at first to side more with the position of the

---

believed it would be improper to utilize the Bible in the schools (except to inculcate the morals of Jesus).

13. Robert N. Bellah has discussed the shared religious assumptions of Americans from a sociologist's viewpoint in "America's Civil Religion," W. G. McLoughlin and Robert N. Bellah, eds., *Religion in America*, 3–23. From my point of view here, Americans in the Revolutionary period shared more avowedly Protestant assumptions than Bellah, covering the whole of American history since 1789, subsumes under our "civil religion."

conservatives and to believe that their duty to God was perhaps rightly enforced by the state for the general good.

The ambiguity of the Revolutionary generation toward religious duties (which were to be enforced) and religious liberty (which was to be untrammeled) has so often been noted that it hardly bears summary: laws requiring respect for the Sabbath and even church attendance were passed but seldom enforced; clergymen were admitted to state office despite prohibitions against it;[14] Jefferson, Madison, and John Leland opposed the payment of federal and state chaplains although many Baptists and other evangelicals proudly accepted such posts; the Northwest Ordinance and Southwest Ordinance utilized federal funds for religious purposes despite the First Amendment; "In God We Trust" was placed on the coins but not in the Constitution;[15] tax exemption was granted to all church property and often to ministers; national days of fasting, thanksgiving, and prayer were regularly proclaimed by some presidents and governors but objected to strenuously by others; and laws against gambling, dueling, theatergoing, and intemperance were debated with varying degrees of religious intensity in various parts of the country for the next century. Few pietists opposed days of fasting and thanksgiving (though notable exceptions like Eleazar Wheelock, John Leland, and Henry Grew may be cited). Some pietists wanted government assistance for the support of denominational colleges, missionary activities, and the printing of the Bible. Baptists and Congregationalists in New England joined in 1791 to request Congress to set up a committee to license the publication of the Bible. Heated argu-

14. While several state constitutions prohibited ministers of the gospel from holding office, the only instance I have seen in which a legislature tried to eject a legislator on these grounds (in New York in 1784) was unsuccessful. The alleged offender, incidentally, was a Baptist preacher.

15. There were of course many objections raised in the ratifying conventions to the absence of a religious test for federal officeholding, but the fact that a Baptist minister in North Carolina found this dangerous, while a Baptist minister in Massachusetts found it a guarantee of religious liberty, only confirms the ambiguity on this issue. See Cecilia M. Kenyon, ed., *The Antifederalists* (Indianapolis, 1966), 418–419, and Jonathan Elliot, ed., *The Debates in the Several State Conventions* . . . (Philadelphia, 1876), II, 148–149.

ments took place in the age of Jackson over the right of the state to deliver the mail on Sunday. Courts prosecuted citizens for blaspheming against the Christian religion until 1836,[16] and most jurists throughout the nineteenth century believed that Christianity was part of the common law, Jefferson notwithstanding.[17] Isaac Backus, one of the leading spokesmen for the extreme Baptist position regarding voluntaryism, nevertheless insisted that there must always be a "sweet harmony" between church and state while he praised and voted for the man who wrote to the Danbury Baptist Association calling for a "high wall of separation."[18] Caleb Blood, a leading Baptist minister in Vermont, said in an election sermon before the state legislature in 1792 that, while "religion at all times is a matter between God and individuals," nonetheless he welcomed "those friendly aids to the cause of our holy religion which may justly be expected from our political fathers"; liberty of conscience, he said, "by no means prohibits the civil magistrate from enacting those laws that shall enforce the observance of those precepts of the Christian religion the violation of which is a breach of the civil peace."

The heart of these indecisions, inconsistencies, and contradictions lay in precisely what kinds of "friendly aids" the political fathers might give to the cause of Christianity. And, logically enough, the first great debate about the proper relationship of church and state in the new nation concerned a general assessment for the support of religion. The essence of this debate was encapsulated in the contrast between Jefferson's assertion in

16. See *People* v. *Ruggles* in New York in 1811 for Chancellor James Kent's famous statement that blasphemy was "inconsistent with the peace or safety of the State." Cited in Perry Miller, *The Life of the Mind in America from the Revolution to the Civil War* (New York, 1965), 66. See also the famous case of Abner Kneeland, who was sentenced to two years in prison for blasphemy in Massachusetts in 1836. Henry Steele Commager, "The Blasphemy of Abner Kneeland," *New England Quarterly*, VIII (1935), 29–41.

17. Howe, *Garden and the Wilderness*, 28, and Carl Zollmann, *American Civil Church Law* (New York, 1917), 15–16.

18. Backus also deplored that Roman Catholics could hold positions in the Massachusetts legislature. William G. McLoughlin, *Isaac Backus and the American Pietistic Tradition* (Boston, 1967), 148–150.

the preamble to his act for religious liberty "that even the forcing [a citizen] to support this or that teacher of his own religious persuasion is depriving him of the comfortable liberty of giving his contribution to the particular pastor whose morals he would make his pattern," and George Washington's negative reply to Madison's "Remonstrance": "I must confess that I am not amongst the number of those who are so much alarmed at the thoughts of making people pay toward the support of that which they profess. . . ."[19]

According to the general-assessment concept every citizen would be required to pay a tax in proportion to his wealth for the support of religion (specifically for some form of Protestantism), but each taxpayer could specify to which particular church or minister he wished his religious assessment allocated (presumably to the church or minister he attended upon). Nothingarians, atheists, Roman Catholics, Jews, and other non-Protestants were equally responsible for paying such taxes, but sometimes in order to preserve their rights of conscience various alternatives were suggested for the allocation of their monies. In Virginia one general-assessment plan stated that the non-Protestant might allocate his money to the support of the poor, while another said his taxes would be allocated to public education; the Maryland plan exempted any Jew or Mohammedan who made a declaration of his belief before two justices;[20] in Massachusetts those who did not attend any church had their taxes allocated to the oldest church in their parish

19. Both statements are printed in Anson Phelp Stokes, *Church and State in the United States* (New York, 1950), I, 390, 393.

20. It is worth noting that Chancellor Kent in the Ruggles case expressly denied the same rights to Mohammedans and Buddhists as to Christians. The founders of their religions he called "imposters" who did not merit protection from blasphemy in a Christian country. Howe, *Garden and the Wilderness*, 29. See also the statement of John Swanwick, a conservative Episcopal merchant of Philadelphia, who wrote in condemnation of Jefferson's religious freedom act that its passage meant that "the legislature of Virginia may be held by men professedly atheists, Mahometans, or of any other creed, however unfriendly to liberty or the morals of a free country." *Considerations of An Act of the Legislature of Virginia* (Philadelphia, 1786), iii. Ironically, Swanwick later became the first Jeffersonian Republican elected to Congress from the city of Philadelphia.

(invariably the Congregational church—a fact that led many to assert that the Massachusetts general-assessment plan favored the old establishment).

The plans also varied in terms of whether the tax was to be laid by the local unit (parish or town) or by the state legislature, whether it was to support Christianity generally or only Protestant Christianity, and whether it was to support only "learned" ministers or any minister.[21] Significantly none of the plans proposed giving these taxes to the denominations as a whole and letting their officers allocate these funds as they thought best; the taxes were to go either to individual ministers or to the elected lay officers of each congregation. The desire to keep the citizen's taxes as close to his own local use and control as possible pervaded the discussions. To grant money to a denomination came much too close to the old form of an establishment, i.e., to aiding an ecclesiastical hierarchy.

The most troublesome aspect of the general-assessment idea was of course the definition of a Protestant (or Christian) church or ministry. In New England this was left to the courts to define. Massachusetts went through a generation of litigation over the matter, extending the benefit of the law first to include such unorthodox Protestants as Universalists and then, by a special act of the legislature in 1811, to any Protestant sect.[22] The first plan for a general assessment to be submitted for legislative action in Virginia, in 1779, attempted a five-point creedal definition of Christianity that, while seeming dangerously close to a state establishment, was so vaguely worded that it would

21. The general-assessment plans in South Carolina and the old Puritan states were designed to support only Protestant Christianity; those in Virginia and Maryland would have permitted the support of any form of Christianity. It is interesting that none of the opposition to the general-assessment plans in Virginia or Maryland was based on the fact that Roman Catholic churches would benefit from them.

22. For one of the most involved legal decisions regarding the definition of which denominations were entitled to be considered bona fide dissenters from the parish churches in New England, see the case of *Muzzy* v. *Wilkins* (1803) cited in *Decisions of the Superior and Supreme Courts of New Hampshire* . . . (Boston, 1879), 2–38. For the problems of Universalists, Methodists, and Roman Catholics in Massachusetts, see John Cushing, "Notes on Disestablishment in Massachusetts," *William and Mary Quarterly*, 3d Ser., XXVI (1969), 169–190.

have included Roman Catholics, Universalists, and Shakers—in fact any church that believed in God and the New Testament.

In addition to the four New England states (and the District of Maine) that transformed their old Congregational establishments into general-assessment systems for the support of Protestant churches during the Revolutionary years, there were at least four other states that contemplated this system between 1776 and 1786: Georgia, South Carolina, Maryland, and Virginia. Had the debates on this plan in Maryland and Virginia produced a majority in favor, doubtless other states would have followed their examples.

In Georgia the constitution of 1777 provided that "all persons whatever shall have the free exercise of their religion . . . and shall not, *unless by consent,* support any teacher or teachers except those of their own profession." The word "teachers" obviously meant ministers (public teachers of piety, morality, and religion), while the clause "unless by consent" indicated that the people of Georgia seriously considered authorizing their legislature (to which only Protestants were eligible) to pass a general-assessment tax.[23]

The constitution of South Carolina, adopted in 1778, had a much more elaborate system built into it. It not only declared that "the Christian Protestant religion" was to be "the established religion of this State" but provided that, "whenever fifteen or more male persons, not under twenty-one years of age," professed "the Christian Protestant religion and" agreed "to unite themselves in a society for the purposes of religious worship," they should be entitled to petition the legislature for incorporation as a religious society. Such a group would be "esteemed a church of the established religion of this State," provided that "each society so petitioning shall have agreed to and subscribed in a book the following five articles:

1st. That there is one eternal God, and a future state of rewards and punishments.

23. See Stokes, *Church and State,* I, 440; Swanwick, *Considerations,* 22; and William C. Webster, "Comparative Study of the State Constitutions of the American Revolution," *Annals of the American Academy of Political and Social Science,* IX (1897), 89.

2d. That God is publicly to be worshipped.

3d. That the Christian religion is the true religion.

4th. That the holy scriptures of the Old and New Testaments are of divine inspiration and are the rule of faith and practice.

5th. That it is lawful and the duty of every man being thereunto called by those that govern, to bear witness to the truth.[24]

The constitution went on to specify that each religious society should have the right to choose its own minister and that "no person shall, by law, be obliged to pay towards the maintenance and support of a religious worship that he does not freely join in."

When this aspect of the constitution was being debated, the Reverend William Tennent III spoke before the South Carolina legislature opposing it. His speech has generally been taken as a plea for religious liberty, but in fact it simply opposed the concept of territorial parishes. In its published form it accepted the principle of general assessment. Tennent was a New Light Presbyterian minister in Charleston, the grandson of the founder of the famous Log College in Neshaminy, Pennsylvania. He spoke on behalf of petitions opposing what the Presbyterians took to be a plan that would permit the majority of inhabitants in every parish to lay religious taxes for the support of the church of the majority. He opposed such a plan as an infringement upon the religious liberty of the minority. Furthermore, even though such a system would leave each parish free to support whatever denomination had a majority (presumably this would often be Presbyterian in the western part of the state), it would permit many parishes in the tidewater area to reestablish the Episcopal church. Hence Tennent argued in broad terms that religious establishments "are an infringement of Religious Liberty" because "they amount to nothing less than the legislature's taking the consciences of men into their own hands." He believed that "the State may enact good laws for the punishment of vice and the encouragement of virtue." He even admitted that "the State may do anything for the support of religion without partiality to particular [religious]

24. Stokes, *Church and State*, I, 432–433. This section of the constitution derives from the constitution that John Locke drafted for the Carolinas in 1669. See *ibid.*, I, 399.

societies or imposition on the rights of private judgment." But "to establish all denominations by law and to pay them all equally" was "impracticable" (he did not say "unscriptural"), at least as he understood the plan under consideration. For "as people of different sentiments lived intermingled [within each parish], and there could be no possible distinction of parishes so as to accommodate different denominations," the minority within each parish would be forced against their consciences to support the religion of the majority.

However, after Tennent delivered his speech, someone pointed out to him that the proposal under discussion was designed to let each individual citizen pay his religious tax to the support of his own church and minister and not to that of the majority of his parish. Hence, when Tennent published his speech a few weeks later, he appended a footnote stating that he now had "the pleasure to find, that a general establishment, or rather incorporation of all denominations" was what was proposed. Since this "makes all parties happy" and "is not liable to the above objections," he withdrew his opposition. In fact he rejoiced that this happy plan "opens the door to the equal incorporation of all denominations—while not one Sect of Christians in preference to all others, but Christianity itself is the established religion of the State."[25] Since Tennent, and presumably the dissenters for whom he spoke, had no objection to a "general establishment of Christianity" supported by the state, it seems that he would have supported the laying of a general-assessment tax under the formula proposed in the constitution. The substitution of the incorporated poll parish for the old territorial parish as the basis for religious support was one of the basic innovative principles of the unique relationship of church and state that Americans were to develop over the ensuing half century. But as in Georgia there is no record of any attempts being made to levy a general-assessment tax in South Carolina.

The general-assessment idea came to a head in Virginia, and the other states in the South seem to have taken their cue from

25. William Tennent III, *Speech on the Dissenting Petition Delivered in the House of Assembly* (Charlestown, Mass., 1777), 15.

her. J. Franklin Jameson wrote that "disestablishment in Virginia was a natural consequence of the doctrine laid down in the Virginia Declaration of Rights of 1776. . . . such principles led inevitably to the equality of all religious bodies before the law. . . ."[26] But there was "inevitability" only in hindsight. As Jameson admitted, Patrick Henry, though he supported George Mason's article on religious liberty in 1776, specifically denied from the floor that it was, as some Anglicans feared, "a prelude to an attack on the established church." It was another three years before the legislature in Virginia voted that the Anglican church should be deprived of its right to lay taxes for the support of its ministers, and during those years the non-Anglicans continued to be legally defined as "dissenters."[27]

In the same year that the Anglican church was stripped of its former power to assess and levy parish taxes, a general-assessment bill was brought forward by James Henry as an alternative. Henry's bill was very similar to the provisions on religion in the South Carolina constitution except that it specified that "the Christian religion [not Protestantism] shall in all times coming be deemed and held to be the established Religion of this Commonwealth."[28] It contained the same provisions for forming religious societies and incorporating them on precisely the same five creedal points. But it went beyond the South Carolina constitution in requiring that a specific sum of money or poundage of tobacco "shall be paid annually for each Tithable by the person enlisting the same for and towards the Support of Religious teachers and places of Worship" according to his taxable property. Every taxpayer could state "what [religious] Society or denomination of Christians he or she would choose to contribute" his tax to. Those who did not specify any church would have their taxes distributed proportionally among the various religious societies in the parish where they lived. The bill passed two readings, but consideration of it was finally postponed, and it died in that session. Nevertheless the principle of a general

26. Jameson, *American Revolution*, 86.
27. H. J. Eckenrode, *Separation of Church and State in Virginia* (Richmond, 1910), 50–53.
28. James Henry's bill is quoted, *ibid*., 58–60.

assessment continued to find strong support, and in 1784 Patrick Henry brought forward another such bill.

Patrick Henry's "Bill Establishing a Provision for Teachers of the Christian Religion" was much simpler than that of James Henry. It contained no statement about incorporation, for that issue was being debated separately at the time. It contained no statement about the general establishment of the Christian religion and no creedal definition of Christianity. But it specified that "for the support of Christian teachers" a tax on property shall be paid by every person "chargeable with the said Tax" and that the taxpayers should give a receipt to the tax collector "expressing to what society of Christians the person from whom he may receive the same shall direct the money to be paid." The vestry, elders, or directors of each religious society were then to use the money "for a Minister or Teacher of the Gospel of their denomination or the providing places of divine worship." Those who failed to specify a religious society to which they wished their tax allocated would have their money used by the legislature "for the encouragement of seminaries of learning within the counties whence such sums shall arise."[29]

The preamble to the act states, in terms strikingly similar to those of Article III of the Massachusetts Constitution of 1780, the philosophy behind the general-assessment concept. It is interesting also for its specific statement regarding the importance of a "learned" ministry (which could not help offending the Baptists and Methodists, who put more store in spiritual gifts than academic degrees), thereby revealing a more conservative approach to the problem than that of the former Puritan states:

Whereas the general diffusion of Christian knowledge hath a natural tendency to correct the morals of men, restrain their vices, and preserve the peace of society; which cannot be effected without a competent provision for learned teachers, who may be thereby en-

29. I have quoted the version of the bill printed on handbills and distributed around the state in the summer of 1785. "A Bill Establishing a Provision for Teachers of the Christian Religion" [Richmond, 1784], Early American Imprints microcard #44619.

abled to devote their time and attention to the duty of instructing such citizens, as from the circumstances and want of education, cannot otherwise attain such knowledge, and it is judged that such provision may be made by the Legislature without counter-acting the liberal principle heretofore adopted and intended to be preserved abolishing all distinctions of pre-eminence amongst the different societies of communities of Christians. . . .

There is no need to reiterate the familiar story of Madison's desperate fight against this bill, but two points concerning the debate are important here: first, the kinds of arguments offered by broad-church Anglicans who supported Henry's bill and, second, the fact that, as in South Carolina, Presbyterians and other dissenters seemed willing to acquiesce in the plan.[30] The broad-church arguments for a general assessment are epitomized in a letter that Richard Henry Lee wrote to Madison from New York on November 26, 1784, when he learned that Henry's bill was under debate:

It is certainly comfortable to know that the Legislature of our country is engaged in beneficial pursuits—for I conceive the Gen. Assessment and a wise digest of our militia laws are very important concerns; the one to secure our peace and the other our morals. Refiners may weave a fine web of reason as they please, but the experience of all times shews Religion to be the guardian of morals— And he must be a very inattentive observer in our Country who does not see that avarice is accomplishing the destruction of religion for want of a legal obligation to contribute something to its support. The Declaration of Rights, it seems to me, rather contends against forcing modes of faith and forms of worship than against compelling contribution for the support of religion in general.[31]

Lee expressed here several important points shared by many Americans: that compulsory religious taxes for the support of

30. For Methodist and other petitions in support of the general-assessment system, see Eckenrode, *Separation*, 47, 72, 76, 79, 83–84, 99. Charles F. James offers evidence that there was considerable Presbyterian support for a general-assessment system from 1776 to 1784 and cites several other petitions in its favor. *Documentary History of the Struggle for Religious Liberty in Virginia* (Lynchburg, Va., 1900), 180–189.

31. James C. Ballagh, ed., *The Letters of Richard Henry Lee* (New York, 1914), II, 304. George Washington thought Henry's bill "impolitic" but not improper. See Eckenrode, *Separation*, 105.

religion were essential to secure the well-being of the Repub-lic;[32] second, that the moral welfare of the community had been seriously undermined by the absence of compulsory sup-port since 1776; and third, that a declaration of rights guaran-teeing the free exercise of religion in no way prohibited the general establishment of Christianity.[33]

As for the acquiescence of dissenters, this was demonstrated by the petition which the Reverend John Blair Smith, the leading spokesman for the Presbyterians in Virginia and the president of Hampden-Sydney College, submitted on Novem-ber 12, 1784. Smith's petition, on behalf of the Hanover Pres-bytery, followed the same reasoning as Lee's letter, expressing hope that in passing the bill "no attempt will be made to point out articles of faith that are not essential to the preservation of society, or to settle modes of worship, or to interfere in the in-ternal government of religious communities, or to render the ministers of religion independent of the will of the people whome they serve." Smith also asserted that "it is a wise policy in legislatures to seek its [religion's] alliance and solicit its aid in civil view because of its happy influence upon the morali-ty of its citizens. . . . It is on this principle alone, in our opin-ion, that a legislative body has a right to interfere at all, and of consequence we suppose that this interference ought only to extend to the preserving of the public worship of the deity and the supporting of institutions for inculcating the great fundamental principles of all religion without which society could not easily exist."[34]

The willingness of the Presbyterians to accept Henry's bill astounded Madison, who had counted on the non-Anglicans to oppose it and support Jefferson's bill. He called the petition a "shameful posture for dissenters to take; the Presbyterians

32. For a typical statement at this time about the particular importance of civic virtue in a republic as opposed to a monarchy or aristocracy, see Varnum W. Collins, *President Witherspoon* (Princeton, 1925), II, 128.

33. Lee went on to say in his letter that he believed "Mahometans" and "Hindoos" had a perfect right to worship according to their beliefs in Virginia.

34. Eckenrode, *Separation*, 89.

seem as ready to set up an establishment which is to take them in as they were to pull down that which shut them out."[35] Jefferson also recorded his annoyance at "some of our dissenting allies, having now secured their particular object [the overthrow of Anglican pre-eminence], going over to the advocates of general assessment."[36] But in many respects it was Jefferson and Madison's position that was eccentric at this time. They later admitted that, had not Patrick Henry, confident of victory for his bill, accepted the governorship at this point and so left the legislature, the bill would have passed.

More interesting in some respects than the famous Virginia debate over general assessment was that in Maryland at the same time. Though it has received little attention from historians, it demonstrates even more conclusively that the deciding factor against the general-assessment plan in the southern states was not so much a principled commitment to voluntaryism as a combined fear of Anglican preeminence and an unwillingness to accept additional taxation even for such a desirable goal.

In 1776 Maryland had adopted in its Declaration of Rights the usual assertion of the fundamental right of religious liberty, but it seemed to make Christians more equal than others: "As it is the duty of every man to worship God in such manner as he thinks most acceptable to him, all persons professing the Christian religion are equally entitled to protection in their religious liberty." The clause went on to state that "no person ought by any law to be molested in his person or estate on account of his religious persuasion or profession or for his religious practice . . . nor ought any person to be compelled to frequent or maintain or contribute, *unless on contract*, to maintain any particular place of worship or any [particular] ministry."[37] Presumably by being "on contract" the state meant simply to assert that congregations that made civil contracts with their ministers were bound to uphold these.[38]

35. *Ibid.*, 90–91.
36. *Ibid.*, 64.
37. Stokes, *Church and State*, I, 440 (my italics).
38. The whole question of "impairment of contract" in regard to

So far the Maryland Declaration of Rights was typical enough, but it then added this important qualification, which made explicit what in Virginia, Georgia, South Carolina, and other states at this time was implicit: "Yet, the legislature may, in their discretion, lay a general and equal tax for the support of the Christian religion, leaving each individual the power of appointing the payment over of the money collected from him to the support of any particular place of worship or minister, or for the benefit of the poor. . . ."

On May 6, 1783, Gov. William Paca and the council of Maryland sent to the legislature a message calling their attention to "the sufferings of the ministers of the gospel of all denominations during the war" and reminding them of the above clause: "Anxiously solicitious for the blessings of government and the welfare and happiness of our citizens and thoroughly convinced of the powerful influence of religion, when diffused by its respectable teachers, we beg leave most seriously and warmly to recommend" that the legislature make some provision for the compulsory support of the ministry.[39] Two years later, on January 6, 1785, the legislature obliged by drafting a bill "to lay a general tax for the support of the ministers of the gospel of all societies of christians within this state."[40] The bill did not define a congregation or church in theological terms. It merely stated "that every society of christians, consisting of thirty or more male persons not under twenty-one years of age, desirous to receive the benefit of this act as a society for the purpose of religious worship, shall give themselves a name or denomination, by which they shall be known in law. . . ." This left to the courts the problem of defining which such de-

---

disestablishment needs more consideration. For Zephaniah Swift's view of of this, see his *A System of the Laws of the State of Connecticut* (Windham, Conn., 1795–1796) I, 141–142. I have also alluded to it in "The Bench, the Church and the Republican Party in New Hampshire," *Historical New Hampshire*, XX (1965), 3–31.

39. For evidence that Gov. Paca may have been led to support this measure through his connection with Rev. William Smith of the Episcopal church, see Horace W. Smith, *Life and Correspondence of Rev. William Smith* (Philadelphia, 1880), II, 93.

40. The bill was printed on handbills and also in the newspapers. See the *Maryland Gazette* (Annapolis), Jan. 20, 1785.

nominations were and were not truly "christian." However, because the vote to draw up this bill was so close (26 to 24), the legislature resolved to reserve final consideration of it until the next session in November. Meanwhile the proposed bill was printed on handbills and distributed throughout the state. One of the issues left undecided in the bill was how large the tax should be. Estimates ranging from 4s. (by proponents) to 48s. (by opponents) per poll were made.

Immediately the legislature was deluged with petitions about "the religious bill" or "the clergy bill." The newspapers became filled with letters pro and con. By the time a new legislature was elected and seated in November, the opposition was so great that the House resolved on November 18 "that any law imposing a general tax for the support of ministers of the gospel of all or any denomination, is unnecessary and impolitic and that instead of promoting the cause of religion, it would be an injury thereto."

It has generally been assumed that the people of Maryland were influenced in rejecting this bill by the simultaneous debate over Patrick Henry's bill in Virginia and that the arguments for religious liberty put forward by the dissenters of Maryland were the principal causes for its defeat. But a study of the newspaper debate indicates that the radical whigs' fear of a reviving Episcopal hierarchy was the dominant factor and opposition to increasing taxes a close second. Unfortunately most of the debate was conducted anonymously, and no identifiable leaders on either side emerged. With typical "paranoid style" the opponents of the bill described it as "an insidious design" to reestablish the Anglican church; the clergy were using "sinister" means to reimpose "an oppressive ecclesiastical establishment."[41] The villains behind the plot were said to be the Reverend William Smith (president of Washington College), "the Maryland Sachervell," and Samuel Chase (a member of Congress and leading Episcopalian), "an insidious lawyer."[42] Smith, "the Champion of the Episcopal Party," had come to

41. See *Maryland Gazette* (Baltimore), Feb. 18, 1785; *Maryland Journal* (Baltimore), Mar. 1, 1785.

42. *Md. Jour.* (Baltimore), Jan. 21, 25, 28, 1785.

Maryland in 1780 from Philadelphia where he had been president of the College of Philadelphia; his loyalist (or neutral) views made him doubly suspect among dissenters and his efforts in Maryland to revive the Episcopal church, to codify its articles and practices, to obtain its incorporation, and to become the first bishop of Maryland were all cited as proofs that he was "an officious priest," leading his body of "designing ecclesiastics" crying "for the fleece."[43] That Governor Paca (also an Episcopalian) had been a pupil of Smith's at the College of Philadelphia and was very friendly with him added to the suspicions of a conspiracy.

The legislators, wrote one opponent of the bill, were predominantly Anglicans who want "you to think it is the cause of the [Christian] Church" they seek to assist by this bill, "when in fact, it is to slyly have you brought under a yoke to the [Anglican] clergy, as formerly."[44] Some of the bill's opponents were themselves Anglicans who feared that "it will not stop here" with a bill to support pastors—"for we must have a BISHOP and the different orders of the Clergy. . . . A Bishop, Arch-deacon, Deacon, Dean, Prebends, and the Lord knows *all*, will require the Lord knows *what* to support them."[45] A tax that began at 4s. would soon leap to 24s. and then to 40s. as the hierarchy grew in size and influence. One irate pietist denounced the legislature for finding it easier to "meddle with a *Saviour* than a surplice."[46]

Some proponents of the bill, however, believed that if there "were such an establishment possible in favour of any religious persuasion, the design is not for the members of the *episcopal church* but those of another denomination [Presbyterian] who are known to be of the most intolerant principles and still seeking by every possible means to exalt their party. . . ."[47] Thus the shades of seventeenth-century Puritans and Cavaliers still hovered over Maryland.

Members of the smaller sects (Baptists, Quakers, Dunkers,

43. See H. W. Smith, *William Smith*, II, 100.
44. *Md. Jour.* (Baltimore), Feb. 8, 1785.
45. *Ibid.*
46. *Ibid.*, Feb. 25, 1785.
47. *Md. Gaz.* (Annapolis), Sept. 29, 1785.

Moravians, and Mennonites) disliked the fact that they could receive no benefit from the bill unless their churches had at least thirty male members. Roman Catholics were said to oppose the bill because all but one of their twenty ministers were already supported by endowment.[48] The debate was complicated by fears of a poll tax (which the constitution specifically prohibited) and by the recent creation of two publicly endowed colleges (Washington College, 1782, and St. John's College, 1784). Many letters opposed the bill on the ground that taxes were already too high or that the holders of slaves would have to pay the most taxes even though slaves would not benefit from the act: "What! 48s [tax] for a lad sixteen year's old or a wench of that age or for a decrepit, old, useless slave! a slave rents for £12 per year. . . . yet the owner must pay the parson, whom he [the slave] neither hears preach nor sees at his habitation as his instructor, one fifth part of it, besides paying his state and country taxes!"[49] A petition from the Salisbury Baptist Association protested, "Your Remonstrants conceive the establishment of Religion at this time is premature, as our State debt and the expences arising for the necessary support of civil government" are already very burdensome.[50] Estimates of the number of non-Episcopalians in the state ranged from "nearly one half" to "a majority," but so many nominal Anglicans were opposed because of the taxes required that the measure was defeated in November by a lopsided vote of 41 to 21. The vote may not therefore be a fair estimate of the general sentiment regarding the principle of government support for religion. But as so often happened in America, pragmatic considerations modified avowed ideals.

In view of the defeat of all efforts at general-assessment plans in the southern states, it has frequently been inferred that New England was backward and out of touch with the prevailing current for religious liberty and equality.[51] But seen in

48. *Md. Jour.* (Baltimore), Jan. 18, Mar. 15, 1785.
49. *Md. Gaz.* (Baltimore), Mar. 4, 1785.
50. *Md. Jour.* (Baltimore), Jan. 28, 1785.
51. I have discussed the process of disestablishment in *New England Dissent, 1630–1833: The Baptists and the Separation of Church and State* (Cambridge, Mass., 1971).

the broader context the old Puritan states were going through precisely the same debate and on precisely the same terms. The reasons why the balance tipped in favor of the general-assessment system in New England can be attributed more to historical tradition and practice than to any significant difference of public opinion regarding the importance of compulsory tax support for religion. New England lacked not only the background of Anglican domination that animated the southern dissenters but also the important leadership of semi-deists like Jefferson and Madison who favored the more radical solution of voluntaryism. Such rationalists or religious liberals as New England had were firmly entrenched within the Unitarian wing of the Congregational establishment and had no quarrel with it. Even John Adams, who might have played the part of Madison, lacked the strong feeling that would have been necessary to fight against his fellow Harvard alumni. Moreover, the Puritan heritage had long since taken New England away from the confessional state, and dissenters found it hard to convince their Congregational neighbors that the New England establishment was such a heinous affair. After all, Connecticut and Massachusetts had granted exemption from compulsory support of Congregationalism to Baptists, Quakers, and Episcopalians a half century before the Revolution. The claim of pietistic dissenters, like Isaac Backus, that even presenting a certificate of dissent in order to be relieved of religious taxes was an abridgment of their rights of conscience was difficult to sustain in view of the great benefit to the general welfare that the general-assessment system provided. True, Article III of the Massachusetts Constitution did require all dissenters to pay religious taxes and thereby appeared to revoke their former privilege of tax exemption, but in practice it turned out that most towns and parishes soon reverted to the older custom and preferred to exempt dissenters who provided certificates rather than go to the trouble of collecting their taxes (often by distraint) only to hand them back to their elders.

Other factors may also account for New England's willingness to try the general-assessment plan. First of all, there were far fewer dissenters in New England, probably less than a fifth in

1780; hence they did not have the votes or the influence to defeat it. Second, the New England Congregational system was a solid and thriving one that, despite the separations during the Great Awakening, remained in firm control of almost every parish. Third, the Congregational clergy, having been staunch supporters of the Revolution, attained increased respect and allegiance during that crisis. And finally, the rulers of Connecticut and Massachusetts may have been somewhat more fearful of social disruption than those of Virginia, where the upper class felt sufficiently secure to accept the dissolution of an ecclesiastical system that had never been very effective anyway. As Shays's Rebellion was to show, the Revolution had unleashed currents of popular self-assertion and centrifugal forces of local self-government to a much greater degree in New England. Perhaps also, given the more firmly indoctrinated Calvinistic principle of innate human depravity in New England, even the average voter preferred to maintain the older institutions a while longer amidst the flux of change. The Congregationalists wished to be fair to dissenters; they had no desire to oppress them. But neither did they, as an overwhelming majority, feel that they should give up all of their traditional ecclesiastical practices to please a minority that seemed to place its own interest before that of the commonwealth.

Connecticut continued its established system without even writing a new constitution in the Revolutionary era, though it did grant a very liberal certificate system to enable dissenters from the Congregational majority to obtain exemption from religious taxes. Massachusetts adopted a new ecclesiastical system that in principle, though not in practice, granted equality to all Protestant denominations. Vermont and New Hampshire, while retaining territorial parishes in which the majority voted religious taxes for the support of their own church, had so many dissenters that often the Congregationalists were the dissenting minority; as a result Baptists, Methodists, Universalists, and other small denominations found little to complain of in these states, and their efforts for disestablishment were sporadic.

The parish system in New England was gradually whittled

away by increasingly permissive grounds permitting individuals to opt out of the parish church and join another (usually one where religious support was voluntary), until scores of parishes in New England had too few persons left to support the established church and its minister by taxes upon themselves. As a result of this tendency the New England states were constantly trying to find other means to supplement the direct taxation of property for the support of religion.

One common means widely used in the Revolutionary era to raise money for building or repairing churches of all denominations was to conduct a lottery (an indirect form of assistance by the state, since lottery schemes had to be incorporated by acts of the legislature).[52] Another expedient, somewhat less common, was the pooling of the resources of a number of local churches by forming a "union" or "catholic" church out of the combined membership.[53] Many New England towns and parishes voted after 1790 to share the use of the meetinghouse, formerly limited to Congregationalists, among all the various Protestant sects in the community. The Connecticut legislature sought on two occasions, in 1793 and in 1816, to supplement the general-assessment taxes raised locally by creating a state endowment fund for the support of religion. But by far the most common expedient, and one not limited to New England, was to rent or sell outright the pews in the meetinghouses of all denominations.

Pew rents had been allowed in Boston from early in colonial days because Boston was never part of the parish system.[54] In 1755 a law granted every parish in Massachusetts the power to lay assessments on pews according to valuation and to sell the pew of any man who failed to pay his rent. This privilege was confirmed by other statutes in 1786 and 1800 as other cities fol-

52. I have discussed this and the other expedients mentioned in this paragraph, *ibid.*, I, 660–697, 962–984, 1034–1042.

53. See for example Ellen Larned, *History of Windham County* (Worcester, Mass., 1880), II, 313–314, and Arthur Wilson, *Weybosset Bridge* (Boston, 1947), 208.

54. It is sometimes forgotten that John Cotton and many other early Puritans opposed the system of parish taxes (a system adopted only after the Puritans found that voluntaryism would not work).

lowed Boston and abandoned the parish system. Because mobile populations and frequent rebuilding made parish zoning and parish tax collecting difficult in the cities, pew rents became increasingly popular. We shall return to the social significance of supporting religious worship by pew rents or taxes levied on pew valuations, but it is impossible to discuss this expedient for the support of religion without a careful consideration of the question of incorporation of religious societies that arose simultaneously. For a church could not enforce its contractual arrangements with its congregation unless it had the force of law behind it.[55]

Since incorporation gave the backing of the state to the group incorporated, making it a "body politic" in law and endowing it with special privileges and powers that the state was obliged to enforce, this effort to deal with the relationship of church and state was as fraught with controversy as the general-assessment concept. However, it proved more amenable to pragmatic adjustments and avoided the more obvious bugbears of a state-church alliance.

Technically, of course, all territorial parishes were quasi-corporations or bodies politic, for they were all empowered by the legislatures to perform certain actions for the state: levying and collecting taxes for the support of ministers, the building and repair of meetinghouses, the care of the poor, and the maintenance of schools. In colonies with an established church every new parish came into being by an act of the legislature, and under English law Anglican vestries were considered to be corporations.[56] Cotton Mather wrote in 1726 that every Congregational minister in New England though "chosen by the People is (not only Christ's but also) in Reality the King's Minister, and the Salary raised for him is raised in the King's name and is the King's allowance unto him."[57]

55. For an example of a Baptist church in the colonial period that was willing to take its members to court if they did not honor their promises to contribute to the support of the church, see the articles of faith adopted by the Second Baptist Church of Groton, Mass., in 1765, Church Records Manuscripts, Connecticut State Library, Hartford.

56. Zollmann, *Church Law*, 64.

57. Cotton Mather, *Ratio Disciplinae Fratrum Nov-Anglorum* (Boston,

Incorporation of religious and charitable bodies started before the Revolution in most colonies but only in a very limited way. Usually an act of incorporation was passed in order to clarify the ownership and management of trust funds and property donated or bequeathed to a religious society for its support. The licensing of dissenting bodies under the Toleration Act of 1689 or similar colonial statutes was also a form of incorporation since it granted official status in law to the congregations so recognized. During the Great Awakening, when so many of the post-Revolutionary issues of church and state first arose, a few groups of individuals were licensed or incorporated in New England as bona fide established churches in order to solve otherwise intractable disputes among New Lights and Old Lights; such congregations were poll parishes, permitted to perform all the functions of territorial parishes among the members named in the licensing act but operating within a territorial parish that retained the right to lay ecclesiastical taxes upon all inhabitants not associated with the poll parish by name.[58]

Prior to 1780, however, incorporated poll parishes were always considered exceptional in New England. They were temporary expedients that hopefully would disappear with the special circumstances that created them. Sectarian dissenters—Baptists, Separates, Quakers—did not seek incorporation since they believed in voluntaryism and did not wish to exercise taxing powers over their congregations. But Anglicans in non-Anglican colonies, the Dutch Reformed Church in New York, and some Presbyterians (who followed the establishmentarian principles of the Church of Scotland)[59] sought and were granted incorporation for this purpose. Generally, however, a self-

1726), 21. Mather was arguing here against the claims of Anglicans, but his words were used against the Congregational establishment by Baptists during the Revolutionary era.

58. For the creation of one of the first poll parishes in Massachusetts, see John M. Bumsted, "The Pilgrim's Progress: The Ecclesiastical History of Southern Massachusetts, 1620–1776" (Ph.D. diss., Brown University, 1965), 214ff. For the licensing of schismatic New Light congregations in Connecticut during the Awakening, see Goen, *Revivalism and Separatism*, 86–88.

59. Notably those in New Hampshire.

selective immigration process minimized this practice in the colonial period. Anglicans and Presbyterians settled in the southern colonies, where they considered themselves part of the establishment; Congregationalists went to New England; and nonconformists to Rhode Island, Pennsylvania, and New Jersey, where there seemed no need for corporate power for religion. The few dissenters within the established colonies could be, if the occasion warranted, allowed incorporation as exceptions to the rule or, in the case of Anglicans in New England, as evidence of the latitudinarian establishment of these colonies.

But the Revolution changed all this. The abolition of the old establishments raised the possibility of replacing all territorial parishes with poll parishes. If members of Anglican, Presbyterian, or Congregational churches wanted the power to levy and collect taxes for the support of their worship, let them have it, and if Baptists, Separates, and Quakers considered this unscriptural, let them continue to support their churches by voluntary gifts. Some conservative religionists, however, wanted a policy of compulsory incorporation forcing everyone to support some form of Christian or Protestant worship but leaving each citizen free to choose his own church. As we have noted, something like this approach lay behind most of the experiments with a general-assessment system, and it is not surprising that radical pietists and deists saw in a general-incorporation system precisely the same specter of state encroachment upon religious liberty and the beginnings of a new league between rulers and priests; they did not believe that incorporation was permissible even upon individual choice. No religious group had the right to enslave itself to or seek special privileges from the state. Furthermore, as Madison said, what the state could create, it could also destroy.

The best example of these dangers was the act of general incorporation passed in South Carolina in 1784. Based on the article in the constitution of 1778 that asserted the right of any fifteen males over twenty-one to unite and seek incorporation for Protestant worship, this system was tried for six years and then abandoned with the revision of the constitution in 1790. It proved unpopular partly because fifteen males seemed an

arbitrary number, twenty-one an arbitrary age, and the elimination of females a discrimination against small congregations
where female members were important; partly because the
article established the right of those incorporated to elect their
own ministers, a commitment to congregational polity and lay
control that obviously threatened the episcopal principles of the
Anglicans and Methodists, not to mention the Roman Catholics; but most important of all because under this system the
state defined the theological tenets upon which all incorporation was to be based, thereby creating a confessional state.

Similar problems curtailed the experiment with incorporation tried in Virginia in 1784 to 1786. This involved incorporating denominations rather than individual churches or congregations. The effort to incorporate the Protestant Episcopal Church
as the successor to the Anglican church and inheritor of its
property, rights, and privileges, though at first receiving the
support of Madison, was repealed within two years (also with
Madison's backing). Again it seemed on the surface a logical
adjustment, compatible with denominational equality, since
the legislature expressly stated in a resolution preceding the
act that "a like incorporation ought to be extended to all other
religious societies within this Commonwealth which may apply
for the same."[60] Dissenters and Madisonian liberals became increasingly hostile to the act, however, pointing out that among
other inequities it granted to one denomination the glebelands
that prior to 1776 had been considered the property of all the
people (another striking similarity to the problem of disestablishing ministerial lots and town meetinghouses in New England). In addition the incorporation act created a unique bond
between the Protestant Episcopal denomination and the legislature by continuing the right of the vestrymen in each territorial parish to levy taxes upon all inhabitants for the support
of the poor, even though vestrymen were to be Protestant
Episcopalians and to be elected by members of their own sect.

60. Eckenrode, *Separation*, 92, gives a somewhat different wording than
the House journal. For the attempt of the Protestant Episcopal Church to
obtain incorporation as a denomination in Maryland in 1783, see Nelson
Rightmyer, *Maryland's Established Church* (Baltimore, 1956), 124–128.

The laity felt threatened because the act gave the clergy the power to regulate faith and practice in the denomination, to depose unworthy ministers, and to elect bishops.

Not only was the act quickly repealed, but continued pressure from dissenters finally forced the legislature in 1802 to take the glebelands from the Protestant Episcopal Church and sell them for the benefit of the poor—an extreme example of "impairment of contract" adopted in no other state.[61] In fact the reaction against the incorporation of religious societies was so great that Virginia became the only state to prohibit it in any form—a position that left that state out of the mainstream of American religious development despite its pioneering efforts in establishing the free exercise of religion.[62]

At the same time that Virginians were debating the policy of incorporation, the state of New York tried a third kind of experiment—granting incorporation rights to all voluntary associations for religious purposes but ignoring theological issues and placing the power of managing the churches' temporal affairs (or seeming to) in the hands of elected trustees who might act even against the majority will of the corporation. This concept of the trustee corporation was imbedded in the acts disestablishing the Dutch and Anglican establishments and creating a general-incorporation system in 1784. The act for the "Reformed Protestant Dutch Church" among other things abrogated the right of that church "to make Rates and Assessments upon all and every of the members in Communion of said Church"—an act parallel to George Mason's act in Virginia in 1779 denying the right of the Episcopal church to tax its members as a denomination. The act revising the status of Trinity Episcopal Church also abrogated its power of religious taxation and all other "Immunities, Emoluments and Privi-

---

61. For the manner in which Anglican glebelands were preserved for the use of the Society for the Propagation of the Gospel in Vermont after the Revolution, see Walter T. Bogart, *The Vermont Lease Lands* (Montpelier, Vt., 1950), 72, 216–220, 245, 261.

62. Zollmann, *Church Law*, 25, 38. See also the discussion of the Virginia lawsuit (*Gallegos* v. *Attorney General*, 1832) in which the court ruled that religious trusts could not be enforced by law; Howe, "Problems in Religious Liberty," in Friedrich, ed., *Nomos IV*, 265.

leges," which gave or implied "a pre-eminence of distinction of the said Episcopal Church or Church of England over all other churches and other religious denominations." This act constituted the official disestablishment of Anglicanism in the counties of Queens, Richmond, Westchester, and New York. But the positive complement to these negative acts in 1784 was the simultaneous passage of a law "to enable the Religious Denominations in the State to appoint Trustees who shall be a Body Corporate." The preamble to this act states its purpose:

Whereas many of the Churches, Congregations, and religious societies in this State (while it was a Colony) have been put to great Difficulties to support the public Worship of God by Reason of the illiberal and partial Distributions of Charters of Incorporation to religious Societies, whereby many charitable and well disposed Persons have been prevented from contributing to the Support of Religion for Want of proper Persons authorized by Law to take charge of their pious Donations and many Estates purchased and given for the support of religious Societies now rest in private Hands, to the great Insecurity of the Society for whose Benefit they were purchased or given and to the no less Disquiet of many of the good People of this State; And Whereas it is the Duty of all Wise, Free and Virtuous Governments to countenance and encourage Virtue and Religion and to remove every Lett or Impediment to the Growth and Prosperity of the People and to enable every religious Denomination to provide for the Decent and Honorable Support of Divine Worship agreeable to the Dictates of Conscience and Judgment. . . .

The act then went on to authorize all religious societies or congregations to choose trustees to "take care of the temporalities" of their church, to receive, hold, and invest estates, to build houses of worship, and to have the power "to regulate and order the Rentings of Pews in the said Churches and Meetinghouses," and of course the concomitant power to sue and dispossess those who did not pay their assessed pew rent.

Unfortunately this act (and others like it in other states) failed to clarify the relationship between the trustees and the congregations that chose them.[63] According to some legal decisions in the years that followed, the act had created an eccle-

63. For a discussion of the confused legal status of trustee corporations down to 1854, see Zollmann, *Church Law*, 49–58.

siastical corporation in which those chosen by the congregation (whether vestrymen, elders, deacons, or a committee) were in effect independent of the congregation and responsible only to the state for their actions. Hence it often occurred that what seemed best for a church or congregation according to the trustees was not what seemed best to those whom they ostensibly represented. The state had created a Frankenstein monster that, far from guaranteeing religious liberty to any group of Protestants in their temporalities (including the payment of the minister of their choice), put them under the power of a small minority of their members. Not until Judge Selden's famous decision in *Robertson* v. *Bullions* in 1854 was this aspect of religious incorporation clarified, and we shall return to it in a moment.

Meanwhile the rapidly deteriorating system in New England produced other approaches to incorporation. The New England states tried to engraft the incorporated poll-parish system onto the old territorial-parish system by extending to all dissenters the right hitherto granted only to Anglicans and a few New Light Congregationalists to form incorporated religious societies. The complications arising out of this dual system of territorial and poll parishes operating side by side is most graphically illustrated in Massachusetts.[64] While maintaining a general-assessment system, the constitution of 1780 had "disestablished" Congregationalism by asserting in Article III that no sect should be subordinate to any other, thereby allowing dissenters, if a majority, to control any territorial parish and, where not a majority, to seek incorporation as a poll parish. As of 1785 none of the dissenting sects had seen any need for incorporation, but because of the construction placed upon Article III by the courts at that time, the voluntaryists had the problem forced upon them. Reluctantly acquiescing in the general-assessment system, the non-Congregationalists had paid the religious taxes laid upon them and assumed that the towns and parishes would return their share to the ministers or

64. See Kirk Alliman, "Incorporation of Congregationalism: The Preservation of Religious Autonomy" (Ph.D. diss., Iowa State University, 1970), and Edward Buck, *Massachusetts Ecclesiastical Law* (Boston, 1865).

churches they attended. When some town and parish treasurers refused to do this, the Baptists brought suit against them, only to discover to their surprise that being unincorporated they could not be recognized in law as groups to whom tax money could be properly granted.[65] This placed all voluntaryists in a quandry. Either they could abandon their conscientious scruples against seeking the aid of the state and petition for incorporation or they could let the towns and parishes keep their share of the religious taxes and appropriate them to the oldest church in the parish where they lived (invariably Congregational).

The Baptists debated the issue hotly for a generation, but never came to an agreement. The Quakers, however, were relieved of the problem by a special act in 1800 that granted them exemption from religious taxes. Because the controversy over incorporation was complicated by the general-assessment system, it is not always easy to see how important it was and how similar the position of many New England Baptists was to that of Madison and the Virginia dissenters on this issue. Had they maintained as united a front as the Virginians the outcome might have been different. But because they were not fighting an Anglican system, because they faced the loss of their religious tax money, which they expected to have applied to the support of their own churches, and because some of their leaders, particularly in the eastern urban and suburban areas, were increasingly disillusioned with the system of freewill offerings as a viable means of church support, the Massachusetts Baptists became hopelessly divided. Nevertheless their long and painful arguments over the true meaning of voluntaryism deserve attention, for out of it came the compromise position that created the Protestant establishment of nineteenth-century America.

Defending the Virginia position that incorporation of religion in any form was ipso facto an establishment of religion were men like Isaac Backus, John Leland, and the renegade Baptist, Elias Smith. Defending the position that voluntary incorporation under congregational control was no threat to re-

65. See Cushing, "Notes on Disestablishment," *WMQ*, 3d Ser., XXVI (1969), 169–190, and McLoughlin, *New England Dissent*, I, 653–659.

ligious autonomy and therefore an acceptable, even desirable, means of state encouragement to religion were Baptist ministers like Hezekiah Smith, Thomas Baldwin, and Samuel Stillman. Of course, many Baptist churches that sought incorporation after 1790 claimed to be sympathetic with the former position and insisted that they took this step, not with any intention of laying taxes upon their own members, but only to bring suits, when necessary, to obtain for their own use the taxes levied by their town or parish.

One of the most vigorous debates on this issue took place among the delegates to the Warren Baptist Association meeting in 1791. The first and most important of the evangelical Calvinist associations among the New England Baptists, the Warren Association was looked to to set the standards for the denomination. In this debate Hezekiah Smith, pastor of the wealthy Baptist church in Haverhill, advocated "the propriety of incorporating baptists churches and societies in order to oblige people to pay what they had agreed to give their minister if they refused to do it voluntarily." Smith's church, like many others in urban and suburban areas, followed a policy of subscription, in which each member agreed each year to pay a certain amount for the support of the church. A church might censure or excommunicate a member who failed to contribute the amount he was assessed or had volunteered to pay (for the sin of covetousness), but without incorporation they could not take him to court and sue him for the arrearage or ask the constable to dispossess him of his pew. Smith argued, however, that it was "no hurt to have law enough to make people fulfill their contracts." It was in fact a fundamental tenet of the Protestant ethic to pay one's debts.

Isaac Backus arose to confute Smith. He saw incorporation as unscriptural—an intrusion of the civil sword into spiritual affairs, an appeal to Caesar to enforce religious duties that only God and conscience should be concerned in. In addition he pointed out that incorporation generally included the whole congregation as voting members, while in scriptural usage and Baptist practice only full church members (the converted, baptized believers) had a right to control church affairs (such as choosing or dismissing ministers or censuring brethren). In an incorporated Baptist society the voting majority might consist of nonmembers, who might force the regenerate members to take un-Christian actions.[66] Thus would the world gain victory over the church.

Hezekiah Smith's position was essentially that of the Puritans who, when they first passed compulsory tax laws in the seventeenth century, reluctantly agreed that, if the unconverted members of each parish were required to support the church with their money, then they had a right to have a voice in the selection of ministers, the location of the meetinghouse, and other temporal affairs of the church (it was a right not to be taxed without representation). Technically Smith lost the debate, for the Warren Association voted with Backus to advise all its member churches not to seek incorporation. But actually Backus lost, for the vote was not binding upon the churches of the association, let alone the whole denomination. Smith's church did get incorporated and so did scores of others, including the leading churches in Boston and vicinity, and the association never took any action against them.[67]

How many incorporated churches actually went to law to recover subscription pledges or assessments and how many people paid to avoid the disgrace of such action is unknown, but Elias Smith reported that he knew of Baptist congregations where "cattle and horses were taken by force [i.e., by legal distraint upon court order] to pay baptist ministers for preaching."[68] Still there were many churches that did not become

66. For a description of this debate, see Elias Smith, *The Life, Conversion . . . of Elias Smith* (Portsmouth, N.H., 1816), 233–234. For Backus's views on incorporation, see T. H. Maston, *Isaac Backus: Pioneer of Religious Liberty* (Rochester, N.Y., 1962), 85–86. As Backus wrote in 1795, "If some who are of the church and some who are not are incorporated together to manage estates to support religious ministers, it binds the church and the world together." For John Leland's views on incorporation in 1791, see L. F. Greene, ed., *The Writings of Elder John Leland* (New York, 1845), 188–189. For Elder Henry Grew's opposition to incorporation in Connecticut, see the manuscript records of the First Baptist Church of Hartford, Conn. State Lib.

67. For a list of the Baptist churches in Massachusetts between 1790 and 1815, see Alliman, "Incorporation of Congregationalism," 206.

68. See E. Smith, *Life of Elias Smith*, 234.

incorporated, and when in 1810 Chief Justice Theophilus Parsons permanently closed the legal possibility that unincorporated churches might still receive the public taxes of their members, these conscientious anti-incorporationists tried another approach.[69] They turned to Jefferson's Democratic Republican party for help, and among the Democratic majority returned to the legislature the next year was John Leland.

The issue was confused by the fact that some dissenting churches that sought incorporation had found the Federalist party reluctant to grant them this privilege; the Democratic legislature of 1811 tried to solve the problem by introducing a general-incorporation law to provide a simple procedure by which dissenting congregations could be incorporated without petitioning for a special act of the legislature. But Leland, carrying on Backus's fight, opposed this measure:

The second section of the bill before the house, I object to. It recognizes principles which are inadmissable—invests all non-corporate societies with corporate powers—puts the mischievous dagger [of coercive legal power] into their hands, which has done so much mischief in the world and presents no balm for the wounds of those who cry for help.

The petitioners do not ask to be known in law as corporate bodies [at least the rural Baptists whom he represented did not], but to be so covered that religious corporate bodies shall not know and fleece them. . . . The interference of legislatures and magistrates in the faith and worship, or support of religious worship, is the first step in the case which leads in regular progression to inquisition.[70]

69. Parsons's decision is quoted in Mark DeWolfe Howe, *Cases on Church and State in the United States* (Cambridge, Mass., 1952), 29–35. This decision also expressed very clearly the fear of Madison and Backus that the power to incorporate some and not others enabled the state and its courts to regulate, or at least to favor, some sects over others: "If the society be not incorporated, what rules are prescribed by law by which its character may be defined?" Parsons asked. The state had no wish to assume "the absurd power of directing or controlling the faith of its citizens," but neither did the state wish to use the authority of the law to support any religion whatsoever. The government had asserted its authority in order to raise taxes to maintain Protestant teachers of piety, morality, and religion, but "a public teacher must be a teacher of some public and not of any private religious society. And what society must be deemed a public society is certainly a question of law whether it be settled by a judge or by a jury."

70. Greene, ed., *Writings of Leland*, 357.

As a consequence of Leland's eloquence, the Religious Freedom Act of 1811 did not include the principle of general incorporation. Instead it enabled any dissenting church, "corporate or unincorporate," to bring suit to recover its share of religious taxes if a town or parish treasurer did not return it. But this merely postponed the issue, and many Baptist churches continued to seek separate acts of incorporation.[71]

In 1820, when the dissenters found themselves unable to persuade the constitutional convention to abolish the general-assessment plan, they turned to the general-incorporation system. The leading spokesman for the dissenters at this convention was Thomas Baldwin, pastor of the Second Baptist Church of Boston and one of the most prestigious Baptist leaders in the nation. Baldwin proposed the following constitutional amendment: "Each and every society or denomination of Christians in this State shall have and enjoy the same and equal powers, rights and privileges and shall have power and authority to raise money for the support and maintenance of religious teachers of their respective denominations, and to build and repair houses of public worship by a tax on the members of any such society only to be laid by a majority vote of the legal voters assembled at any society meeting warned and held according to law."[72] Baldwin was ably assisted in this effort to replace the old territorial-parish system with incorporated poll parishes by Nathan Williams, pastor of the Baptist church in Beverly. Williams said "he agreed that contracts between the teachers and societies ought to be enforced, although some gentlemen [among the dissenters] thought otherwise."[73] In other words, these Baptist spokesmen had by 1820 come to agree with those Congregationalists who believed that voluntaryism was not sufficient to sustain a Christian nation. However, this effort to

71. The Congregationalists hoped that the state's Supreme Court would soon find an opportunity to declare the Religious Liberty Act an unconstitutional infringement upon Article III. They were disappointed when, in 1817, Chief Justice Parker, while deploring the bad effect of the act upon the parish system, nevertheless declared it constitutional. For his decision see Howe, *Church and State*, 35–40.

72. *Journal of the Debates in the Convention to Revise the Constitution of Massachusetts* (Boston, 1853), 347.

73. *Ibid.*, 382.

replace the general-assessment system by the general-incorporation system did not pass the convention. But it did come into
being in 1824 as an amendment to the Religious Freedom Act
of 1811.

The Religious Liberty Act of 1824 was introduced into the
legislature by Charles Train, pastor of the Baptist church of
Framingham. Train admitted that formerly most dissenters had
preferred "to support the Gospel by voluntary subscription,"
but now "this mode is gradually going out of use."[74] He therefore proposed that henceforth any congregation "may legally
organize by applying to a Justice of the Peace for a warrant to
call the first meeting without the trouble and expense of applying to the Legislature" for a special act of incorporation. This
act was supported by many Trinitarian Congregationalists who,
following the Dedham case in 1820–1821, found that Unitarian
majorities in many parishes were outvoting Trinitarian Congregationalists; since Trinitarians in such parishes thereby became dissenters, they were taxed to support a parish church that
they considered heretical (unless they filed certificates and became incorporated). Inevitably Massachusetts was forced soon
after to abandon its territorial-parish system entirely.

It is significant that the general-incorporation system was
adopted in Rhode Island and Pennsylvania at about the same
time it was first being debated among the Baptists of the former
Puritan states. Rhode Islanders had written voluntaryism into
law in 1716, stating that maintenance of churches and ministers
in the colony "shall be raised by free contribution and no other
way." Yet, said Isaac Backus, writing in horror to a friend in
London in 1791, "in Providence and Newport, societies have
been incorporated by the special acts of the government, to collect and manage funds for the support of religious ministers,
above the church. The Congregationalists [in Providence] began this practice in 1770 and two or three Baptists societies have
followed it, and Providence [First Baptist Church, under James
Manning] in particular. But what a reproach is cast upon Christ

74. *Christian Watchman* (Boston), Feb. 8, 1823, 33. For the law of 1824, see
Jacob C. Meyer, *Church and State in Massachusetts* (Cleveland, 1930),
213–215.

and his church when an incorporation by his laws, and the influence of his Spirit, is not esteemed a society strong enough to be intrusted with worldly property consecrated to religious uses!"[75] That Rhode Islanders were uneasy about this can be seen in the very defensive tract issued by the Congregationalists of Providence in 1771 to explain why they needed the assistance of the state.[76] The legislature began by simply empowering religious corporations to acquire, sell, and lease property to create an endowment fund, but by 1792 incorporation acts included the right of the majority "to assess the Expence thereof upon the Proprietors of the Pews in the said Meeting-House and, upon the Neglect or refusal of Payment, to levy and collect the same by selling the said Pews for the said purpose"; and further, "that the Society be and hereby is empowered to levy and collect any Tax or Taxes on the Proprietors lots in the Burying Ground. . . . and in case any Proprietor . . . shall neglect or refuse to pay the same, that the Society proceed to dispose of them in such Manner as to them shall appear proper for the best Advantage of said Society."[77]

The subversion of pure voluntaryism under the pressure of maintaining a Christian nation operated in Pennsylvania in a similar fashion. In 1791 the legislature passed "An Act to confer on certain associations of the citizens of this commonwealth the powers and immunities of corporations or bodies politic in law." Designed to relieve religious societies from making individual applications to the legislature for incorporation, it asserted that "when any number of persons, citizens of this commonwealth, are associated or mean to associate for any literary, charitable, or for any religious purpose, and shall be

75. Isaac Backus to John Rippon, Aug. 30, 1791, Florence Backus Papers, John Hay Library, Brown University, Providence, R.I. See also Isaac Backus, *A History of New England*, ed. David Weston (Newton, Mass., 1871), II, 172–173.

76. See *Act of Incorporation of the Benevolent Congregational Society in the Town of Providence* (Providence, 1771).

77. "An Act in Addition to an Act Passed . . . October, 1785 . . . to incorporate certain persons hereinafter mentioned by the Name of the Congregational Beneficent Society in Providence," *Rhode Island Session Laws, October, 1792* (Providence, 1792), 4. See also Wilson, *Weybosset Bridge*, 208–209, 220.

desirous to acquire and enjoy the powers and immunities of a corporation or body politic in law," it shall prepare "an instrument" specifying its objects, articles, and title and submit it to the attorney general; he would approve it and send it to the supreme court; if it approved, the "instrument" went to the governor, who automatically transmitted it to the master of rolls, who enrolled it among the bodies politic of the state. The powers granted to all such corporate bodies were "to sue and be sued, plead and be impleaded," make "by-laws and ordinances, and to do everything needful for the good government and support of the affairs of the said corporations." [78] As Louis Hartz has noted, that this general-incorporation law granting sovereign power to voluntary groups to raise money to support themselves was enacted on behalf of religious and charitable societies long before such a law was enacted for business corporations indicates that the commonwealth thought it had more to gain directly from guaranteeing the support of religion.[79]

As a result of the incorporation of religious societies, the courts in all of the states (except Virginia) were henceforth compelled to adjudicate such issues as whether the assessments in a corporate congregation were binding upon all members or simply upon those who agreed to them; whether the failure to pay one's pew rent entitled the congregation to sue the delinquent or merely to repossess his pew; whether pews were real estate or personal property; whether as personal property pews could be assessed by the state for civil taxes; whether a pewholder could prevent strangers from occupying his pew if he were absent; whether the trustees or other officers chosen by a corporate congregation were responsible only to the state or to the body that elected them. It was this last point that gave the most trouble, and it was not until 1854 that states with a system

78. James T. Mitchell and Henry Flanders, eds., *The Statutes at Large of Pennsylvania from 1682 to 1801*, XIV (Harrisburg, 1909), 50–53.

79. Louis Hartz, *Economic Policy and Democratic Thought: Pennsylvania, 1776–1860* (Cambridge, Mass., 1948), 38–39. Pennsylvania was among those states that wrote into its constitution a religious oath excluding non-Christians from officeholding, just as its laws required punishment for those who blasphemed against Christianity. See Stokes, *Church and State*, I, 438–439.

of trustee corporations resolved the dilemma. Judge Selden's decision in *Robertson* v. *Bullions* is worth quoting not only because it was a precedent-setting decision, in which "the entire theory of an implied trust was . . . brought down in a crumbling mass," but also because it was decided at the height of the Know Nothing controversy in New York and seems clearly to reflect the Protestant bias of American courts in the nineteenth century.[80]

The case concerned a Presbyterian church in Cambridge, New York, whose pastor, Dr. Bullions, was deposed and excommunicated by the presbytery for alleged misconduct (a decision concurred in by the synod). However, the majority of the corporation and the majority of the trustees remained loyal to Bullions and continued to pay his salary from the corporation's funds. Suit was brought by the minority claiming that the trustees had acted improperly by intruding a disqualified minister and excluding from the pulpit a minister whom the local presbytery approved. The court of first instance granted their plea, but upon appeal by the trustees Judge Selden made several important points in reversing the lower court's decision: "These officers," he said, "are trustees in the same sense with the president and directors of a bank or of a railroad company. They are the officers of the corporation to whom is delegated the power of managing its concerns for the common benefit of themselves and all other corporators; and over whom the body corporate retains control, through its power to supersede them at every recurring election." They are "not to be regarded as ecclesiastical corporations, in the sense of English law" but as civil corporations; they are not "subject to ecclesiastical judicatories" whether a church, a presbytery, a bishop, or other denominational authority.

This did not mean that the members of a corporation could not be spiritually disciplined by appropriate spiritual authorities, but the spiritual status of the corporators in no way affected their voting power as members or trustees of a civil

80. Selden's decision is printed in Howe, *Church and State*, 113–120. See also Zollmann, *Church Law*, 57. Zollmann cites five other states that followed the Selden precedent. See Howe, *Garden and the Wilderness*, 47.

corporation. "The majority of the congregation [that has been incorporated] may be composed of persons of any religious faith, or of no particular faith, and still their right to vote and to control the election, is not affected. . . . The salary of the minister is put absolutely, and at all times, under the control of the majority of the congregation." It followed that "neither presbytery or synod had any control over the Associate Congregation of Cambridge in respect to the minister whom they should employ." In a statement that, despite its pejorative tone, would have been thoroughly approved by Backus and Leland, Selden went on: "If a [religious] society wishes to devote its property to an unchangeable form of worship and to tie down its members to a Procrustean bed of creeds and confessions of faith, it must remain a voluntary association and not commit the management of its affairs to a corporation."

Selden's decision reaffirmed on one hand the anti-Erastian nature of the American commonwealth by treating religious corporations as purely temporal arrangements and on the other hand the danger to spiritual authority when it allied itself with the state. Imbedded also in this decision was an evangelical Protestant bias that implied that congregationalism, or democratic control of a church's affairs (including its choice of a minister), was the unwritten law of the land or, as he put it, "what the public sentiment of this country would seem to demand." Roman Catholic and other churches based upon an episcopal (hierarchical) form of church polity were assumed to be undemocratic and hence inimical to the cultural consensus (just as the Anglican hierarchy had been after 1776). Congregations of these denominations henceforth sought incorporation at their peril, for the state would support the lay majority against their bishops. Coming at the height of the trustee controversy in New York and other parts of the nation, Selden's decision was tantamount to denying equality to the Catholic church. Or, as he probably saw it, it was designed to assist that church and its "alien" adherents to adjust or assimilate to "the American way of life" by encouraging lay trustees (as the ones who paid for the building and support of Catholic churches and parish priests) to assert their popular will against a hierarchy appointed by a foreign power.

Not until after the Civil War, when Roman Catholics had proved their willingness to fight and die for their new nation and had become so numerous that they were, willy nilly, acquiring political power, did the states begin to consider including them as participating equals. The various judicial decisions and statutes that led to the creation of the corporation sole and other arrangements acceptable to Catholic canon law represent the entrance of the Roman Catholics into the American consensus just as disestablishment represented the acceptance of Baptists and other sectarian dissenters after 1776. But beyond a Judeo-Christian consensus Americans were not willing to move.[81]

It may seem at first glance as though the dispersal of government power to voluntary religious associations was anything but an effort to encourage religion. Rather it appears like an effort by the state to abdicate all responsibility for the maintenance of a Christian commonwealth. Because the conscience of the individual was left free, because all citizens were allowed to worship as they chose (or not at all), because the spiritual autonomy of the churches was untouched, because no overt state aid was given to religious institutions, it has been easy to assume that either the Jeffersonian or the radical Baptist position on church-state relations has prevailed in America. But, as I have tried to indicate, such was not the case. The kind of voluntaryism that we have traditionally described as "the separation of church and state" was neither conceived of nor carried out as an abdication of state action. Far from being left to itself, religion was imbedded into every aspect and institution of

81. For a discussion of the corporation sole as an adjustment to Roman Catholic ecclesiastical needs, see Zollmann, *Church Law*, 33–49. For a discussion of the lay trustee problem, see Ray A. Billington, *The Protestant Crusade* (New York, 1938), 38–41, 295–300. Legal authorities differ as to just how rapidly the various states modified their religious corporation laws to meet Catholic needs; Zollmann, *Church Law*, 59, implies that this was well taken care of by 1917, but Howe, *Garden and the Wilderness*, 32–33, 59–60, implies that it was not until after 1925.

American life. From the moment they became a nation, or thought of themselves as a nation, Americans defined Christianity in terms of their own cultural values and did their best to encourage the arrangements that sustained them. The result was individual freedom for the believer, cultural captivity for the Christian churches, and exclusion or subordination for non-Christian faiths.

It is a misreading of American history to see voluntaryism as a theory of religious laissez-faire, at least as voluntaryism worked out in and after the Revolution. Writing about Massachusetts in 1947, Oscar and Mary Handlin pointed out that Americans were by no means committed to a policy of laissez-faire during these years. The state of Massachusetts (Louis Hartz found the same situation in Pennsylvania) believed that it had an obligation to the commonwealth—the general welfare—to promote certain activities such as turnpikes, banks, bridges, canals, railroads, and industries. But as in the case of religion the people did not want to pay the heavy taxes that state control and administration of these activities would necessitate. Hence the state, following the old practices of mercantilism but adapting them to new American needs, granted franchises, charters, and incorporation to groups of private entrepreneurs willing to undertake these activities on behalf of the commonwealth. In exchange the state offered them certain safeguards and rewards. Sometimes it granted them monopoly rights (at least for a specific period), sometimes it granted them subsidies, sometimes it guaranteed them against financial loss, often it granted them tax exemption (again for specific periods), and always it gave them the prestige of the state and the "coercive power of assessment" upon their own members in order to give "the corporation a more efficient fund-raising mechanism." The virtue of incorporation under the aegis of the state was that "the corporation controlled its own purse strings, drawing funds from members obliged to contribute."[82]

The Handlins were concerned to demonstrate the concept of

---

82. Oscar and Mary Handlin, *Commonwealth: A Study of the Role of Government in the American Economy: Massachusetts, 1774–1861* (New York, 1947), 115, 151.

"the state as a positive force in the economy," but their delinea-
tion of the commonwealth ideal, the concern for the overriding
interest of the general good versus the self-interest of individuals
or factions, applies with equal force to the development of
American religious institutions. It may be that in discussing
the separation of church and state and the concept of religious
liberty in a "Christian commonwealth" we should speak in
terms of the economic "take-off point" of American Protestantism. As the Handlins pointed out, public corporations became
private when they became sufficiently prosperous to make profits in competition with each other. It was at this point that
general-incorporation laws for business purposes were enacted
by the Jacksonians, who concluded that special franchises provided too many possibilities for favoritism. So it was, *mutatis
mutandis*, with religious incorporation. The Massachusetts law
of 1860 that summarized the rights of parishes and religious
societies indicates clearly the derivation of voluntary incorporation from the territorial parish: "The qualified voters of each
religious society . . . may grant and vote such sums of money as
they judge necessary for the settlement, maintenance, and support of ministers or public teachers of religion, for the building
and repairing of houses of public worship, for sacred music, for
the purchase and preservation of burial grounds, and for all
other necessary parish charges; which sums shall be assessed on
the polls and estates of all the members of the society in the
same manner and proportion as town taxes are by law assessed."[83] In short, incorporated religious societies, whether
conceived of as private or public, ecclesiastical or civil corporations, were as integral to the community—the commonwealth—
as the towns.

The symbiotic relationship between church and state (or
churches and states) was still so strong in 1917 that Carl Zollmann, a lawyer writing an analysis of American civil church law,
could state flatly that "these relations do not rest on antagonism or indifference but on cordial cooperation. While the state
by its legislative, judicial, and executive powers creates, guards,
and enforces the civil, contract, and property rights of all the

83. Quoted in Buck, *Massachusetts Ecclesiastical Law*, 213–215.

various denominations, these in turn, by their charitable, religious, and moral influences, save, protect, and preserve the state from an overgrowth of pauperism, delinquency, and crime. These mutually advantageous relations have grown out of the very life of the American people as a nation and have crystallized one of the fundamental principles of their political philosophy into concrete form."[84] That principle he defined as the belief that "our nation and the states composing it are Christian in policy to the extent of embracing and adopting the moral tenets of Christianity as furnishing a sound basis upon which the moral obligations of the citizens to society and the state may be established."[85] The crowning evidence of this policy was the subsidy granted to all religious societies by local, state, and federal authorities in the form of exemption from civil taxes.[86]

But if we follow up the assumption that Americans felt the state had an obligation to maintain Christianity for the benefit of the general welfare, how did the system of voluntary incorporation do this? By treating religious societies in the same manner as it treated townships or business affairs, the state encouraged what we have called "free enterprise." And free enterprise, bent upon the creation of a Christian commonwealth defined in terms of the beliefs and values of the evangelical majority, simply created a new form of establishment. The self-confidence and self-assertion that provided the cutting edge of

84. Zollmann, *Church Law*, 3. See also 15, 16, 29, 237.

85. *Ibid.*, 13. Zollmann maintained that the position expressed in decisions of the Nebraska and Wisconsin courts prohibiting Bible reading in the schools "harks back to a conception of religious liberty which is Jacobinical rather than American" (p. 33). And he defended prosecution for blasphemy on the grounds that such acts "may in a rash hour lead to a riot or other breach of peace" (p. 16). The law rightly "punishes persons who vilely attack the legitimacy of Christ and the virginity of his mother. To hold that such an attack is protected by the constitutional guarantee of religious liberty would be an enormous perversion of the meaning of the constitution." And he cites cases to prove it.

86. As Zollman said, quoting a court decision, "It has, therefore, been the policy of the various states by tax-exemption laws 'to encourage, foster, and protect corporate institutions of a religious and literary character because the religious, moral and intellectual culture afforded by them were deemed, as they are in fact, beneficial to the public, necessary to the advancement of civilization, and the promotion of the welfare of society.'" *Ibid.*, 29.

revolution against the colonial established order rapidly entrenched itself in its own institutions within which insiders vied for status and from which outsiders were debarred. Witness the following typical pew deed from an early nineteenth-century Baptist church:

KNOW ALL MEN BY THESE PRESENTS, that Mr. Jonathan Wales, Jun. and Zelba Spear of Randolph, and Seth Alden of Stoughton, all in the Country of Norfolk and Commonwealth of Massachusetts, *Gentlemen*, said Wales as agent for the Proprietors of the North Baptist Meeting house and Spear and Alden for and in behalf of the North Baptist Church, being Deacons of said church, *in Consideration of One hundred and Nineteen dollars* to us paid by Daniel Alden of Randolph in the Country of Norfolk and State of Massachusetts, *Gentlemen*, the Receipt whereof we do hereby acknowledge, have remised, released, and forever quit-claimed, and do, for ourselves and our Heirs, by these present, remise, release, and forever quit-claim unto the said Daniel Alden, his Heirs and Assigns,

A Pew in the Meeting house called the North Baptist No. 27—on the lower floor,

The Conditions at Vendue were such that the Purchasers shall not sell, lease, let or give his Pew to any person of Colour on forfeiture of his Pew and damages....[87]

The values imbedded in this official religious system were neither the universal principles of the rights of man nor the absolute ideal of neighborly love but the relative culture-ethics of property rights and white supremacy.

And even among white men the measure of a man's worth in a legally incorporated house of worship was money. Men competed with each other in financial terms to hear the Word of their tribal God. Witness an article in the Baptist *Watchman Reflector* in 1854 entitled "Renting Church Pews": Its anonymous author addressed himself to the current debate as to the most effective way for a church to raise the funds for its support. Some churches preferred to ask for subscriptions, some to levy taxes or assessments upon pew holders, some to sell the pews outright as personal property. The writer, however, found an annual rental system far more satisfactory, "because it gives a

87. This pew deed is among the Baptist Papers at Andover Newton Theological School, Newton, Mass., in a folder marked "1819." Italics added.

man the same right in religion that he claims in temporal things, viz., of getting what he is willing to pay for. . . . We know this has been the practice in our cities for many years and this we deem one of the causes of their spiritual prosperity. We know too it has succeeded admirably in the country where it has been followed. . . . the renting process gives every person the privilege of taxing himself for just such a place in the house of God as he wants" or can afford, the rents being fixed in advance in terms of the pew's convenience and nearness to the pulpit. Unlike a system in which pews are bought or inherited and remain in the same spot for the lives of their owners, a system in which pews are rented annually "promotes enterprise," for a man can change his pew (like his home) to fit his improving social condition and (though the writer did not say so explicitly) his sense of his own social status.[88]

It is true, of course, that in the established churches of the colonial period the seating in parish meetinghouses was also arranged according to status. But there were important differences between the corporate and the individualistic concept of worship in a Christian commonwealth. In the first place, parish meetinghouses were large enough to seat all inhabitants, for all were required to attend. And when, in a New England parish, a committee was appointed to "dignify" the pews—assign seats according to social status—special consideration was given to the aged or hard of hearing; "dignity" was assigned for reasons other than wealth; and most important a sense of total contribution to the community underlay the assignments. Under the free enterprise system, money and money alone was the basis of a man's worth in the community. It is little wonder that by the third quarter of the nineteenth century the Protestant churches were alarmed at the increasing gap between the churches and "the masses."[89]

While the avowed commitment of Americans to religious equality gradually produced a kind of tolerated status for

88. *Watchman and Reflector* (Boston), Nov. 7, 1854, 177.

89. It is a measure of the vitality of American Protestantism, however, that a third Great Awakening took place to meet this new crisis, just as the religious impulse behind the antislavery movement indicates that all Protestants were not culture-bound.

Roman Catholics and Jews within the prevailing establishment (similar to that of Presbyterians in colonial Virginia or Anglicans in colonial Massachusetts), Americans were unable to stretch their concept of religious liberty to include such extremes as Mormonism, the American Indian religions, Mohammedanism, or the various Oriental religions. The last two were prevented even from entering the country by one means or another (sometimes called "gentlemen's agreements") on the grounds that they were so outlandish as to be "unassimilable." The Mormons and Indians were forced to conform, the former by a combination of mob, martial, and judicial law, the latter by being treated as incompetent wards of the state whose education was turned over to the various denominations.

If religion in America, institutionalized as incorporated voluntaryism and the Protestant ethic, became so culture-bound as to constitute by the mid-nineteenth century a new form of official establishment, this does not mean that religion became one of the less important aspects of American life. If the American Revolution was a revival, the new nation became a church. Far from being an opiate, religion was an incredible stimulus to the American people. Religious free enterprise inspired a vast variety of organizations and activities to which thousands of men and women dedicated their lives, often at great sacrifice: the foreign mission movement to bring Christian civilization to the heathen; home missionary societies to bring religion to the unchurched frontiers; Bible and tract societies to supplement or stimulate individual and family devotions; education societies to subsidize the training of ministers; professional evangelistic societies to promote mass revivals; temperance and reform societies to bring the leaven of Christian faith to the poor, the criminal, the hopeless.

Yet it is true that American churchgoers and their ministers became less interested in theology than in winning souls; less interested in denominational distinctions than in evangelical homogeneity; less interested in religious education than in "nonsectarian public schools." In a sense the public school movement might be seen as a failure of religious nerve.[90] But

90. Sidney Mead has argued that "perhaps the most striking power that

leaving aside the strong counterargument that the public schools were essentially Protestant parochial schools (though perhaps evangelically "nonsectarian") and the claim that if America is a church then its schools are rightly considered religious in function, I still think that the churches retained the most important institutional role in the culture. For at the same time that mere academic and moral training was given over to the "godless" public school system, the Sunday school movement and professional mass evangelism arose to perform (quite outside the educational sphere) the important *rite de passage* by which a child or adolescent entered adulthood. Schools and colleges suspended formal classes for prayer meetings when a revival broke out. Every church expected to have an annual revival meeting at which its more advanced Sunday school scholars were converted and joined the church. If we combine this aspect of American society with the religious reforms, philanthropic activities, and missionary efforts, it seems to me that the ideal of a Christian nation, like that of the Jewish nation, while ethnocentric was by no means secular. Witness here the profoundly felt contemporary view of the Civil War as God's judgment upon the nation for which a bloody sacrificial atonement had to be made to expiate its sins; the many comparisons of the martyred Lincoln to the crucified Christ seem to confirm the church-like quality of American culture in the nineteenth century.[91]

Only the scientific challenge to the heart of Protestant faith—its reliance upon the revealed truth of the Bible—succeeded in undermining the institutionalized establishment of the Christian nation. And that did not occur until the twentieth century. Since 1892 no Supreme Court justice has officially repeated

---

the churches surrendered under religious freedom was control over public education which traditionally had been considered an essential aspect of the work of an established church if it was to perform its proper function of disseminating and inculcating the necessary foundational religious beliefs. . . . In this sense the public-school system of the United States *is* its established church." *Lively Experiment*, 68.

91. I have expressed elsewhere my views on the fundamentally pietistic nature of the American character. See "Pietism and the American Character," in Hennig Cohen, ed., *The American Experience* (Boston, 1968), 39–63.

David Brewer's proclamation that "this is a Christian nation" (though William O. Douglas in 1952 called it "a religious nation"). The application of the First Amendment to the states since 1925 has considerably extended Jefferson's and Madison's concept of "neutrality." But in so doing, as Mark Howe has pointed out, the Supreme Court is very directly attacking "the de facto [religious] establishment which prevails." [92] And it is doing so in terms that distort the historical context in which Americans developed their religious institutions. For all the evidence seems to me to indicate that the role of religion in the Revolution was to create religious liberty for Protestantism in order to provide the cultural cohesion needed for the new nation. [93]

92. Howe, *Garden and the Wilderness*, 11–12.
93. Again, see *ibid.*, 59: "Everywhere in the nation [in the years after 1776] the impulse toward religious liberty was working to provide institutions through which Protestant Christianity could fulfill itself."

7

Feudalism, Communalism,

AND THE

Yeoman Freeholder

*The American Revolution
Considered as a Social Accident*

by

ROWLAND BERTHOFF

and

JOHN M. MURRIN

The star of social history has been in the ascendant, especially in the American sky, for several years past. Defined, more precisely than formerly, as the history of the institutional structure of society, it has indicated one way in which historians might move on from the points arrived at by the economic interpretations of the 1920s and 1930s and the intellectual history of the 1940s and 1950s. Political history in particular is being rewritten in terms of social class, ethnic and religious affiliation, and a social psychology that may even restore the family to its old importance for our understanding of the political commonwealth.[1]

1. See Eric Hobsbawm, "From Social History to the History of Society," *Daedalus*, C (1971), 20–45.

From this new social perspective a variety of conventional topics—the democratic and humanitarian movements of the age of Jackson, half-a-dozen seemingly ill-assorted phases of Progressivism, and even that perennial enigma, the Civil War—appear in a new light. It may be the more noteworthy, then, that so far the American Revolution has *not* been similarly reinterpreted. Was the eighteenth-century context so unlike the society of the mid-nineteenth and early twentieth centuries that the great event of that age, the Revolution, cannot be seen as having been generated from within, as Jacksonian egalitarianism or the Civil War were, but rather as being imposed from without? So most historians, like most of the revolutionaries, have believed. Did the Revolution, furthermore, leave unaltered the direction and the rate of social change? Was colonial society already moving ineluctably, whether a political revolution occurred or not, into its nineteenth-century patterns?

I

Until very recently few historians argued that the causes of the Revolution lay in the structure of colonial society. Neither J. Franklin Jameson, when in 1925 he broached the question of the Revolution as a social movement, nor Frederick B. Tolles, in reassessing the matter in 1954, paid any attention to the possibility that social causes impelled the political events of the years 1763 to 1775.[2] It has recently occurred to several historians, however, that the deepest roots of the Revolution may indeed have tapped the social subsoil of colonial America. Gordon S. Wood has suggested that a "social crisis within the gentry" of Virginia in the mid-eighteenth century, sometimes taking the form of excessive independence and disobedience of sons toward parents, may help explain the near unanimity of that class in support of the political revolution.[3] In his study of Andover, Massachusetts, Philip J. Greven, Jr., detects a subtle

2. J. Franklin Jameson, *The American Revolution Considered as a Social Movement* (Princeton, 1926); Frederick B. Tolles, "The American Revolution Considered as a Social Movement: A Re-Evaluation," *American Historical Review*, LX (1954–1955), 1–12.

3. Gordon S. Wood, "Rhetoric and Reality in the American Revolution," *William and Mary Quarterly*, 3d Ser., XXIII (1966), 29–30.

connection between social change and revolution. An emerging gap between the third and fourth generations of settlers impelled the colonists to extend to the king himself "the idea of independence from parental authority." Somehow, Greven implies, the inner structure of the family had already anticipated the ideology of Thomas Paine.[4] The crumbling of old communal ties may have worked to the same end. The practical pluralism and individualism among the no longer homogeneous townsmen of New England, according to the variant accounts of Kenneth A. Lockridge and Edward M. Cook, Jr., were leading to social and political revolution and also, as a kind of reaction during the conflict, to the patriotic imposition of a forced unanimity.[5] Jack P. Greene contends that Americans of the pre-Revolutionary generations were suffering from an identity crisis and that independence pointed a way out of their self-doubt.[6] The gross rhetorical exaggerations by which they expressed their grievances against the mother country, Wood has suggested, were stimulated by a basic reality: "*Something* profoundly unsettling was going on in [their] society."[7] That something, according to Edmund S. Morgan, was a fear that old social and economic virtues were being lost in the march of material affluence during the eighteenth century; hence the colonists' nonimportation and nonconsumption agreements of the 1760s and 1770s were aimed not only at gaining redress from Parliament but at self-reformation—doing without luxuries, supplying their own essential wants, and cutting themselves off from the unproductive services of English merchants.[8] As Bernard Bailyn, J. G. A. Pocock, and Gordon Wood have pointed

4. Philip J. Greven, Jr., *Four Generations: Population, Land, and Family in Colonial Andover, Massachusetts* (Ithaca, N.Y., 1970), 281–282.

5. Kenneth A. Lockridge, *A New England Town, The First Hundred Years: Dedham, Massachusetts, 1636–1736* (New York, 1970), 161–163, 179–180; Edward M. Cook, Jr., "Social Behavior and Changing Values in Dedham, Massachusetts, 1700 to 1775," *WMQ*, 3d Ser., XXVII (1970), 578.

6. Jack P. Greene, "Search for Identity: An Interpretation of the Meaning of Selected Patterns of Social Response in Eighteenth-Century America," *Journal of Social History*, III (1970), 218–220.

7. Wood, "Rhetoric and Reality," *WMQ*, 3d Ser., XXIII (1966), 31. Emphasis added.

8. Edmund S. Morgan, "The Puritan Ethic and the American Revolution," *WMQ*, 3d Ser., XXIV (1967), 8–18.

out, this recrudescence of Spartan self-denial invoked not only the Calvinist economic ethic but also old English "country" or commonwealth ideas of classical civic virtue that appeared to shield the colonies from the "corruption" into which the British government was sinking.[9]

For the most part these hypotheses remain in the realm of ingenious conjecture and fragmentary afterthought appended to studies of other eighteenth-century matters. The meagerness of the evidence adduced for them could about as easily lead back to the contrary conclusion that, as Thomas C. Barrow has put it, "such tensions and divisions as did exist within American society were relatively minor and harmless"—and that the Revolution basically was the colonial war for political independence that most historians, like most people of that time, have supposed it was.[10] By comparison with the social tensions and divisions of the nineteenth century, those of the eighteenth, though real enough, recede to a level that may be considered about normal in human affairs.

The Civil War, the great cataclysm of the nineteenth century, can more convincingly be explained in terms of the pervasive social anxiety of that later time, an uneasiness that through a peculiar chain of circumstances and events aggravated every political dispute, made sectional and racial divisions seem intolerable, and so combined to produce an irreconcilable conflict.[11] That war has never been satisfactorily explained, at any

9. Bernard Bailyn, *The Ideological Origins of the American Revolution* (Cambridge, Mass., 1967); Gordon S. Wood, *The Creation of the American Republic, 1776–1787* (Chapel Hill, 1969); J. G. A. Pocock, "Machiavelli, Harrington, and English Political Ideologies in the Eighteenth Century," *WMQ*, 3d Ser., XXII (1965), 549–583; Pocock, "Virtue and Commerce in the Eighteenth Century," *Journal of Interdisciplinary History*, III (1972–1973), 119–134.

10. Thomas C. Barrow, "The American Revolution as a Colonial War for Independence," *WMQ*, 3d Ser., XXV (1968), 464. Barrow's attempt to link the Revolution to modern struggles for colonial independence has its own pitfall. No recent war for independence has involved colonies as closely tied to the mother country by culture, language, and direct descent as were the original thirteen states. The American Revolution was different and must be explained on different grounds, because it did *not* involve a major ethnic antagonism.

11. Rowland Berthoff, *An Unsettled People: Social Order and Disorder in American History* (New York, 1971), chap. 18.

rate, in terms simply of economic interest, partisan advantage, or even the social peculiarities of North and South—certainly not by reiterating the abstract constitutional theories upon which the sectional leaders laid such weight. The contrast to the eighteenth century on the last point is especially significant. The question of the proper constitutional relationship of the colonies to the empire seems, especially to a historian of the society of the later United States, to have been a sufficient cause of the political revolution that did occur; the revisionist attentions of social historians and psychologists do not appear to be required.

It is the older question of the social effects of the Revolution, however, that most concerns us here. If it may be said that the Civil War resolved few of the underlying social tensions that had led to it, is it possible that the Revolution, even though it did not spring from such causes, nevertheless had a greater impact upon the structure of society? The general understanding of recent historians has been that it did not. Most of the social effects that Jameson adduced might better be called *economic* effects—changes in the distribution of wealth and in legal patterns of landholding, confiscation of tory estates, the opening of new land, the impetus to industrial development—as well as such changes in political forms as the disestablishment of churches that were already splitting into "denominations." Professor Tolles, in summing up another thirty years' work on the matter, concluded that it had added less proof to Jameson's hypothesis than it had taken away; virtually nothing new on the structure of society had been unearthed. Whoever possessed the wealth of the country when the Revolution was over, the economic class structure remained about what it had been; reforms in landholding were mainly symbolic; the Industrial Revolution awaited a still later generation.

The general understanding of the matter has changed little since Tolles's article. Recent historians of the early national period have implicitly assumed that social data drawn from different decades between 1750 and 1825 can be used quite interchangeably, the basic structure of society having altered so little during that age.[12] The conclusion prevails, evidently, that American society in the half century after 1775 was substantially what it had been in the quarter century before.

II

Like any epoch—certainly any in the history of American society—the century from 1725 to 1825 was far from static. The direction of change, however, was confused and sometimes contradictory. In certain ways economic growth and greater social maturity were making the New World resemble the Old more closely. Long-settled districts were approaching the demographic pattern of Western Europe: a denser population, both urban and rural; more pronounced stratification of economic classes; more specialization of labor; and less vertical mobility than before. At the same time, however, the rapid extension of settlement into the remote backcountry—a new kind of frontier that Frederick Jackson Turner dated from about 1730—continually renewed the earlier sources of mobility and made it difficult to impose the degree of social stability that the earlier seaboard settlements had once enjoyed.[13] As the frontier advanced, the social circumstances of the West, which seemed ever less like those of European tradition, also affected the eastern districts from which the migrants came; after 1825 industrialization and mass immigration further intensified the radical impact of the frontier. In a society thus becoming both more like and more unlike that of Europe, more settled and more unsettled, more complex and less homogeneous, a revolutionary war—even one conducted for the most narrowly political ends—could hardly fail to stimulate certain kinds of change and to inhibit others.

At the least, however glacial the changes in the social structure, the American Revolution marked a major turning point in the perception that Americans had of their society. As

12. E.g., Sidney H. Aronson, *Status and Kinship in the Higher Civil Service: Standards of Selection in the Administration of John Adams, Thomas Jefferson and Andrew Jackson* (Cambridge, Mass., 1964).

13. Frederick Jackson Turner, *The Frontier in American History* (New York, 1920), chap. 3.

colonials they had adhered to English values and conformed to old-country institutions—both often of a rather archaic sort— as closely and as soon as their growing resources of population and wealth permitted. The recurrent tension between this conservative, even reactionary, ideal and the practical liberty and individuality that their new circumstances stimulated is a familiar theme of colonial history—Puritanism against secularism, communalism eroded by economic progress, hierarchic authority challenged by antinomianism. Recently the same sort of conservative-liberal tension has been observed as a central element of the "Jacksonian persuasion" half a century after the Revolution.[14] By 1825 the liberal-individualist side was clearly dominant, and conservative caution recessive, among a people who now thought of themselves as establishing new social models for the Old World to imitate. It is a reasonable hypothesis that the shift from one set of values to the other had been accelerated by the political events of the 1760s and 1770s. From that time on the kind of instability that had been conventionally deplored in colonial society as a sad "declension" from proper standards was instead accepted as setting a new and better model, and standards that were too obviously English were rejected. It was not in commercial affairs alone that Americans cast off the "great reluctance to innovation, so remarkable in old communities," as was observed in 1785, and moved ahead on "a line far beyond that to which they had been accustomed."[15]

This redressing of the conservative-liberal balance affected some parts of the social structure more than others. Some social values and institutions to which the course of events drew attention were explicitly forsworn, while others were just as explicitly rallied around, and the development of still others quietly proceeded no matter how poorly they fit the new circumstances. American society between the Revolution and 1825—in many respects, indeed, right down through the nine-

14. Marvin Meyers, *The Jacksonian Persuasion: Politics and Belief* (Stanford, 1957).

15. Robert A. East, *Business Enterprise in the American Revolutionary Era* (New York, 1938), 323.

teenth century and into the twentieth—was an odd mixture of archaic and modern elements.

This is not surprising. National independence, although sought for the sake of preserving certain accustomed political patterns, required rapid development of new ones. On the other hand, the Revolution provided a radical justification for various archaic elements that were also carried along, consciously or unconsciously, into the nineteenth century. Some of the archaic ideas, as they were incongruously applied to their modern circumstances, inadvertently hastened change more than they retarded it, just as radical ideology sometimes retarded social change rather than advanced it. Confusion necessarily resulted in the minds of historians as well as contemporaries, both native and foreign, between what was truly new on the American scene and what was a vestige of another age. Just as American speech was studded with old English expressions that Englishmen took for fresh (or barbaric) new coinages, some of the archaic elements in American society were in a modern context the most radical.

III

Certain developments in the late colonial era, especially during the generation after 1725, suggest that without the Revolution nineteenth-century America might have become a very different place from that with which we are familiar. If American society in 1825 did not differ sweepingly from the social order of 1725, the Revolution and particularly its idealization of social anachronisms may have been the chief reason. Revolutionary ideology powerfully stimulated a nostalgic attachment to a seventeenth-century simplicity that the eighteenth century had been doing its best to erode. Most notably, perhaps, colonial society had been far closer to a state of practical equality in the seventeenth century than it became in the eighteenth. Except for New England, contemporary critics often associated this lack of social differentiation with acute social disorder. Before 1700 the colonists were more nearly equal, but thought they should be less. They moved steadily toward this goal in the eighteenth century until by the Revolution they were indeed less equal, only to discover that they should be more. In this regard the Revolution challenged what was perhaps the main social trend of the previous half century.

Most colonies in the eighteenth century experienced what European specialists would recognize as a "feudal revival." A conspicuous example is South Carolina's demand for a lifetime "nobility" or upper house in the early 1770s, but since South Carolina planters were much wealthier than other colonial elites, this proposal is less surprising than the absence of other feudal relics in the colony, such as entail.[16] Elsewhere the revival took different forms.

By 1630, after the commercial corporation had demonstrated the unprofitability of founding colonies, proprietary projects on a feudal model dominated virtually all seventeenth-century attempts to plant English settlements in the New World. By the end of the century all of them had failed quite decisively, although in Carolina the proprietary regime struggled on for another twenty years. Lord Baltimore's Maryland, ducal New York, and the Jerseys had been royalized, while William Penn was reduced to pathetic impotence in his own colony on the Delaware, and the Culpepers and their heirs had failed to derive any significant benefit from their claim to the Northern Neck of Virginia. Historians accordingly conclude that feudalism was too anachronistic to survive in the free air of a new world.[17]

The opposite explanation is more compelling. Feudal projects collapsed in the seventeenth century, not because America was too progressive to endure them, but because it was too primitive to sustain them. A feudal order necessarily implies a differentiation of function far beyond the capacity of new so-

16. Jack P. Greene, *The Quest for Power: The Lower Houses of Assembly in the Southern Royal Colonies, 1689–1776* (Chapel Hill, 1963), 406–407; Bailyn, *Ideological Origins*, 279–280; Jackson Turner Main, *The Upper House in Revolutionary America, 1763–1788* (Madison, 1967), 18–20. For earlier attacks upon South Carolina's appointive council, see M. Eugene Sirmans, *Colonial South Carolina: A Political History, 1663-1763* (Chapel Hill, 1966), 261, 306.

17. The best example is the general levity with which virtually every history of the colonial period treats Lord Shaftesbury's Fundamental Constitutions of Carolina. For a similar attitude toward early Maryland, see Louis B. Hartz, *The Liberal Tradition in America* (New York, 1955), 64–66.

cieties to create. In every colony the demographic base was much too narrow. Even in New France the rationalized feudal order that Colbert attempted to impose in the Saint Lawrence valley produced an impressive number of paper seigneuries by 1700, but not feudalism in any recognizable sense. Only by the middle of the eighteenth century would the population of New France expand sufficiently to make the seigneurial system profitable—and quite durable thereafter.[18]

In this regard the English colonies were not drastically different from French Canada. Although the seventeenth century had not created a workable feudal regime in a single English colony, it did bequeath its feudal charters and land patents to the next century. Charters and land patents are legal documents that can always be revived, provided someone has sufficient reason to do so. By 1730 the older colonies had become populous enough to make the old feudal claims incredibly lucrative. The data from each colony have long been familiar; taken together, a truly striking pattern emerges.

As late as the 1720s the New York manors were largely untenanted and profitless to their owners. The East Jersey proprietors had abandoned the effort to derive a steady income from their patent.[19] The claims of the Carolina proprietors became almost worthless when Charleston revolted in 1719, and a decade later all but one proprietor—Lord Carteret, later Earl Granville—sold out to the crown.[20] Lord Fairfax, the Culpeper heir, netted only £100 from the Northern Neck in 1721, nothing in 1723, and another £100 in 1724.[21] Years later Pennsylvania

18. Cf. Sigmund Diamond, "An Experiment in 'Feudalism': French Canada in the Seventeenth Century," *WMQ*, 3d Ser., XVIII (1961), 3–34, with Richard C. Harris, *The Seigneurial System in Early Canada* (Madison, 1966), esp. 63–81.

19. The most recent account is Gary S. Horowitz, "New Jersey Land Riots, 1745–1755" (Ph.D. diss., Ohio State University, 1966), esp. 39, 48.

20. Edward McCrady, *The History of South Carolina under the Proprietary Government, 1670–1719* (New York, 1897), 645–680; Sirmans, *Colonial South Carolina*, 103–128; Christopher C. Crittenden, "The Surrender of the Charter of Carolina," *North Carolina Historical Review*, I (1924), 383–402; William L. Saunders, ed., *The Colonial Records of North Carolina (1662–1776)* (Raleigh, 1886–1890), III, 32–47.

21. Stuart E. Brown, Jr., *Virginia Baron: The Story of Thomas 6th Lord Fairfax* (Perryville, Va., 1965), 39; Louis B. Wright, ed., *Letters of Robert*

still returned perhaps £100 clear profit to the heirs of the first proprietor. Maryland alone was beginning to show signs of a profitable future following the restoration of the proprietary regime shortly after the Hanoverian succession.[22]

Between 1730 and 1745 old claims were revived and consolidated from Carolina to New York. Thomas Penn sailed to Philadelphia to put his affairs in order in 1732, and Lord Baltimore visited Maryland in 1732–1733, where he negotiated a number of financial arrangements highly favorable to himself.[23] Rather than visit the Carolinas, Carteret first relied on the royal governments of the two colonies to collect his quitrents and then, when this arrangement proved disappointing, prevailed on the crown in 1745 to consolidate his claim into a single holding, later called the Granville District, that took in over half the land and about two-thirds of the population of North Carolina.[24] In 1745 Lord Fairfax obtained an exceptionally favorable court decision that enlarged his claim in the Northern Neck to 5,200,000 acres, which soon encompassed twenty-one counties of Virginia.[25]

As in France, the feudal revival in the English colonies employed old legal and social forms for quite single-mindedly modern purposes. Old charters, which at one time had assumed a mutuality of obligations and responsibilities, were revived only because they had become profitable. In the colo-

---

Carter, 1720–1727: The Commercial Interests of a Virginia Gentleman (San Marino, Calif., 1940), 69, 108.

22. On the Penn revenues, see Lawrence H. Gipson, *The British Empire before the American Revolution*, rev. ed. (Caldwell, Idaho, and New York, 1936–1969), III, 180. Lord Baltimore was willing to lease his right to quitrents for only £300 sterling per year as late as 1716, but by 1729 he knew that they were quite valuable. Cf. Newton D. Mereness, *Maryland as a Proprietary Province* (New York, 1901), 80, with Charles A. Barker, *The Background of the Revolution in Maryland* (New Haven, 1940), 130–134.

23. Robert Proud, *The History of Pennsylvania, in North America, from the Original Institution and Settlement of that Province* . . . (Philadelphia, 1797–1798), II, 206–208; Barker, *Background of the Revolution in Maryland*, 134–144.

24. See G. F. R. Barker in *DNB* s.v. "Carteret, John, Earl Granville"; E. Merton Coulter, "The Granville District," *James Sprunt Historical Studies*, XIII (1913), 33–56.

25. Douglas S. Freeman, *George Washington, A Biography* (New York, 1948–1957), I, 501–510; Brown, *Virginia Baron*, 94–98.

nies, as in France, these claims aroused resentment precisely because they divorced the pursuit of profit from any larger sense of community welfare. Historians miss the point when they reject the notion of feudalism in America on the grounds that no one seriously intended to resurrect the Middle Ages. On both sides of the Atlantic the revival ripped feudal relationships out of their original social context and seized what surviving obligations could be enforced for the income they might produce.[26] And, in fact, exploitation of legal privilege became the greatest source of personal wealth in the colonies in the generation before Independence. By the 1760s the largest proprietors —and no one else in all of English America—were receiving colonial revenues comparable to the incomes of the greatest English noblemen and larger than those of the richest London merchants. Indeed the Penn claim was rapidly becoming the most valuable single holding in the Western world.[27]

26. Alfred Cobban, *The Social Interpretation of the French Revolution* (Cambridge, 1964), 25–53; George V. Taylor, "Types of Capitalism in Eighteenth-Century France," *English Historical Review*, LXXIX (1964), 478–497; Taylor, "The Paris Bourse on the Eve of the Revolution, 1781–1789," *AHR*, LXVII (1961–1962), 951–977; Taylor, "Non-Capitalist Wealth and the French Revolution," *ibid.*, LXXII (1966–1967), 469–496; Elizabeth L. Eisenstein, "Who Intervened in 1788? A Commentary on *The Coming of the French Revolution*," *ibid.*, LXXI (1965–1966), 77–103. See also the acrimonious discussion of the problem in Jeffrey Kaplow, Gilbert Shapiro, and Elizabeth L. Eisenstein, "Class in the French Revolution," *ibid.*, LXXII (1966–1967), 497–522. Two excellent discussions of the feudal revival, both broader in scope than the seigneurial reaction and old-regime France, are Penfield Roberts, *The Quest for Security, 1715–1740* (New York, 1947), chap. 3; and R. R. Palmer, *The Age of the Democratic Revolution: A Political History of Europe and America, 1760–1800* (Princeton, 1959–1964), I, chaps. 1–3. Alexis de Tocqueville's observations of a century ago are also quite pertinent. He argued that feudalism had become intolerable in France precisely because it was no longer feudal. Lordship had almost completely disappeared, while feudal relationships in general had been converted to fiscal obligations and advantages that did not correspond at all to the social division between noble and bourgeois. The system was hated because it was mercenary and because of the dependency it symbolized. *The Old Regime and the French Revolution*, trans. Stuart Gilbert (New York, 1955), 22–23. After 50 years of attempts to interpret the French Revolution in terms of a clash between a feudal and a capitalistic order, many historians are now moving quite decisively back toward Tocqueville.

27. Only about 400 English landed families had annual incomes exceeding £4,000 in 1760; a few were as great as the £30,000 to £40,000 of the

The feudal revival was as divisive as it was profitable, provoking more social violence after 1745 than perhaps any other problem. Wherever the revival was strong, response to the Revolution was mixed or divided. Pennsylvania and Maryland, where feudal charters conveyed immense political power to the proprietors, both developed royalist movements that hoped to replace proprietary government with a royal regime. By 1755 Franklin in particular had grown utterly disgusted by the Penns' habit of protecting proprietary revenue while ignoring the colony's most urgent needs. His bitter campaign to bring in the crown eventually destroyed the Quaker party and seriously weakened the Revolutionary movement in Pennsylvania.[28]

---

dukes of Newcastle and Bedford, but the average was around £6,000. By then Lord Baltimore's income from Maryland surpassed £30,000 a year, which was equal to an 18% duty on the exports of the colony. By the 1770s the Penns had probably caught up with the Calverts. Averaging about £10,000 sterling a year in land sales, they increased the quitrents from about £500 in 1732 to over £10,000 by 1774, besides £6,000 from various royalties and a sizable amount from rents on their 80 manors, which contained about 600,000 acres. The Granville District, despite poor management, returned about £5,000 in quitrents alone by the 1760s.

These English levels of wealth in 1760 have been calculated at two-thirds of the 1790 levels discussed in G. E. Mingay, *English Landed Society in the Eighteenth Century* (London, 1963), chaps. 1–2, esp. 10, 20–21, 23. For Newcastle's fortune, see *ibid.*, 78. For Bedford's, which was about the same as Baltimore's, see Gladys Scott Thomson, *The Russells in Bloomsbury, 1669–1771* (London, 1940), 301. On Baltimore's revenues, see Barker, *Background of the Revolution in Maryland*, 142–144, and his "The Revolutionary Impulse in Maryland," *Maryland Historical Magazine*, XXXVI (1941), 135. Data on the Penns have been compiled from William R. Shepherd, *History of Proprietary Government in Pennsylvania* (New York, 1896), 88, and from William H. Kain, "The Penn Manorial System and the Manors of Springetsbury and Maske," *Pennsylvania History*, X (1943), 240. For the revenue of the Granville District, see Saunders, ed., *N. C. Col. Rec.*, IX, 49, 261, 262. For the sake of useful comparison, all of the above statistics have been reduced to sterling. In addition, they reveal gross rather than net income. In England, the net return on land was usually two-thirds to three-fourths the gross earnings, but for political families it was less. Mingay, *Landed Society*, 52–54. Lord Baltimore undoubtedly had the highest overhead among the great proprietors, and his net income was 35 to 40% of his gross, or about £13,000 per year, which was still well within the upper level of England's wealthiest 400 families.

28. James H. Hutson, "Benjamin Franklin and Pennsylvania Politics, 1751–1755: A Reappraisal," *Pennsylvania Magazine of History and Biography*, XCIII (1969), 303–371; and his "The Campaign to Make Pennsylvania

Similarly in Maryland the leaders of both parties showed exceptional reluctance to embrace the Revolution.[29] Practically all of the violence in North Carolina in the twelve years before the Battle of Alamance occurred within the Granville District. The earliest riots were directed against the proprietor's land policy, which remained a grievance throughout the Regulator disturbances. His claim to quitrents deprived the colony of a leading source of revenue and forced it to resort to other taxes that also contributed to the war of the Regulation.[30]

In large part, however, these disputes were due to the fact that the greatest colonial proprietors were absentee landlords. The colonial social structure was not graced with a resident upper class of the eminence that their income and rank could have supported. But there was a second rank of resident proprietors whose position suggests what both the strengths and weaknesses of an American landed aristocracy might have become had the development of such a social class not been cut off after the Revolution. Unlike the absentee Calvert, Carteret, and Penns, Lord Fairfax established his seat in the Northern Neck, where by 1768 he was receiving £4,000 in quitrents, besides revenue from manor rents, land sales, and other sources.

a Royal Province, 1764–1770," *ibid.*, XCIV (1970), 427–463, and XCV (1971), 28–49.

29. More study of both the proprietary and antiproprietary movements in Maryland is needed, but see Barker, *Background of the Revolution in Maryland*; Aubrey C. Land, *The Dulanys of Maryland: A Biographical Study of Daniel Dulany, the Elder (1685–1753), and Daniel Dulany, the Younger (1722–1797)* (Baltimore, 1955); Bernard C. Steiner, *Life and Administration of Sir Robert Eden* (Baltimore, 1898); and David C. Skaggs, "Maryland's Impulse Toward Social Revolution, 1750–1776," *Journal of American History*, LIV (1967–1968), 771–786.

30. Saunders, ed., *N. C. Col. Rec.*, VII, 513–514, VIII, 524, IX, 262, 358–359. William K. Boyd, ed., *Some Eighteenth Century Tracts concerning North Carolina* (Raleigh, 1927), 308–312. See also, Marvin L. Michael Kay, "Provincial Taxes in North Carolina during the Administrations of Dobbs and Tryon," *North Carolina Historical Review*, XLII (1965), 440–453; his "The Payment of Provincial and Local Taxes in North Carolina, 1748–1771," *WMQ*, 3d Ser., XXVI (1969), 218–240; and his "An Analysis of a British Colony in Late Eighteenth Century America in the Light of Current American Historiographical Controversy," *Australian Journal of Politics and History*, II (1965), 170–184. This last piece uses the Regulator controversy to challenge the Hartz thesis about the liberal tradition in America.

The governor and the House of Burgesses had fought the Fairfax claim into the 1740s, but once the crown had determined every disputed point in the baron's favor, the colony accepted him without violence of the sort that occurred elsewhere. Doubtless a major reason for this acquiescence was Fairfax's willingness to become a resident proprietor, an ornament of provincial society. Throughout the Northern Neck large landholders were increasingly turning to leases and rents as a primary source of revenue. For example, Robert Carter of Nomini Hall was able to live exclusively off rents (about £2,250 a year) by 1790. Fairfax was simply the most spectacular example among many, and his physical presence lent a genuine title and real dignity to the social life of the region. George Washington, for one, remained quite loyal to the baron throughout the Revolution.[31]

Residency did not ensure as happy an outcome in New York, where the seventeenth-century manors also were becoming profitable in the middle third of the eighteenth century. Scarsdale, Philipsborough, and Livingston returned between £1,000 and £2,000 a year, Rensselaerswyck probably more, and Cortlandt Manor less.[32] The manor lords would have qualified as middling gentry in England, while their income greatly exceeded that of the provincial nobility of Toulouse.[33] The

31. H. R. McIlwaine, ed., *Journals of the House of Burgesses of Virginia, 1727–1734, 1736–1740* (Richmond, 1910), 82, 83, 92–96, 125, 155; Brown, *Virginia Baron*, 155, 160, *passim*; Willard F. Bliss, "The Rise of Tenancy in Virginia," *Virginia Magazine of History and Biography*, LVIII (1950), 427–441; Louis Morton, *Robert Carter of Nomini Hall: A Virginia Tobacco Planter of the Eighteenth Century*, 2d ed. (Williamsburg, Va., 1945), 78.

32. Main, *Upper House*, 55; Beatrice G. Reubens, "Preemptive Rights in the Disposition of a Confiscated Estate: Philipsburgh Manor, New York," *WMQ*, 3d Ser., XXII (1965), 440. Because Cortlandt Manor was divided among ten joint proprietors, the income available to any one of them was never very large. Rents apparently varied from about £30 to something over £100 a year, but they did tend to rise over time and leases tended to be made shorter. Sung Bok Kim, "The Manor of Cortlandt and Its Tenants, 1697–1783" (Ph.D. diss., Michigan State University, 1966), 91–92, 120–124, 128–133, 140, 144, *passim*. Iron, a source of income overlooked by Kim, may have been as important as rents. See *New-York Weekly Journal*, Apr. 2, 1744; *New-York Weekly Post-Boy*, June 17, 1745.

33. Mingay, *Landed Society*, 23, again allowing a reduction by one-third to reach the level of 1760; Robert Forster, *The Nobility of Toulouse in the*

tenant rising on Livingston Manor in 1753–1754 and the much larger New York tenant revolt of 1766 challenged the manorial system in the most direct way.[34]

In terms of genuine feudalism the revival was thus grossly imperfect, more a matter of economic profit for the proprietor than of mutual obligations between lord and man or landlord and community that might have harmonized the relationship. Where a sense of genuine mutuality did exist, the system sometimes acquired powers of endurance that outlasted the Revolution, but elsewhere it was destroyed. In the Hudson-Mohawk valley it survived both the tenant riots and the Revolution, partly because the manor lords provided some genuine economic benefits for their tenants. The developmental function of manorialism and its ethnic role among Dutch farmers probably helped it to survive there into the 1840s.[35]

Absenteeism was a different matter, especially when it conveyed tremendous political power. Lord Baltimore built the most elaborate and most expensive patronage system in English America out of his proprietary revenues.[36] In Pennsylvania the Proprietary party dominated the council, the closed corporation of the city of Philadelphia, the college, the courts, and most other political offices.[37] The East Jersey proprietors, most of whom lived in Perth Amboy or New York, used their dominance of the council to protect their interests against both the

Eighteenth Century: A Social and Economic Study (Baltimore, 1960), 178–188. French *livres* converted into pounds sterling at a ratio of about 23:1 on the eve of the French Revolution. Arthur Young, *Travels in France during the Years 1787, 1788, and 1789*, ed. Constantia Maxwell (Cambridge, 1929), 405.

34. Oscar Handlin, "The Eastern Frontier of New York," *New York History*, XVIII (1936), 50–75; Irving Mark, *Agrarian Conflicts in Colonial New York, 1711–1775* (New York, 1940).

35. Sung Bok Kim, "A New Look at the Great Landlords of Eighteenth-Century New York," *WMQ*, 3d Ser., XXVII (1970), 581–614; David M. Ellis, *Landlords and Farmers in the Hudson-Mohawk Region, 1790–1850* (Ithaca, N.Y., 1946), esp. 225–312.

36. Barker, *Background of the Revolution in Maryland*, esp. 267–274; Donnell M. Owings, *His Lordship's Patronage: Offices of Profit in Colonial Maryland* (Baltimore, 1953).

37. G. B. Warden, "The Proprietary Group in Pennsylvania, 1754–1764," *WMQ*, 3d Ser., XXI (1964), 367–389.

assembly and the tenant rioters of Newark and Elizabeth-town.[38] In all of these cases the feudal revival differed from mere land speculation in two respects. It involved a legal or customary claim to the exercise of political power regardless of the wishes or interests of the community as a whole. And rather than profit only from the opening of new lands to settle-ment, it also imposed its fiscal demands upon older areas with-out offering any benefits in return. In both respects it distinctly resembled the feudal reaction in Europe far more closely than the good American habit of pure land speculation.

We can only guess what sort of society the feudal revival might have produced had it gone unchecked for another half century. The trend towards tenancy, which helped to legitimate Lord Fairfax, continued after independence in Virginia until by 1830 it had disfranchised about half of the adult white males. Could Virginia have assumed the same revolutionary posture in 1810 or 1830 that it found easy to adopt in 1776?[39] At the very least the destruction of the revival during the Revolution was socially and perhaps politically significant. The growth of mercenary feudalism for another generation or two might *possibly* have divided some colonies beyond the point at which they could have revolted successfully from the Empire, and it might have made a political union of the continent on common principles much more difficult to achieve. But because the Revolution happened when it did, the feudal revival was truly destroyed.

For obvious reasons the absentees lost most completely. The Granville and Calvert proprietorships were confiscated; the Penns were allowed to retain their "manors" or private estates, but the proprietorship itself was abolished at a cost to the commonwealth of £130,000 sterling voted by the legislature.[40]

38. Edgar J. Fisher, *New Jersey as a Royal Province, 1738–1776* (New York, 1911), 58–71.

39. Chilton Williamson, *American Suffrage from Property to Democracy, 1760–1860* (Princeton, 1960), 230, 234.

40. Brown, *Virginia Baron*, 176–191; William Waller Hening, ed., *The Statutes at Large; Being a Collection of All the Laws of Virginia, from the First Session of the Legislature, in the Year 1619* (Richmond and Philadel-phia, 1823), XI, 128–129; James T. Mitchell and Henry Flanders, eds., *The*

Tory landlords lost their estates in New York, but whigs did not, which suggests that confiscation was designed chiefly to punish political loyalism rather than to create a new egalitarian order. Nevertheless the impact was considerable. The number of freeholders increased significantly, especially in areas that had been heavily tenanted before. Even the few large-scale beneficiaries were usually new men who in one way or another made life difficult for the old landlords.[41] The East Jersey situation was less complex. There the proprietors lost their privileged political position, but they still exist today as a legal entity. They survived because they had already ceased to matter; they had failed to make good their claim to quitrents even before the Revolution broke out.[42]

The geographical limits to the feudal revival are quite instructive. In particular New England and New Englanders displayed a striking immunity to the whole phenomenon. Old charters were also revived around mid-century in Maine and New Hampshire, but no one used them to claim quitrents or to press demands upon older settled regions. Instead their function was developmental, rather similar to the Ohio Company of Virginia in their own day and to numerous speculative enterprises of the nineteenth century with perhaps a greater admixture of responsibility to the community. But when proprietors attempted to impose feudal obligations upon Yankee settlers outside New England, the results were invariably explosive. Almost all the East Jersey tenant rioters of 1745–1754 were Yankees. So apparently were most of New York's rioters of 1745–1754 and 1766. In each of these cases neighboring Dutch farmers accepted identical feudal impositions with few quarrels. Obviously Yankee behavior requires special explanation.[43]

Statutes at Large of Pennsylvania from 1682 to 1801 (Harrisburg, 1896–1908), X, 33–39.

41. For an excellent summary of recent research on confiscations in New York, see Alfred F. Young, *The Democratic Republicans of New York: The Origins, 1763–1797* (Chapel Hill, 1967), 62–66.

42. John E. Pomfret, *The New Jersey Proprietors and Their Lands* (Princeton, 1964), 107–120.

43. Horowitz, "New Jersey Land Riots," *passim.* On the ethnic base of the New York riots, see Handlin, "The Eastern Frontier of New York,"

If a modern land system is one that desymbolizes and disencumbers land in the interest of the freest possible exchange, New England resisted the feudal revival because in several important respects it was rather less modern than the rest of English America. As in Tudor and Stuart England, freehold proclaimed a man's independence by ensuring that he was not subject to the will of another. For New Englanders, consequently, the freehold system helped to bind the town together as a community of consenting individuals. Since the town elected its officers and governed its own affairs through a general meeting of the freeholders (the great majority), it has usually been taken for an early form of the democracy of the nineteenth and twentieth centuries. But if the form seems familiarly modern, it embodied an archaic English tradition.[44]

The early New England town, Kenneth Lockridge has recently argued, was not only a Puritan utopia but also a peasant utopia, a "Utopian Closed Corporate Community," ordering its own affairs by the "common consent of the neighbors" that had been customarily invoked by English villagers of the Middle Ages, though in the New World all the lesser peasant tenures had been transformed into simple freehold.[45] Because it distilled the communal side of medieval peasant experience—with lordship quite deliberately excluded—it could resist feudal claims with furious energy during the middle third of the eighteenth century. John Adams elevated this antagonism to the level of high ideology in his *Dissertation on the Canon and Feudal Law* (1765), which explained New England history

---

58, 73. Roy H. Akagi, *The Town Proprietors of the New England Colonies: A Study of Their Development, Organization, Activities, and Controversies, 1620–1770* (Philadelphia, 1924), chap. 8, is still extremely helpful, especially for comparing New England with other areas in terms of the uses to which ancient patents were put. See also Otis G. Hammond, "The Mason Title and Its Relation to New Hampshire and Massachusetts," American Antiquarian Society, *Proceedings*, N.S., XXVI (1916), 245–263.

44. Michael Zuckerman, "The Social Context of Democracy in Massachusetts," *WMQ*, 3d Ser., XXV (1968), 523–544.

45. Lockridge, *New England Town*, 18–22; Warren O. Ault, "Open-Field Husbandry and the Village Community: A Study of Agrarian By-Laws in Medieval England," American Philosophical Society, *Transactions*, N.S., LV, Pt. 7 (1965), 41.

as an emancipation from feudal restraints. By contrast, the more atomized pattern of settlement in other colonies failed to generate the communal cohesion and the consistent belief necessary for sustained resistance to the feudal revival. Jefferson, by inventing a mythical contract between the Jamestown settlers and James I, developed his own antifeudal interpretation of Virginia history in 1775, but as he himself admitted, few Virginians agreed with him at the time.[46]

Ultimately the Revolution would announce an ideology of natural rights in the name of which the feudal revival would be all but obliterated, even from historical memory. Yet despite obvious similarities, the nation's triumph was not New England's. By exploiting the fiscal side of lordship the revival had triumphed where communalism was weak. Although, conversely, the social communalism of New England had prevented the feudal revival from making headway there, self-government based upon the joint consent of all the responsible inhabitants of the town had been breaking down in the course of the eighteenth century, as the population grew denser, less homogeneous, more individualistic, and more European. The town meeting still sought the appearance of consensus through a process of accommodation that muted and obscured, as far as possible, the rising level of conflict. In some degree the Revolution accelerated the transformation from truly communal consensus to the explicitly majoritarian democracy of the nineteenth century in which political parties institutionalized and even promoted conflict by appealing to the self-interest or prejudice of the individual voter. The steps in this process after 1775 need to be investigated with the same care that Lockridge and Cook have given to the earlier years, but it is likely that the Revolutionary generation, by declaring political home rule to be the guiding principle of government, inadvertently lost sight of the end that it had served: the maintenance of communal consensus.[47]

46. Thomas Jefferson, *A Summary View of the Rights of British America* . . . (Williamsburg, Va., 1774); Merrill Peterson, *Thomas Jefferson and the New Nation: A Biography* (New York, 1970), 71.

47. Lockridge, "Land, Population and the Evolution of New England

Freshly released from bonds of social community as well as of "feudal" lordship, the new democratic individualism harked back to yet a third old English model that had persisted more successfully in eighteenth-century America than in England itself—the yeoman freeholder, a figure most typical of the back-country settlements of Pennsylvania, the new Southwest, and northern New England. Increasingly he would be taken as the archetype of the American everywhere. Instead of peasant communities the new nation preferred to idealize the peasant himself or rather the yeoman of English folk memory: self-reliant, honest, and independent, the classic figure of eighteenth-century English "country" ideology that the American revolutionaries appropriated to describe themselves—and the backbone of Jeffersonian democracy, the common man of Jacksonian rhetoric. The immediate origins of the explicit doctrines both of social egalitarianism and political democracy that were articulated in the post-Revolutionary half century may reasonably be sought in the political revolution declared on the principle that all men are created equal.

IV

How decisive a turning point in the development of the American social structure the Revolution was can only be guessed. It summarily put an end to one archaic element of eighteenth-century society, the feudal revival, and inadvertently turned away from a no less ancient communalism while beginning to exalt a third traditional figure, the virtuous yeoman freeholder, into an ideal detached from its older, more organic social and civic context. Perhaps Alexander Hamilton, like certain English politicians and writers of the eighteenth century, perceived that that old-fashioned ideal was no longer sufficient to govern the modern world of commerce, banks, factories, and specialized professions, but to a growing majority of citizens of the new republic his ideas smacked of the parliamentary and royal "corruption" of civic virtue against which the Revolution had been declared.[48]

The Federalist party found itself in the awkward position of fostering what amounted to traditional "court" policies—a national debt, a bank, executive patronage, an army, an expanded judicial system—in a nation of "country" ideologues. By excluding hereditary orders the Constitution had consciously divorced its balance of governmental powers from any corresponding division of society into estates or orders. Yet somehow, Federalists believed, they had to combine revolutionary ideology with an organic and deferential social order. The new Constitution provided the necessary opportunity. Federalists could truly defend the document as more radical, more republican than the Articles of Confederation, if only because the new House, unlike the old Congress, was directly elected by the people. But since congressional constituencies would be much larger than existing electoral districts within the states, Federalists also expected the new system to return to office "the wise, the rich, and the good"—the sort of man who could count on being generally known throughout a wide geographical area. From this perspective the rise of a disciplined opposition party was socially quite significant because only systematic organization of the electorate could make other kinds of candidates available.[49]

While the national capital remained at Philadelphia, Federalists set a dizzying social pace characterized by splendid new houses, fashionable equipages, frequent balls, dinners, and parties—what Harrison Gray Otis called "the annual fatigue." Only through a conspicuous display of wealth, Federalists

48. See Isaac Kramnick, *Bolingbroke and his Circle: The Politics of Nostalgia in the Age of Walpole* (Cambridge, Mass., 1968); Gerald Stourzh, *Alexander Hamilton and the Idea of Republican Government* (Stanford, 1970); and Pocock, "Virtue and Commerce," *Jour. Interdis. Hist.*, III (1972–1973), 119–134. Lance G. Banning, "The Quarrel with Federalism: A Study in the Origins and Character of Republican Thought" (Ph.D. diss., Washington University, 1972), traces the impact of country ideology upon the Jeffersonian Republicans in the 1790s.

49. Wood, *Creation of the American Republic*, 471–564; Banning, "Quarrel with Federalism," esp. chap. 5.

seemed to believe, could they legitimate the elite role they had assumed in the government of the republic. In effect the federal government tried to engraft itself upon the existing social order of America's leading city, and for a few years the experiment showed signs of endurance. Nothing of the kind was even conceivable once the government removed itself to the wilderness village of Washington, where under frugal Jeffersonian stewardship it rapidly became "a government out of sight and out of mind." There the divorce of government from distinct social orders, already announced in Revolutionary ideology, became a political reality. Republican virtue eliminated the threat that a Federalist government had posed for the new equality, but the cost was severe. The government found itself embarrassingly irrelevant to the social needs and concerns of America in general.[50]

Thus whatever chance the economic and demographic growth of the eighteenth century had offered for a complex but well-integrated social structure was cut off, not all at once, to be sure, but irreversibly nonetheless with the ultimate decline of the Federalist party and the later failure of the Whig program for governmental direction of an "American system." Economic growth continued in the nineteenth century, of course, but Americans found it excessively awkward to maintain a reasonable degree of harmony, stability, and equity among economic classes and other social groupings while thinking of themselves as so many self-reliant, unconstrained individuals on the yeoman-freeholder model.

To build a modern commercial and industrial economy on that archaic premise was to undermine such yeoman equality as had in fact persisted from colonial to nineteenth-century America. Recent studies leave little doubt that the eighteenth-century trend toward economic stratification continued almost unaffected by the new egalitarianism of 1775 to 1825. We know

50. Cf. Wood, *Creation of the American Republic*, 475–483, 593–615; Ethel E. Rasmusson, "Democratic Environment—Aristocratic Aspiration," *Pennsylvania Magazine of History and Biography*, XC (1966), 155–182; and James Sterling Young, *The Washington Community, 1800–1828* (New York, 1966).

far more, indeed, about economic class than about any other social category, because of the almost exclusive preoccupation of social historians with it.[51] There has always been a close correlation between economic class and social status in America (though perhaps wealth translated less directly into social standing during the century between 1725 and 1825 than before or after), and the acquisition and distribution of wealth has usually seemed the central social question, though again rather more so since 1825 than before.

Historians have usually taken the question of socioeconomic class, or rather socioeconomic equality, to be central to the existence of political democracy. But they have too easily assumed that the egalitarianism of the oncoming "age of the common man" ought properly to have been based on a general increase of actual equality of wealth and social classlessness. Evidence that not a few ardent egalitarians were in fact rather uncommon men has been regarded as a paradox at best and at worst a blot on the democratic purity of the Jacksonian era. It may be, however, that social egalitarianism was a not very surprising reaction to the irresistible growth of economic and social inequality. The image of a golden age of republican equality, of a society of yeoman freeholders (abstracted from their place among the various interrelated classes of English social tradition and colonial reality), had its greatest appeal at a time when there was solid reason to feel things were going too far the other way.

Historians have only recently begun to make precise calculations of the distribution of wealth before and after the Revolution, and these at widely separated points in time. It seems likely that the long-accepted impression will stand: that, as the wealth of the country increased between 1725 and 1825, so did the extremes in its distribution between rich and poor. In the seaboard cities and in eastern rural districts the upper class of great merchants or landowners was growing much richer, and a lower class of tenant farmers and laborers was getting both

51. E.g., Jackson Turner Main, *The Social Structure of Revolutionary America* (Princeton, 1965), esp. 4–6.

poorer and more numerous.[52] The characteristically American middle class of independent farmers, tradesmen, and professional men, however, still outnumbered all the rest in most parts of the country. In newly settled districts close behind the frontier the availability of cheap land fostered a fairly equal division of property for a time, while at the other extreme certain of the oldest areas, where the customarily careless farming methods had worn down the soil, fell back into a lower level of general and individual poverty. In Virginia the whole cycle worked itself out from east to west during the eighteenth century, from the exhausted soil of the tidewater to the settled but still thriving fall-line and piedmont counties and the rapidly developing frontier of western Virginia and Kentucky.[53] Elsewhere too the "long-term tendency seems to have been toward greater inequality, with more marked class distinctions," reversed only temporarily, at certain points, by the economic vicissitudes of the Revolutionary years.[54] As the wealth of the country continued to increase—in the Middle Atlantic states the $213 per capita of 1774 almost doubled by 1850—the actual distribution of wealth grew more uneven wherever the frontier circumstances of the generation of settlement had been outgrown.[55]

By any objective measurement the class structure did not change radically. The growth of more tangible extremes of wealth and poverty in effect gave substance to the eighteenth-century belief in hierarchy that the nineteenth century no longer accepted. The personnel of the upper class of the commercial ports kept changing, most rapidly during and after the Revolution, but the rising merchant families of Boston, New York, or Philadelphia, and of smaller places like Newburyport, slipped quite credibly into the social status—and sometimes the

52. E.g., James A. Henretta, "Economic Development and Social Structure in Colonial Boston," *WMQ*, 3d Ser., XXII (1965), 75–92.

53. Jackson Turner Main, "The Distribution of Property in Post-Revolutionary Virginia," *Mississippi Valley Historical Review*, XLI (1954), 241–258.

54. Main, *Social Structure of Revolutionary America*, 286.

55. Alice Hanson Jones, "Wealth Estimates for the American Middle Colonies, 1774," *Economic Development and Cultural Change*, XVIII, No. 4, pt. 2 (1970), 128.

very houses—of those who failed in business or suffered confiscation and exile for loyalty to the crown.[56] Although the redis-
tribution of property that followed confiscation of certain loyalist estates in New York, Maryland, and elsewhere did put much
of it in the hands of smaller landholders, the extent of change
fell far short of social revolution.[57] The families of the colonial
gentry, or the close counterparts who succeeded some of them,
not only improved their relative advantage as an economic
elite—investing in new western lands and the industries of the
early factory age—but maintained their position as the de facto
upper class of early nineteenth-century society.[58]

But they were progressively less accepted as a gentry by right.
The precise stages whereby the old hierarchic ideal of the
English colonists gave way to the new egalitarianism of the
Jacksonian persuasion remain obscure, like so much else in the
social history of the period. Historians have been more interested in the democratic political applications of egalitarianism than in its specifically social gestation. Although hierarchy
was rejected and social equality taken to be the thoroughly
modern ideal, the new egalitarianism made a conscious principle out of the widespread practical equality of condition that
had prevailed among the small landowners, independent artisans, and petty businessmen of the simpler age that was now,
except in various recently settled frontier districts, being rele-
gated to the past. In effect the archaic English "country" tradition of the virtuous yeoman freeholder was thereby sustained,
although it was increasingly commingled with the broader leveling strain that much humbler kinds of Englishmen had voiced
from time to time since John Ball in the fourteenth century
questioned the authority of the gentleman's pedigree. Such

56. East, *Business Enterprise in the American Revolutionary Era*, 222–
237; Benjamin W. Labaree, *Patriots and Partisans: The Merchants of
Newburyport, 1764–1815* (Cambridge, Mass., 1962), chaps. 4–5.

57. Young, *Democratic Republicans of New York*, 62–66; Philip A. Crowl,
*Maryland During and After the Revolution: A Political and Economic
Study* (Baltimore, 1943), 54; Richard D. Brown, "The Confiscation and
Disposition of Loyalists' Estates in Suffolk County, Massachusetts," *WMQ*,
3d Ser., XXI (1964), 549.

58. Stow Persons, "The Origins of the Gentry," in Robert H. Bremner,
ed., *Essays on History and Literature* (Columbus, Ohio, 1966), 83–119.

egalitarianism as had been most explicitly asserted in America down to the Declaration of Independence had had more to do with political parity among constituted governing bodies—of towns, counties, or provinces—than with the social equality of persons. But during the next half century the claim to the equal right to home rule was explicitly enlarged to include the democratic right of each citizen to social equality as well as to a voice in government.

American egalitarianism eventually assaulted every artificial barrier to equality, not so much to equality of material or social condition as to the individual's equal opportunity to establish superiority over his peers. Perhaps the reason that baseball was rapidly developed out of the archaic English village game of rounders, to become the national pastime of the new republic, was that more than any other sport it symbolized how Americans thought equality ought to work. Every player bats and fields as a conspicuous individual, thus reflecting equality of opportunity, and then his performance is measured to three decimal places in order to sort everybody out according to a precise hierarchy of achievement. As in the national economy, relatively slight statistical differences pay heavily disproportionate rewards.

In society at large the number of "artificial" impediments to equal competition was capable of infinite expansion, a possibility that endowed the doctrine of equality with its own powerful, inherent dynamic of reform. The Revolution rejected birth and legal privilege as proper criteria for setting some people apart from others. Later reformers could add education, family connections, wealth, race, and gender to the proscribed list, usually so that Americans could compete ever more furiously and, reformers believed, ever more fairly—for the joy of outdoing their neighbors. So long as government remained all but irrelevant to society and the economy, the pursuit of equality was frustrating and often self-defeating. Only with the reassertion of government in later generations could the doctrine assume a more consistent and effective reformist role.

For a people to think of their society in terms drawn from

the objective conditions of a simpler but outdated age is neither unusual nor necessarily harmful. Inherited values shape present circumstances even while being reshaped by them. For Americans to find themselves confronting a new polarization between great wealth and widespread poverty would conceivably have been reason enough to articulate a contrary standard, even if they had never had occasion to hear the egalitarian phrases of the Declaration of Independence. Having declared their political liberty in egalitarian terms, however, they were too easily persuaded, when declaring for social equality, to do so in libertarian terms that made their efforts more symbolic than effectual. Partly because of their Revolutionary heritage Americans could not really face the possibility that their liberty—their freedom to compete—was undermining their equality.

Some notable reforms of the time raised this dilemma. Abolition of entail in Virginia, which J. Franklin Jameson—like Thomas Jefferson—thought a mortal blow to the old order, is now generally understood to have been little more than an egalitarian gesture, since entail had not been required to ensure the existence of great estates in a country where land was easily obtained and usually profitable. But if the abolition of entail had any practical effect in such a country, it was libertarian rather than truly egalitarian.[59] The freedom to seize the speculative opportunities of the market in land had been a main source of the greatest fortunes of colonial days; it was certainly

59. C. Ray Keim, "Primogeniture and Entail in Colonial Virginia," *WMQ*, 3d Ser., XXV (1968), 585–586. It may be, however, that as wealth became more concentrated after the 1780s, entail would have been more useful had the law still allowed it. Even before that time its position is still uncertain. To count the number and percentage of wills creating entails, as Keim has done, is insufficient. Because descent by fee tail was automatic, such an estate would not appear in a will after the first-generation testament that created it. Since entails were cumulative, the counting of wills cannot determine the proportion of estates held in fee tail as against fee simple at any given moment. Certainly for the tidewater, where most entails were located, the system grew in importance between 1705 and the Revolution. Entailed estates were in general the larger ones; the quantity of land so held was greater than indicated by the mere number of entails. We lack comparable English data from which to estimate Virginia's approximation to or deviation from the norm of the mother country. For other colonies the question has never been seriously studied.

worth more in the nineteenth century than the right to tie up particular tracts of land in perpetuity would have been. It is true that the freedom to speculate helped many ordinary farmers to acquire a modest competence in one new district after another as settlement advanced across the continent. But after a new district had been fully settled, liberty from legal restraints on landholding sooner or later had the opposite effect of concentrating ownership in fewer hands. The unwelcome growth of permanent tenancy and a fixed class of farm laborers in the midwestern regions of free soil and homesteads, as well as in the South and East, challenged the egalitarian tradition as the nineteenth century advanced.[60]

Other reforms of the post-Revolutionary half century also promised to make men more equal, on the model of the yeoman freeholder, but instead made them free to become unequal, and on a far grander scale than was possible through land speculation. During the first half of the nineteenth century governmental regulation of the economy, hitherto accepted when required for the general welfare of the commonwealth, was progressively abandoned, first in practice and finally in principle. The new, liberal principle of laissez-faire was supposed to be egalitarian as well; it may have been in some degree a reaction to the steady increase of inequality among the economic classes of the time. Overt egalitarianism, which came to a head in the Anti-Masonic movement of the late 1820s and

60. To some extent 19th-century law had to recognize the practical necessity of certain kinds of concentration of wealth that the Revolutionary generation had rejected. Outside New England colonial law had imposed primogeniture in cases of intestacy, but this provision apparently had little impact because most estates of any size were bequeathed by will. For this reason most scholars now regard its abolition as more symbolic than substantive, despite the explicit egalitarian intent of the reform. By contrast, colonial Massachusetts had permitted primogeniture only through direct testimentary action. The law required partible inheritance, with a double share to the eldest son, in all intestacy cases. But repeated subdivision of the land had proceeded so far by the end of the 18th century that the courts began to impose primogeniture even on intestate estates. All of the land was awarded to the eldest son, who was required to settle cash on his brothers and sisters. "Massachusetts estates are very rarely divided," Tocqueville observed in the 1830s; "the eldest son generally takes the land, and the others go to seek their fortune in the wilderness." Alexis de Tocqueville, *Democracy in America*, ed. Phillips Bradley (New York, 1945), I, 293.

overnight made fervent democrats of such recent opponents of universal suffrage as the gentlemen of the Albany Regency, was directed in particular against the artificial privileges of state-chartered and state-regulated monopolies. Yet for Andrew Jackson to strike down the regulatory power of the central Bank of the United States because it represented aristocracy—personified as it was by an undoubted Philadelphia gentleman, Nicholas Biddle—was to open the way as time went on to far greater and far less restrained concentrations of economic power. The transportation revolution, after an initial stage of public capitalization and control, and the Industrial Revolution from its inception were allowed to proceed as though an unregulated modern economy would distribute the wealth it produced as satisfactorily as the simple agricultural and mercantile economy of the colonial past had done—or as parts of the contemporary but old-fashioned West were still doing. Of course it did not. In the second half of the nineteenth century the current egalitarian dogma, based upon the increasingly archaic figure of the yeoman freeholder, helped produce modern extremes of inequality far beyond anything attained by the pre-Revolutionary feudal revival.

The sheer size of wealth and the extent of poverty in the latter part of the nineteenth century were not the most untoward results. Men spoke of the new conditions in terms borrowed from the rejected past—of industrial "barons" and a "new feudalism"—but the old feudal balance between baronial obligations and privileges was not easily restored to a dogmatically egalitarian society. The spirit of noblesse oblige persisted among the successors to the colonial merchant gentry, in Boston and Philadelphia if not New York or Chicago, but with diminishing practical force in economic and political affairs.[61] Landed gentlemen established themselves on the midwestern prairies somewhat as Lord Fairfax had done in the Northern Neck, but like the captains of industry they were considered to be only the most conspicuous exemplars of the material success to which the common man aspired, rather than

61. Paul Goodman, "Ethics and Enterprise: The Values of a Boston Elite, 1800–1860," *American Quarterly*, XVIII (1966), 437–451.

a distinctive social class with special responsibilities to their inferiors.[62] The nineteenth-century elite was increasingly a mere plutocracy, insistent upon the absolute rights of property; the working classes reluctantly but inevitably had to acknowledge that in such a changed situation "capital" and "labor" no longer shared a common interest. In the twentieth century the chief effort of social reformers, seeking to come to grips with this problem, would be to level economic classes up or down to something like the relative equality of material condition of an age now long vanished, rather than to restore that age's forgotten ideal of an equitably related hierarchy among existing social classes.

The stratification of economic classes had been going on, however, since long before the American Revolution. Soon after that time, as the Revolutionary mixture of political egalitarianism and liberalism was extended to a doctrine of social equality, the further development of structural ties between social classes was cut off. In rejecting social hierarchy, as a relic of the feudal past, in favor of the equally archaic and far less recoverable practical equality of a simpler age, the reformers of later generations repeatedly condemned themselves to frustration.

v

The reinvigoration of certain old social institutions and the suppression of others during the Revolutionary era has other implications. Louis Hartz has tried to explain all of American history in terms of the absence of a feudal past. Lacking the old dialectic between feudalism and liberalism that made socialism possible in Europe, America is imprisoned in a liberal present that seems to allow no escape.[63] Hartz derived his perception

---

62. Paul Wallace Gates, *Frontier Landlords and Pioneer Tenants* (Ithaca, N.Y., 1945).

63. Hartz, *The Liberal Tradition in America*, and his *The Founding of New Societies: Studies in the History of the United States, Latin America, and South Africa, Canada, and Australia* (New York, 1964), 1–122. Cf. the symposium on the Hartz thesis by Hartz, Harry Jaffa, Leonard Krieger, and Marvin Meyers in *Comparative Studies in Society and History*, V (1962–1963), 261–284, 365–377, and the comments by Sydney James, "Colonial

from the nineteenth century, particularly the Jacksonian era.[64] For that period his emphasis is surely correct. As of 1825 America no longer had a feudal past because the Revolution had put social hierarchy on the road to obloquy and then to oblivion, just when it might have achieved significant dimensions. But he exaggerates his case by reading the phenomenon backward through the whole of American history.

The profundity of Revolutionary thought owed something to the growing relevance, up to that point, of social ideology to the social order and to the perception by 1790 of the limits of that relevance.[65] Conversely the victory of the Revolution over "feudal" hierarchy helps account for the banality of Jacksonian thought, when political and constitutional rhetoric (mostly borrowed from the Revolution itself) seldom bore any meaningful relation to social realities.

This painful gap between political loyalty and social reality became, perhaps, the central tension of the nineteenth century, and it helps to define and to limit the social significance of the American Revolution. Especially in its Jeffersonian variety the Revolution provided a "national" political framework in which very different societies, or remnants of societies, could pretend to share a common loyalty and common interests. So long as the government did nothing important the illusion could last, but whenever it pursued a vigorous policy the nation threatened to fall apart. Hamilton's program antagonized too many interests to endure. Jeffersonian foreign policy after 1807 drove New England to calculate the value of the Union. The Republican program of reconstruction in 1816 was totally dismantled within twenty years and produced a nullification crisis along the way. By loudly doing nothing the Jacksonians restored the Jeffersonian illusion of a harmonious nation, but Polk's active

Rhode Island and the Beginnings of the Liberal Rationalized State," in Melvin Richter, ed., *Essays in Theory and History: An Approach to the Social Sciences* (Cambridge, Mass., 1970), 167–168.

64. Cf. Louis B. Hartz, *Economic Policy and Democratic Thought: Pennsylvania, 1776–1860* (Cambridge, Mass., 1948).

65. Wood, *Creation of the American Republic*, esp. 383–390, 475–499, 593–615.

foreign policy destroyed the dream and began the final descent toward actual Civil War.

The Revolution created a national government, but not a national community. The imperatives by which that government survived may even have weakened the sense of community within each of its member societies without providing a convincing substitute. To an extent not easily measured disembodied Revolutionary rhetoric made hard problems difficult to define, much less resolve. Perhaps the ultimate impact of the Revolution was to divorce power from politics and politics from social reality. Not until after the Civil War and an irresolute "Reconstruction" were over would America begin to draw them all together again.

8

Conflict and Consensus

IN THE

American Revolution

by

EDMUND S. MORGAN

During the past fifteen or twenty years a division has emerged
among historians of the American Revolution, a division between those who emphasize the consensus achieved by the
revolting colonists and those who emphasize conflicts among
them. The division has excited attention and has perhaps been
exaggerated because of the special position occupied by the
Revolution in our national consciousness. As the noises of the
approaching bicentennial grow louder, it is scarcely necessary
to point out that most Americans, including historians, seem
to think the Revolution was a good thing. If any episode in our
past is enshrined in our consciousness, this is it. By consequence any group or cause that can affiliate itself with the
Revolution may hope to have some goodness rub off on it.
As an example, some of us can remember vividly the campaign
of the 1930s to make the Revolution and its Founding Fathers
rise to the support of Stalinism. Under the slogan "Com-
munism is twentieth-century Americanism," Washington, Jefferson, and Franklin were enrolled posthumously in the popular

front. We have similarly had, long since, Catholic interpretations of the Revolution and Calvinist interpretations, Massachusetts interpretations and Virginia interpretations, and a host of others, each somehow concerned with reflecting American-Revolutionary glory on Catholicism or Calvinism, on Massachusetts or Virginia, or whatever.

The alacrity with which the current division among scholars has been recognized, if not promoted, I believe, lies in this sanctifying power of the Revolution and its Founding Fathers. Those who contend that the Revolution bore few marks of social conflict or social upheaval seem to be denying the blessing of the Founding Fathers to present-day struggles against the establishment, while those who emphasize conflicts seem to be suggesting that conflicts, or at least conflicts against an upper class or established system, are sponsored by the Founding Fathers, consecrated in the fires at Valley Forge. No such power attaches to other episodes in our history. The New Deal, for example, has not achieved sanctifying power in the national memory. Hence no one would think to classify as conservative those historians who deny that the New Deal achieved or aimed at radical social change. But to say that the Revolution did not achieve or aim at radical social change and lacked the conflicts that generally accompany such change is taken as a denial that radical social change is a good thing. Hence those who give the Founding Fathers failing grades as social revolutionaries are greeted, sometimes to their astonishment, as conservative.

But conservative and radical are relative terms, and so are consensus and conflict; and relative terms, if I may be allowed to follow for a moment the logic of Peter Ramus, can be understood only in relation to each other. Those impressed by the achievement of consensus among the Revolutionists can scarcely hope to understand the nature of that consensus without understanding the conflicts that had to be overcome or repressed in order to arrive at it. Nor can those who emphasize conflict gauge the force of the movements they examine without considering the kind of consensus that later grew out of those movements or that succeeded in subduing them. Therefore, in attempting to assess the meaning of the American Revolution, it may be worthwhile to survey the various points of consensus and conflict that can be discerned in the Revolutionary period, to weigh their effect on the Revolution, and then to examine the kind of consensus that emerged at the end, even if that consensus is thought to be no more than a sullen acquiescence in the measures of a ruling class.

The type of internal conflict that historians have most eagerly searched for among Americans of the Revolutionary period is class conflict. The search is handicapped by a problem of identification. With the struggle of the colonies against the mother country dominating the scene, how does one distinguish a class conflict within that larger conflict?

Not by the side a man chose to support. Although the first historians of the loyalists did assume that they represented an upper if not a ruling class, subsequent investigations have revealed that loyalists, like patriots, were drawn from all classes. That a man sided with the mother country or against her tells us little about his social position. Although it seems altogether likely on the latest evidence that a larger percentage of the well-to-do could be found among the loyalists than among the Revolutionists, the Revolution cut sharply across nearly all previous divisions, whether regional, ethnic, religious, or class. It was not a conflict in which one side was predominantly upper class and the other predominantly lower class.

If, then, we look only at one side, at the Americans who supported the Revolution, or who did not oppose it, can we there find that lower-class rebels were bent on the overthrow or reduction of ruling-class rebels? A moment's reflection on the nature of the Revolutionary War may moderate our expectations. The Revolutionary effort against Great Britain tended to suppress or encompass social conflicts. Where it did not, where hostility between social groups rose to a level of intensity approximating that of the conflict with the mother country, one group or the other would be likely to join with the loyalists. Some merchants in New York City, for example, felt that the local Revolutionary leaders threatened their interests more than the mother country did; and similarly some tenant farmers of the Hudson valley felt more bitter toward their patriot landlords than they did toward king and Parliament. But these men, whether merchants or tenants, by joining the loyalist side deprived themselves of a part in any contest about who should rule at home. Loyalism in this way tended to absorb social groups that felt endangered or oppressed by the Revolutionary party. It operated as a safety valve to remove from the American side men who felt a high degree of social discontent. Or to change the figure, it drew off men at either end of the political spectrum, reducing the range of disagreements. It removed from the scene the intransigents, of whatever persuasion, who might have prevented the achievement of consensus.

Disputes did occur, of course, among those who remained on the Revolutionary side, but the extraordinary social mobility characteristic of eighteenth-century American society usually prevented such disputes from hardening along class lines. Although recent statistical samplings point to a narrowing of economic opportunity in the latter half of the eighteenth century, Americans still enjoyed an upward mobility unknown in other societies. In a land of rising men a political group formed along lower-class lines had little prospect of endurance.

The Revolution probably increased social mobility temporarily both upward and downward, ruining the fortunes of many established families and opening opportunities for speedy ascent by daring upstarts. This very mobility engendered, as it always has, political disputes, but seldom along class lines. An American who had moved up from the lower ranks carried with him the expectation of sharing with those who had already arrived the offices of government traditionally exercised by the economically and socially successful. If he found himself excluded, he could call upon a wide electorate of his former equals but present inferiors to help him achieve the kind of office that they, no less than he, considered proper for successful men. But the fact that the lower ranks were involved in the contest should not obscure the fact that the contest itself was generally a struggle for office and power between members of an upper class: the new against the established. We must be wary of seeing such struggles, like Patrick Henry's successful bid for power in Virginia, as a rising of the oppressed against their masters.

I do not mean to argue that hostility between classes did not exist at all among those who supported the Revolution or that it cannot be discerned or recognized. In the antirent riots of 1766, for example, New York tenant farmers expressed a hostility to their landlords that was not entirely absorbed by loyalism after 1775. More than one scholar has found clear expressions of class conflict in the conduct of the war and of politics in Revolutionary New York. But in assessing class conflict as a Revolutionary force, we shall be hard pressed to find many instances outside New York in which antagonism rose to the level of actual fighting or even to openly expressed hostility of the kind that might be expected to lead to fighting.

American social structure was so fluid that to talk about social classes at all in most colonies or states requires the use of very loose economic categories such as rich, poor, and middle class, or contemporary designations like "the better sort" or "the poorer sort," or occupational categories like merchant, planter, lawyer, farmer, artisan, and seaman. Americans were no less skilled than other peoples in measuring the degree of deference due to each of their neighbors for the host of reasons and prejudices that confer honor or contempt on the members of any community. But such distinctions were local, seldom negotiable beyond the neighborhood where a man was known, and not always easy to discern even there.

Nevertheless, one absolute, clearly defined, and easily recognized division did exist, that between freeman and slave. Half a million Americans, perhaps a fifth of the total population, were slaves, and slavery is so direct an assault by one group of men on another that it can properly be considered as a form of class conflict in itself. In the American Revolution, however, slaves were unable to mount any serious uprising against their masters. Although the armies of both sides sooner or later made use of slaves and gave some of them freedom for their services, neither side provided the help necessary for large-scale insurrection. Both felt more need to woo masters than slaves. Perhaps the possibility of insurrection was even lessened by the few efforts of the British to promote it. When Lord Dunmore invited the slaves of Virginia to desert their masters and join his forces, he probably drew off many of the bolder individuals, leaving behind those who were less likely to rise in revolt later. Again loyalism tended to absorb men who might otherwise have directed their energies more radically against a local ruling class.

That the American Revolution did not produce an uprising of the group in colonial society that was most visibly and legally oppressed, and oppressed with the explicit or tacit approval of the rest of the society, is itself an instructive comment on the nature of social conflict and consensus during the Revolution.

The absence of any massive revolt, white or black, may perhaps be put in perspective if we compare the labor force of the Revolutionary period with that a century earlier, when Bacon's Rebellion had terrorized the first families of Virginia. In the seventeenth century as in the eighteenth the greater part of the colonial labor force, that is, of men who worked for other men, was concentrated in the South and especially in Virginia. In 1676, when Bacon's Rebellion occurred, the laborers were mostly imported servants, English, Irish, Scottish, or Welsh, whose terms of service generally expired when they reached the age of twenty-four. They were imported at the rate of eight hundred to a thousand or perhaps as many as fifteen hundred or two thousand annually; they were mostly male, and they had come in expectation of a better life once their terms of service were up.

For a variety of reasons, in the ten or fifteen years before 1676, Virginia underwent a depression that severely curtailed the opportunities for a newly freed servant to make his way in the world. Tobacco prices were low. Land in the settled areas had been taken up in large quantities by earlier comers, and men either had to rent land at prices that left no room for profit or else they had to move to the frontiers, where Indians mounted guerrilla attacks on them. The officers of government lived high off the hog in spite of depression, by levying high taxes and voting each other generous fees, salaries, and sinecures. The result was the presence of a clearly distinguishable privileged class and a clearly distinguishable lower class, composed not merely of servants who made tobacco for their betters but of former servants who were trying to make it for themselves. These freedmen were likely to be single. They were likely to be without land of their own. But they were not likely to be without guns, especially those who had moved, as many had, to the frontier.

As early as 1673 Governor Berkeley recognized the dangers of this situation. At least one-third of Virginia's militia, he estimated, were single freedmen, who would have nothing to lose by turning their arms against their superiors for the sake of plunder. Three years later, goaded by Indian raids, they did it. Bacon's Rebellion swept across Virginia, starting among the penniless pioneers of the frontier counties and gathering momentum from the adherence of other men who had nothing to lose in a free-for-all scramble for the accumulated wealth of the privileged few. In the midst of it Berkeley wrote to England, understandably raising his estimate of the numbers of the disaffected. "How miserable that man is," he complained, "that Governes a People wher six parts of seaven at least are Poore Endebted Discontented and Armed."

A hundred years later the situation had changed radically in at least one important respect. In the South, where a large labor force still furnished the way to wealth for plantation owners, the laborers were not continually emerging into the status of independent, poverty-stricken, discontented freemen trying to make a start against heavy odds. By the middle of the eighteenth century the majority of the entire labor force in the plantation colonies was held in permanent slavery. The development of slavery is perhaps the key to the consensus that prevailed in colonial America, for slavery meant the substitution of a helpless, closely guarded lower class for a dangerous, armed lower class that would fight if exploited too ruthlessly. The slave had more reason to revolt than the servant or the new freedman. But he was less able to. He had no hope, no rising expectations, and no arms. On top of that he was black. His status in the community was proclaimed by his color and maintained by a tyranny in which white men of all ranks and regions consented and approved. The consensus on which colonial society rested was a racist consensus.

Had the southern plantations not shifted from free to slave labor, had the planters continued to import masses of indentured servants and continued to pour them into their own and other colonies a few years later as indigent freedmen, then the picture of social mobility in the colonial period and of class conflict in the Revolution might have been quite different. The minutemen of 1775 might have been truly a rabble in arms, ready to turn from fighting the British to fighting their well-to-do neighbors, just as Bacon's men turned from fighting the Indians to fighting Berkeley and his crew. But in the century between 1676 and 1776 the growth of slavery had curbed the growth of a free, depressed lower class and correspondingly magnified the social and economic opportunities of whites. It is perhaps the greatest irony of a Revolution fought in the name of freedom, a Revolution that indeed advanced the cause of freedom throughout the world, that the men who carried it out were able to unite against British oppression because they had so completely and successfully oppressed the largest segment of their own laboring population.

To be sure, there were those among the Revolutionists who felt uncomfortable about rebelling against what they chose to call the threat of slavery, while they themselves held some 20 percent of their own population in slavery. But such feelings were translated into legal action only in states where slaves were few in number. Those were not the states where an enslaved labor force grew the country's principal exports. And if northerners freed their own slaves, they did not propose at this time to free their neighbors'. The racial consensus on which colonial society had rested was shaken a little but not broken by the Revolution.

There of course continued to be indentured servants and servants who worked for wages both in the plantation colonies and in the North. But the great majority of men who worked for other men were probably the slaves of the plantation colonies. The growing economy, in spite of periodic depressions

like that of the 1670s, could absorb the number of indentured
servants who turned free each year and could offer most of
them an independent and comfortable if not affluent existence
on the land. Only a small minority fell permanently into the
servant class, like some of the sailors whom Jesse Lemisch has
described, and even they reacted more visibly, violently, and
vociferously against iniquities of the British government than
against whatever oppression was visited upon them by their
compatriots.

In sum, the evidence of Revolutionary class conflict is scanty,
and for good reason. With a majority of laborers in chains and
with the most discontented freemen venting their discontent in
loyalism, the struggle over who should rule at home was unlikely to bear many of the marks of class conflict. Class conflict was
indubitably present, but it did not surface with an effective
intensity until a later day, after the Revolution had built a
consensus that could both nourish and contain it, and after
social, political, and economic change had produced greater
provocations to it.

Let us turn now to another kind of conflict that was more intense and also, I believe, more significant for the Revolution. If
we examine the occasions when Americans fought with one another or came very close to fighting between 1763 and 1789, excluding battles between loyalists and patriots, we find a number
of episodes, all of them involving men who had moved from the
older coastal regions into the interior: the march of the Paxton
Boys against Philadelphia, the Regulator movement in the
Carolinas with its Battle of Alamance, the activities of the
Green Mountain Boys in Vermont, the skirmishes of Pennamite
and Yankee in the Wyoming Valley of Pennsylvania, and
Shays's Rebellion in Massachusetts. However diverse in immediate cause and attendant circumstance, these conflicts had
one thing in common: they were all manifestations of the
discontent of western settlers or settlers on new lands against
governments dominated by or subservient to the interests of
older or eastern regions.

Americans of the Revolutionary period were less successful in
repressing sectional conflicts than conflicts arising from class or

race. Though this fact is obvious and though the westward movement has received its full share of attention, historians considering the Revolution as a social movement have not always borne in mind two conspicuous conditions of life in eighteenth-century America, conditions that lay at the root of East-West conflict: first, the extraordinary rate of population growth and, second, the abundance of land, unoccupied or only thinly occupied by the native Indians.

Although the rate of population growth in the colonies varied a good deal from place to place and from year to year, the overall long-range trend is clear. The total population of the thirteen colonies that participated in the Revolution more than doubled every twenty-five years during the eighteenth century. Beginning at about 250,000 in 1700, it rose to over 5,000,000 by 1800. As we learn more about the role of population growth in history, it may ultimately appear that the most significant social fact about America in the eighteenth century was this fearful growth, unlike anything that had been known in Europe in recorded history. Every twenty-five years the colonies had to absorb numbers equal to their total population. The result by the last quarter of the eighteenth century was explosive emigration out of the older settled regions into the West. Consider the westward thrust into the Kentucky-Tennessee area alone: the population there could scarcely have amounted to 10,000 in 1781; by 1790 it had soared to 110,000. If we note that this migration over the mountains in the 1780s by itself dwarfed the so-called Great Migration over the ocean in the 1630s, when probably no more than 50,000 left England for all parts of the New World, if we note also that migration was simultaneously occurring into other western areas, then we may begin to appreciate the magnitude of a western factor in the Revolutionary period.

The westward population explosion probably relieved the East from social conflicts that might have arisen from overcrowding; but it generated other conflicts potentially as dangerous. It set rival groups of speculators into contests for control of the richest western lands, contests that drew in and corrupted state governments and the national government. And it created a block of Americans who by moving west acquired different needs and interests from eastern Americans, but who by the same move lost their political ability to make their needs heard or attended to. People moved west so rapidly that even with the best of intentions a government could scarcely have kept up with them in furnishing the town or parish or county organization that formed the units of representation in the legislature. Because representation did not keep up with the expansion of population into new territory, governments remained under the domination of easterners and frequently neglected the needs of westerners. Even where representation was fairly proportioned, the location of the legislature subjected it to eastern influences that could bring it into serious conflict with the West.

Eastern insensitivity to western needs was the source of the Paxton incident, as it had been in part of Bacon's Rebellion. The prime western need in the early years of a settlement was to cope with the Indians, who gathered to attack the invaders of their land. Indian raids were no longer part of life in the East. The very existence of westerners furnished a buffer zone to easterners, enabling them to view the rights and wrongs of the situation with an objectivity that westerners could not achieve or afford. We need not assume that the Paxton Boys were righteous. Benjamin Franklin called them "Christian White Savages," and the epithet was deserved. They were armed thugs, terrorists, murderers; but they were also westerners, and as westerners they had grievances against an eastern-dominated legislature that spent its time arguing about who would pay the bills while it neglected the defense of the frontier.

The Regulator movement represents another phase of the same East-West conflict: the eastern-dominated governments of South Carolina and North Carolina failed to extend the machinery of law enforcement into the West as rapidly as the needs of the settlers required, and so the West took the law in its own hands. In Shays's Rebellion the Shaysites, who also called themselves Regulators, hoped to gain by direct action what the government in Boston had denied them. The Pennamite-Yankee conflict and the activities of the Green Mountain Boys offer a variation on the theme. In these cases two colonial governments, representing different speculative interests, were engaged in a contest for western lands, and the actual settlers fought with each other. The significance of the frontier in early American history, if we may borrow that phrase, was that it kept Americans in conflict. Movement of the exploding population into new lands was continually generating new communities with interests differing from those of the older communities that retained, or at least claimed, control over them.

This kind of internal conflict among Americans was far more visible during the Revolutionary period than was class conflict. Although there were overtones of class conflict in any contest between established eastern interests and the interests of pioneer western farmers, the contest was primarily geographical, created by the problem of stretching the social and political apparatus that bound one group of people to another in the expanding American universe.

That this form of conflict produced more active hostility in the Revolutionary period will seem no more than natural if we view the Revolution itself from the same perspective. The English colonies in America stood to England in the way that the western parts of the colonies stood to the eastern parts, but with even stronger grievances and correspondingly stronger hostility. The institutions that England devised for her overseas emigrants in the wake of the Great Migration were even more inadequate by 1776 than the institutions that they had devised for themselves. While many colonial legislatures had too few representatives from their western areas, Parliament, which could legislate for all the colonies, had not a single representative from them. When the colonists cried out that Parliament without American representatives knew nothing about their needs and had no right to tax them, they spoke to England in the voice of westerners speaking to easterners. In the Declaration of Independence they announced that the social and political bonds that tied them to an eastern government were severed. The American Revolution was itself a revolt of settlers in a new land against a government that by its location and

composition could not be properly acquainted with their needs
and could not keep up with their growth.

After 1776, in seeking to sustain the new nation they had
just proclaimed themselves to be, the Americans had to contain
the very force that had impelled their revolt against the mother
country. If the colonies could secede from England, the West
could secede from the East for the same reasons. The danger
was aggravated by the fact that slavery and loyalism, which
helped to lower tension between classes, perversely heightened
tension between East and West. Since slavery did not move
westward as rapidly as freedom, the much higher concentration
of slaves in the East served to emphasize the difference in sectional interests. And since loyalism had as much appeal for
disaffected regions as for disaffected individuals, it could become a catastrophic ingredient in sectional conflicts. If an entire region became sufficiently hostile to a government dominated by easterners, it might choose to rejoin the mother
country. The result, as in the defection of individuals or groups,
might be a greater harmony among those remaining. But the
defection of a whole region could have jeopardized the viability
of the Union; and a consensus formed by the secession of all
dissident elements would scarcely deserve the name.

The British were not slow to recognize the advantages for
them of sectional conflict and kept hoping for it after the war
was over. In violation of the treaty they clung to their northwest trading posts, flirted with the disgruntled leaders of Vermont, and made plans for detaching the whole Northwest. Nor
was Britain the only recourse for discontented westerners:
Spain had eyes on the whole Southwest. She came uncomfort-
ably close to detaching Kentucky when the Spanish minister
maneuvered the Continental Congress into what appeared to
westerners as a gross display of eastern indifference to western
interests. If Congress had actually ratified the Jay-Gardoqui
Treaty, with its seeming recognition of Spanish control of the
Mississippi, the Americans who marched across the mountains
into Kentucky and Tennessee in the 1780s might well have
marched right into the arms of Spain.

In sum, while class conflict tended to be muted during the

Revolutionary period by social mobility among whites, by the enslavement of blacks, and by loyalism, sectional conflict was aggravated. The gravest form of sectional conflict was East-West, but it was not the only form. The greater North-South conflict had already cast its ominous shadow in congressional voting alignments, in the uneasiness of both northerners and southerners over the continuance of slavery, and in steps taken toward abolition of slavery in the North, but not in the South. The most farsighted Americans sensed already that North-South differences as well as East-West differences might one day lead to secession. Indeed in the late 1780s so many sectional disagreements were festering that men who had led their states to a united independence fifteen years earlier now predicted the breakup of the American nation.

We know that it did not break up. What, then, other than the superior wisdom of the Founding Fathers, prevented the breakup? What sort of consensus enabled Americans to contain not only the immediate threats to their Union perceived in the 1780s but also the threats that grew with time from sectional and class conflict? The question in some measure answers itself. The Americans did achieve nationality during the Revolutionary period, and nationalism has proved to be the most powerful, if the least understood, social force of modern times. In the shrinking world of the twentieth century it has often been a sinister force, confining the vision of its devotees to a single country when they should be looking at the entire globe. But for Americans of the Revolutionary period the world was expanding instead of shrinking, and nationalism exerted a cohesive influence among the people of the several states, stretching instead of confining their political horizons. Even Jefferson, whose state loyalties proved particularly strong, urged his fellow Virginians to send their best young men to Congress, so that they could acquire the continental vision early. That vision extended not merely up and down the Atlantic seaboard but westward to the areas where Americans were moving so rapidly in the 1780s. It scarcely occurred to Jefferson that the United States might not one day reach to the Pacific and indeed occupy the whole of North America, and perhaps the Caribbean and South America too. If not everyone felt this way, there were enough who did to give American nationalism an expansive quality and to make her statesmen conscious of the need to retain the westward migrants within the national community.

Nationalism was in itself the strongest force binding Americans of the Revolutionary generation together. Devotion to the nation helped to keep both sides in any conflict on speaking terms, helped to make disagreements negotiable within the framework of national politics, and even made possible the creation of a new and stronger framework in 1787 when the old one proved unsatisfactory. But nationalism was not the only force disposing Americans to bury their conflicts. The racial consensus of colonial times, though challenged and diminished, still prevailed and helped to keep the North-South conflict from coming to center stage. The Revolutionists were not prepared to allow the issue of freedom for blacks to threaten the union of whites. By the consent of white Americans the American labor force, concentrated in the South, remained for the most part in slavery, outside the arena where American quarrels and conflicts were expected to take place. Contending factions, whether of class, region, or party, were agreed in not seeking or expecting the participation of men in chains.

The exclusion of most laborers meant that the participants on both sides of any conflict were men who possessed formidable powers, powers that were carefully withheld from slaves. Both sides could negotiate from strength and demand compromise. Although repression might be an effective mode of dealing with discontent or insubordination from slaves, it did not recommend itself as a way of handling men who had the means to fight back either politically or, if necessary, with force. Unlike the peasants of the Old World, Americans, or at least those Americans without black skin, possessed two palpable sources of power: most of them owned the land on which they lived, and a very large number of them owned guns. Land gave them economic and political power; and guns, we may as well admit, gave them firepower.

In the events that led up to the Revolution, England had failed to recognize the strength that these two kinds of power gave to her colonists. The colonists themselves knew at first hand that the ownership of land enabled a man to bid defiance to those who had traditionally controlled society through control of its lands. They had developed a society in which deference to birth and wealth was tempered by constant reminders to the rich and wellborn that their authority rested on the consent of ordinary property owners. Most adult male Americans owned property and could vote for the men who made the laws that affected their property. If they generally voted for a local bigwig, a man who held more property than they did, they did not hesitate to dump him if he neglected their interests. Similarly, within the legislative assemblies lesser men bowed to the leadership of bigger ones. As Robert Zemsky has shown, social status counted for more than seniority in at least one colonial assembly. But when the leaders of the assembly brought in a bill that looked oppressive to the back-benchers, they voted it down and even substituted impromptu measures of their own from the floor.

What alarmed Americans about taxation by Parliament was that they could not vote it down. The program that seemed so conventional and so reasonable from the standpoint of Whitehall appeared to the Americans as a threat to the power that enabled them to direct their own lives. If a legislature to which they elected no member could take their property in taxes, that legislature could ultimately take all their property and reduce them to the impotence of which they had such visible examples in the slaves at their feet. It was consensus on this point that enabled the colonies to unite so suddenly and so successfully against parliamentary taxation. The American reaction to parliamentary taxation seemed to England too hysterical and wicked to be genuine, and her statesmen failed to deal with it adequately, partly because they failed to recognize its existence.

The British failed also to recognize the existence of American firepower. It would perhaps be an exaggeration to say that most Americans had guns and knew how to use them. But it seems likely that nowhere else in the world at the time was there a population so well armed as the Americans. Governor Berkeley had perceived and experienced the implications of this fact in 1676, and as early as 1691 William Blathwayt, the English auditor general for the colonies, who was more conversant in colonial affairs than any other Englishman of the time, recorded with admiration the familiarity of the colonists with guns. "There is no Custom more generally to be observed among the young Virginians," he noted, "than that they all learn to keep and use a gun with a Marvellous dexterity as soon as ever they have strength enough to lift it to their heads." Had Lord North been as keenly aware as Blathwayt of the skills thus acquired, he and George III might not have underestimated so badly the American capacity for resistance.

In order to maintain themselves as a single nation, Americans had to recognize the economic power and firepower that Britain ignored. By the time of the Revolution the proportion of the population owning land in the East may have been somewhat reduced from what it had been fifty or a hundred years earlier, but the westerner by definition was a man who had broken out of the limited acreage of the East. Whether or not he held a secure title, he knew how to make his living from the land and to make life uncomfortable for anyone who tried to stop him. And he was even more likely than the easterner to be armed. The westerner in our history has always been a man with a gun. Eastern-dominated governments simply did not have sufficient power of their own in the long run to impose on the West conditions that armed westerners would not agree to, any more than the Continental Congress could have imposed its edicts on the states, as some members proposed, by the use of military force. American nationalism was obliged to start with the assumption that the population was armed and that no group within it, slaves excepted, could be pushed very hard in any direction it did not want to go.

With a population already equalized to a large degree by firepower and economic power, the United States began its independence appropriately with the declaration that all men are created equal. The immediate purpose was to affirm the equality of England's transatlantic colonists with Englishmen in England, who were taxed only by their elected representatives. But the simplicity of the declaration of equality endowed it with a resonance that was momentous for the whole subsequent history of the nation whose existence it announced.

It could not have been predicted at the time that this would become a national creed. The men who adopted the declaration in 1776 would scarcely have been unanimous if they had been obliged to state precisely what they meant by "created equal." Many of them, including the author of the phrase, held slaves. If the preceding analysis is correct, the fact that they were able to unite at all depended in part on their denial of equality to black Americans. Even when applied only to white Americans, the meaning of equality was hardly as self-evident as Congress declared the proposition itself to be. The equality promulgated by the Congress at Philadelphia had no power to dissolve at once the conflicts and tensions in American society. Westerners were obliged for several years to flirt with Spain and England, while eastern speculators, many of them in Congress, quarreled over the profits they hoped to gain from western settlement if the West could be kept under eastern domination. James Madison tried in vain to secure a guarantee in the Federal Constitution of the equality of western states. Instead the principle was precariously acknowledged only as a result of a shady bargain during the last weeks of the expiring Continental Congress.

But acknowledged it was in the end. The Northwest Ordinance, by stipulating that western states should be admitted to the Union on equal terms with the existing states, saved the nation from future attempts to make subordinate colonists out of its western emigrants. As the Revolutionists gradually became aware of the implications of the creed to which they had committed themselves, they also whittled down, albeit even more gradually, the inequities in their laws governing religion, representation, and inheritance. And as the social structure of the nation changed in subsequent generations, Americans probed further into the meaning of equality.

It has generally taken more than the chanting of the creed to bring about the social justice that it promises. Our history is not the chronicle of steady and continuous application of the principle of equality to match the continuous expansion of the population. The reluctance of easterners to grant equal rights to westerners was prophetic of later contests. Those who have claimed the benefits of equality in America have usually had to press their own claims against stubborn opposition. Men with power over other men have often affirmed their dedication to the principle while denying it by their actions, masters denying it to slaves, employers to workmen, natives to immigrants, whites to blacks, men to women.

Is it fair, then, to call this a point of consensus? Was it not mere rhetoric? Perhaps, if by rhetoric is meant the terms on which men can agree to speak together. An alternative rhetoric and an alternative social creed prevailed before the Revolution both in America and Europe and continued to prevail in most of Europe. That creed also offered a way to consensus, but of a quite different sort. It affirmed divine sanction for a social hierarchy in which every man knew his place and was expected to keep it. The old creed was designed to suppress the aspirations of lower classes, to make them content with their lot. Redress of grievances was not impossible, if superiors failed in their acknowledged obligations to inferiors; but the likelihood was much greater that oppression would go unchecked and that resentment would build into an explosive, revolutionary situation before redress could be obtained. The American Revolution itself was brought on by a British minister who had rejected what he called "the absurd opinion that all men are equal." That absurd opinion became the basis of the American consensus that grew out of the Revolution.

It may indeed seem an absurd sort of consensus that rests upon an invitation to conflict. The creed of equality did not give men equality, but invited them to claim it, invited them, not to know their place and keep it, but to seek and demand a better place. Yet the conflicts resulting from such demands have generally, though not always, stopped short of large-scale violence and have generally eventuated in a greater degree of actual equality. After each side has felt out the other's strengths and weaknesses, some bargain, some equivalent to a Northwest Ordinance, is agreed upon, leaving demands not quite fulfilled, leaving the most radical still discontented with remaining inequalities, but keeping the nation still committed to the creed of equality and bound to move, if haltingly, in the direction it signals.

While the creed invites resistance by the oppressed, it also enjoins accommodation by the oppressor. If it is mere rhetoric, it is a rhetoric that has kept conservatism in America on the defensive. The power that the consensus of equality has wielded over the minds of Americans ever since the Revolution is in fact nowhere more clearly exhibited than in the posture it has imposed on conservatism. To Europeans it may seem odd for conservatism to be garbed in the language of human equality, but conservatives in America quickly learned that this was the only acceptable dress in which they could appear in public. In order to argue for special privilege in the United States it was necessary to show—and it sometimes required considerable legerdemain—that special privilege was somehow the outcome of equality or a device to protect equality. John Adams, for example, contended that Americans should reserve a special place in their governments for the rich, the talented, and the well-born, on the grounds that it was necessary to isolate and thus ostracize and disarm these dangerous men in order to preserve equality. A century later William Graham Sumner argued against every kind of social legislation on the grounds that all Americans were created equal, so that every American who attained wealth and position had done so by his own efforts and therefore deserved to keep what he had earned, while the poor equally deserved their poverty. To aid the poor would threaten equality.

If these arguments today seem ludicrous, it is because conservatism in the United States has often been reduced to the ludicrous by the national commitment to equality. A conservatism based on a more congenial premise can make little headway. When the South, long after the Revolution, attempted to defend slavery on another premise, the attempt generated the greatest crisis American nationality has faced. The resulting conflict did not really destroy the racial consensus among whites and did not achieve equality for Negroes, but it did destroy slavery and it did preserve the national commitment to equality. That commitment is gradually eroding racism. And it continues to serve the oppressed, both black and white, in their efforts to attain what the nation has promised them, just as it also serves to keep most of the oppressed from totally rejecting a society that admits their right to an equal treatment not yet received.

If, then, the American Revolution produced a consensus among the victorious Americans, it was not a static consensus but one with the genius to serve changing times and needs. It was a consensus that invited conflicts and still invites them, a consensus peculiarly adapted to a growing people, a people on the move both geographically and socially. It could not have contained, but it did not produce, the kind of conflict that gave Charles I his Cromwell. It made instead for a society where a Hamilton had his Jefferson, a Hoover his Roosevelt, and a Nixon—might profit by their example. If this be conservatism, it is radicals who have made the most of it.

INDEX

Notes

ON THE

Contributors

BERNARD BAILYN, Winthrop Professor of History at Harvard University, is the author of *The Ideological Origins of the American Revolution* and other books and the editor of *Pamphlets of the American Revolution, 1750–1776*.

RICHARD MAXWELL BROWN, Professor of History at The College of William and Mary, is the author of *The South Carolina Regulators*. He has a special interest in the history of violence.

ROWLAND BERTHOFF, Professor of History at Washington University in St. Louis, has recently published *An Unsettled People: Social Order and Disorder in American History*.

JACK P. GREENE, Professor of History at The Johns Hopkins University, is the author of *The Quest for Power: The Lower Houses of Assembly in the Southern Royal Colonies, 1689–1776*, and the editor of *The Reinterpretation of the American Revolution, 1763–1789*.

H. JAMES HENDERSON is Professor of History at the University of Oklahoma. His book on the politics of the Continental Congress will be published in the near future.

WILLIAM G. MC LOUGHLIN, Professor of History at Brown University, has published most recently *New England Dissent, 1630–1833: The Baptists and the Separation of Church and State*. He is also the author of *Isaac Backus and the American Pietistic Tradition*.

EDMUND S. MORGAN, Sterling Professor of History at Yale University, is the author of *The Stamp Act Crisis: Prologue to Revolu-*

tion, written in collaboration with his wife, Helen S. Morgan; *The Birth of the Republic, 1763–1789*; and numerous other books and articles on early American history.

JOHN MURRIN, Associate Professor of History at Washington University in St. Louis, has been studying the process of Anglicization in the eighteenth-century colonies and is the author of several articles.

JOHN SHY, Professor of History at the University of Michigan in Ann Arbor, is the author of *Toward Lexington: The Role of the British Army in the Coming of the American Revolution.*